Taylor and Politics

THINKING POLITICS

Series Editors: Geoff M. Boucher and Matthew Sharpe

Politics in the twenty-first century is immensely complex and multi-faceted and alternative theorisations of debates that radically renew older ideas have grown from a trickle to a flood in the past twenty years. The most interesting and relevant contemporary thinkers have responded to new political challenges – such as liberal multiculturalism, new directions in feminist thinking, theories of global empire and biopolitical power, and challenges to secularism – by widening the scope of their intellectual engagements and responding to the new politics. The thinkers selected for inclusion in the series have all responded to the urgency and complexity of thinking about politics today in fresh ways.

Books in the series will provide clear and accessible introductions to the major ideas in contemporary thinking about politics, through a focus in each volume on a key political thinker. Rather than a roll-call of the 'usual suspects' it will focus on new thinkers who offer provocative new directions and some neglected older thinkers whose relevance is becoming clear as a result of the changing situation.

Each book will:

- Provide a summary overview of the thinker's contribution
- Position the thinker within the contemporary political field and their intellectual contexts
- Explain key concepts and events
- Balance accessibility with a serious critical treatment of the thinker
- Expose the thinker's ideas to robust tests of empirical and conceptual evidence
- Focus on ideas and debates in relation to real world politics and contemporary political questions with empirical examples
- Include text boxes to highlight key concepts and figures

www.edinburghuniversitypress.com/series/thpo

TAYLOR AND POLITICS

A CRITICAL INTRODUCTION

Craig Browne and Andrew P. Lynch

EDINBURGH
University Press

Edinburgh University Press is one of the leading university presses in the UK. We publish academic books and journals in our selected subject areas across the humanities and social sciences, combining cutting-edge scholarship with high editorial and production values to produce academic works of lasting importance. For more information visit our website: edinburghuniversitypress.com

Edinburgh University Press Ltd
The Tun – Holyrood Road,
12(2f) Jackson's Entry,
Edinburgh EH8 8PJ

Typeset in 11/13 Adobe Sabon by
IDSUK (DataConnection) Ltd, and
printed and bound in the United States of America

A CIP record for this book is available from the British Library

ISBN 978 0 7486 9193 7 (hardback)
ISBN 978 0 7486 9194 4 (paperback)
ISBN 978 0 7486 9195 1 (webready PDF)
ISBN 978 0 7486 9196 8 (epub)

Contents

Acknowledgements vi
Abbreviations of Taylor's Works vii

Introduction 1
1 Charles Taylor: A Thinker for Our Times 17
2 Meaning, Identity and Freedom 33
3 Romanticism and Modernity 55
4 Democracy and Recognition 79
5 Modern Social Imaginaries 107
6 Living in a Secular Age 129
7 *A Secular Age:* Controversies and Critiques 151
8 Charles Taylor's Work after *A Secular Age* 174
Conclusion 193

Bibliography 197
Index 209

Acknowledgements

The authors would like to thank the editors of the Thinking Politics series, Geoff Boucher and Matthew Sharpe, for their support with this book as it has developed. Thanks are also due to the reviewers for their invaluable critical suggestions on the text. Thank you also to the staff at Edinburgh University Press for their assistance, especially Jen Daly for her advice and commitment to this project.

Craig Browne would like to thank Shaun Wilson, Gabrielle Meagher and the editors of *Thesis Eleven* for facilitating his publication dealing with Charles Taylor's interpretation of modern social imaginaries, and Karl Smith, in particular, for his invitation to contribute to a Special Issue that he edited of *Thesis Eleven* on Charles Taylor's recent work. He would also like to thank Daniela Heil for her support and background understanding.

Andrew Lynch thanks Michelle for her encouragement and support while working on the book, and for proofreading portions of the text.

An earlier version of parts of Chapter 5 was published as Browne, C. (2006). 'A Moral Order of Mutual Benefit', *Thesis Eleven* 86: 114–25.

Abbreviations of Taylor's Works

APLS 'Afterword: Apologia pro Libro suo', in Michael Warner, Jonathan VanAntwerpen and Craig Calhoun (eds) *Varieties of Secularism in a Secular Age*. 2010. Cambridge, MA: Harvard University Press, pp. 300–21.

BF *Building the Future: A Time for Reconciliation*. Gérard Bouchard and Charles Taylor. 2008. Quebec: Government of Quebec.

CM *A Catholic Modernity?* 1999. New York: Oxford University Press.

CP *Church and People: Disjunctions in a Secular Age*. Charles Taylor, José Casanova and George F. McLean (eds). 2012. Washington, DC: Council for Research in Values and Philosophy.

DC *Dilemmas and Connections: Selected Essays*. 2011. Cambridge, MA: Harvard University Press.

EA *The Ethics of Authenticity*. 1992. Cambridge, MA: Harvard University Press.

EB *The Explanation of Behaviour*. 1964. London: Routledge & Kegan Paul.

H *Hegel*. 1975. Cambridge: Cambridge University Press.

HAL *Human Agency and Language: Philosophical Papers 1*. 1985. Cambridge: Cambridge University Press.

HMS *Hegel and Modern Society*. 1979. Cambridge: Cambridge University Press.

KP Kluge Prize Acceptance Speech. 2015. Washington, DC: Library of Congress.

LA *The Language Animal: The Full Shape of the Human Linguistic Capacity*. 2016. Cambridge, MA: Harvard University Press.

M *Multiculturalism: Examining the Politics of Recognition*. Amy Gutmann (ed.). 1994. Princeton, NJ: Princeton University Press.

MSI	*Modern Social Imaginaries*. 2004. Durham: Duke University Press.
PA	*Philosophical Arguments*. 1995. Cambridge, MA: Harvard University Press.
PHS	*Philosophy and the Human Sciences: Philosophical Papers 2*. 1985. Cambridge: Cambridge University Press.
RR	*Retrieving Realism*. Herbert Dreyfus and Charles Taylor. 2015. Cambridge, MA: Harvard University Press.
RS	*Reconciling the Solitudes: Essays in Canadian Federalism and Nationalism*. 1993. Montreal: McGill-Queen's University Press.
SA	*A Secular Age*. 2007. Cambridge, MA: Belknap Press.
SFC	*Secularism and Freedom of Conscience*. Jocelyn Maclure and Charles Taylor. 2011. Cambridge, MA: Harvard University Press.
SS	*Sources of the Self: The Making of the Modern Identity*. 1989. Cambridge, MA: Belknap Press.
VRT	*Varieties of Religion Today: William James Revisited*. 2002. Cambridge, MA: Harvard University Press.

Introduction

Charles Taylor is one of the world's foremost thinkers, and he has produced an impressive body of work over a lifetime which focuses on some of the most pressing issues of contemporary politics and social life, including social diversity, religion and secularism, justice, language and philosophical considerations on realism. His work has been noted by academics around the globe, but has also caught the attention of politicians, policy makers and government administrators in a number of countries. His ideas are debated in a range of academic disciplines beyond his own of philosophy, including sociology, anthropology, religious studies, theology, history, political science, cultural studies and literary theory. Whenever big ideas are being discussed that have an impact on social integration and the living of meaningful lives, Taylor's work is soon mentioned. His writings have instigated a large body of secondary literature, including conferences debating the implications of his ideas, journal symposiums, edited volumes on topics he has engaged with, and book length treatises that investigate his work from a range of perspectives.

Furthermore, his writings constitute a substantial alternative to the dominant liberal strand of political theory and offer a novel critique of capitalist society. Taylor's conception of freedom has identifiable links with the aims of contemporary movements for social change. Taylor's writings represent a major account of historical processes of democratisation and a unique interpretation of the attributes of a democratic political culture. Indeed, Taylor is concerned with the moral horizon of politics and with how meanings and values shape political institutions and practices. Taylor's politics is usually characterised as communitarian, but while Taylor is critical of 'atomistic' individualism and 'proceduralism', his politics should be more properly understood as a type of 'holistic liberalism'.

As Nicholas Smith points out, Taylor is not a systems builder; that is, he has not developed one consistent philosophical edifice or framework that attempts to understand the world or reality, and he has not written one particular book that sums up his philosophy.

Rather, Taylor has made many novel, and in some cases groundbreaking, contributions to a wide range of philosophical and social issues, including the work of Hegel, the politics of recognition and multiculturalism, personhood, modernity, the self, language, realism, hermeneutics and science, history and the Romantic Movement, religion and secularism, and freedom. Taylor's approach is problem-oriented (Smith 2002). He believes that many contemporary political debates are not intractable, rather political disputes can be reformulated through revealing their larger moral background. More controversially, Taylor claims that certain questions are inescapable, and he aims to make the basis of evaluations explicit and to reveal how significance is constituted. Furthermore, Taylor's work has not been confined to abstract philosophising; he has also been directly involved in politics for much of his adult life, and this includes stints as a political candidate and academic interventions into political issues.

Throughout his career, Taylor has grappled with a range of problems that stem from the duality that often occurs in intellectual thought, for instance his interest in Romanticism as a countermovement of the Enlightenment; his defence of communitarianism in the face of atomist understandings of social relations; and his deep thinking on secularism as it relates to religion. Our analysis highlights how Taylor's political thought is founded on his general philosophical perspective, and how his arguments develop through participation in major contemporary theoretical debates, like those over the politics of recognition, civil society, secularism and modernity. We will pay particular attention to Taylor's writings over the last decade and their endeavours to develop a perspective that is relevant to the contemporary social and political situation. This will involve a survey of the wide-ranging debate that Taylor's book *A Secular Age* has stimulated, and we will examine the critical response to this work in the social sciences. Taylor's writings represent one of the most important accounts of long-term historical processes of democratisation, especially significant for their clarification of the background frameworks of understanding that shape a democratic culture. Similarly, Taylor's political theory elaborates a distinctive conception of freedom, one that incorporates aspects of romanticism's notions of self-realisation and self-expression, assumptions drawn from his philosophical anthropology and related 'moral ontology', as well as reflecting Taylor's commitment to a holistic version of liberalism. We hope to show how Taylor draws on this perspective in his critical diagnoses of the 'malaise of modernity', which is manifested in alienation, fragmentation and isolation. We will likewise examine Taylor's critiques of certain influential positions in contemporary social and political theory, such as 'proceduralism', and liberal notions of negative liberty.

Furthermore, while our reconstruction of Taylor's positions is generally sympathetic and appreciative, we argue that Taylor's political thought is in considerable tension with itself. This is the source of certain ambiguities concerning the precise implications of his arguments, and these tensions have provoked various critical responses. Namely, Taylor seeks to promote a strong sense of autonomy, yet he equally seeks to limit its implications, being particularly opposed to equating democracy with the idea of the general will. Given the modern experiences of violence, Taylor is right to develop a morally responsible position. Even so, we show that Taylor's positions are more contentious than they might initially appear. This is the case for his recent writings on secularism and his contribution to the debates over the politics of recognition. This analysis explains why Taylor's politics is sometimes at odds with secular perspectives that share similar theoretical assumptions, and we consider whether Taylor effectively addresses contemporary forms of subordination and inequality, which arguably constitute a challenge to his interpretation of the moral order of modern liberal democratic societies. However, although we place particular emphasis on the most recent phase of Taylor's work, we will attempt to explain the continuities and developments in his thought, importantly contextualising his various political arguments. Nonetheless, this book does not focus in detail on Taylor's early arguments concerning epistemology and the methodology of the human sciences. These are referred to in sketching the philosophical underpinnings of his work, but they are not explored in depth here. Other authors have examined these issues in great detail, and we see no need to revisit those arguments (see Tully 1994; Abbey 2000; 2004; Smith 2002). Likewise, our analysis does not attempt to cover all of the various historical details and diverse schools of thought that are sketched in his history of the sources of the self. For similar reasons, we concentrate on the political aspects of Taylor's account of Hegel's philosophy, but do not scrutinise his interpretation of Hegel's metaphysics, although the critical appraisals of Taylor's work that are concerned with these general philosophical themes will be discussed when relevant to the discussion of his political thought.

What we will offer in this book is an analysis of how Taylor's philosophical project is concerned with three broad and politically charged issues: debates about the self and society, the social context of ethics in modern times, and how religion is being reconciled, or not reconciled, to the project of modernity. Most of the other issues that we address, and which hold a place in Taylor's work, from recognition and language, through to Romanticism and secularism, can be said to contribute to these three general areas of investigation. Furthermore, although Taylor's work has largely been scrutinised by philosophers, both of the authors of this book are sociologists, and so we will provide an examination of Taylor that leans towards its relevance for social and political questions pertinent to individuals and communities in the contemporary, modern era. Another feature of this book is that while much of the secondary literature on Taylor deals with the period before or after *A Secular Age*, we will reveal the links between these phases of his project and show how they interconnect. We will also go beyond current commentaries on *A Secular Age* by not only assessing the text itself, but also the debates that it has generated in the scholarly literature. We also offer a more critical comparison of Taylor's notion of social imaginary with that of other authors who work on the concept, leading to new assessments that differ from other commentaries. And we will bring later critiques of recognition theory to bear on Taylor in a way that extends existing discussions.

A foundational idea that informs much of Taylor's work is that society is made up of more than individuals and institutions and the rational rules and laws that organise their interactions. Rather, for Taylor, society is bound together by a moral order, what he sometimes calls an 'order of mutual benefit' (MSI, 21; SA, 171). It is this moral order which serves as the ethical basis of society and human interaction, and in whatever ways it might be perverted by forces such as capitalism, alienation, prejudice or misunderstanding, there is a constant need for us to recover this moral order and recognise its centrality for achieving a more harmonious collective life. Furthermore, for Taylor this moral order is not located in naturalism, and he contests the idea that 'nothing beyond the natural is required to make sense of ethics' (Gutting 1999: 159). Taylor puts forward three alternatives to naturalism, which are strong evaluations (decisions about right and wrong that are based on independent standards); frameworks (the background assumptions in which moral decisions are arrived at and justified, SA, 27; see Chapter 2); and hypergoods (values or commitments which persons place highest in their lives, and which provide a benchmark for assessing other values, SA, 63). Each of these supports Taylor's claim that moral orders are ultimately based on foundations beyond individuals and social constructivism (SS; Gutting 1999: 137–59).

Discussion of moral orders leads some commentators on Taylor's work to raise the issue of his Catholicism, and the influence that it plays in his philosophy. But it is not Catholic dogma, but rather faith that has had an impact on his intellectual output. Although he has maintained a lifetime practice of the Catholic faith, and it no doubt forms some of his background assumptions, Taylor has for the most part steered clear of engaging in specifically Catholic or theological argument. His work certainly does have relevance for those interested in theology and religious studies, but apart from some speeches and essays (see CM; CP) he has remained aloof from topics such as the Catholic Church's place and role in the modern world, and has not written a major work on the Church or on Catholic intellectual history. And he is certainly no apologist for Catholicism or the Christian faith. Along with his contemporary Alasdair MacIntyre, Taylor would best be described as a philosopher who happens to be Catholic, rather than as a 'Catholic philosopher' such as John Haldane may be categorised as being. But faith more generally has had an impact on his thought, serving as a sometimes unseen foundation to the intellectual edifice he has constructed over the course of his career. His interest in moral sources is an example (Connolly 2004). And he holds long-held and deeply thought-out ideas about religion in modern times, and how our ideas about religion are framing much of our current political discourse about individualism, rights and equality.

About the book

In Chapter 1 we provide a biography of Charles Taylor's career that highlights his major works and the key contributions that he has made to contemporary thought. This biographical sketch also tries to highlight some of the political and social changes that were occurring as Taylor worked. In doing so, it is hoped that Taylor's biography shows in some ways the context of his work and the debates that he has contributed to. This context is both international and national, because Taylor is consistently concerned with issues relevant to the world and to his native Canada. Taylor has participated in many political campaigns, and was among the initiators of what became the journal *New Left Review*. He also ran for parliament in Canada four times, and he recently served as a co-chairperson of the Quebec Government's Consultation Commission on Accommodation Practices Related to Cultural Differences, co-authoring its final report. The English language translation of this report appeared in 2008 (see BF). Taylor has played the role of a public intellectual, writing extensively on Canadian society and politics. Although Taylor's political theorising cannot be reduced to the particularities of the Canadian situation, we suggest that significant insights into Taylor's general political thinking can be gained from examining the Canadian context. Indeed, Canadian society and politics provides an accessible and concrete point of reference for the more abstract questions of political theory that will be dealt with in later chapters. Canadian debates arguably pioneered the discussion of recent political topics, like diversity, immigration, citizenship, cultural subordination and post-colonialism. Likewise, Taylor's interest in nationalism and identity, his perspective on the problem of reconciling pluralism and unity, are certainly influenced by various Canadian debates and political struggles, like those over the integrity of the nation and the potential secession of Quebec. The positions that Taylor adopts in these Canadian debates are instructive for understanding his general political orientation and his defence of a holistic version of liberalism. This biographical context provides important insights into not only the positions Taylor endorses, but also into what he considers politically dangerous and opposes. The latter includes certain militant or radical political positions, which Taylor thinks misconstrue popular sovereignty, and the related risk that disenchantment could lead to mistaken political solutions to problems of morality and cultural meaning.

In Chapter 2, 'Meaning, Identity and Freedom', we argue that there are four key philosophical themes that inform Taylor's political thought: the concern with identity, the problem of meaning, the idea of moral ontology, the concern with identity and the notion of effective freedom. This chapter has then a two-fold purpose. First, it will detail some of Taylor's most general notions and categories, noting their specific relevance to his political arguments. Second, it will focus especially on Taylor's conceptions of freedom, meaning and action, as these significantly contribute to his distinctive political perspective. One of Taylor's major concerns has been developing a philosophical anthropology of the human subject and explicating an interrelated, in his terms, moral ontology. This project has its roots in his early work on *The Explanation of Behaviour* and it clearly shapes his landmark study *Sources of the Self*. We will highlight Taylor's links to the tradition of hermeneutic phenomenology, with his claim that humans are 'self-interpreting' animals, for whom meaning is central to the human condition. We hope to show how these ideas are developed in terms of well-known features of Taylor's writings, such as the narrative construction of the self and the idea of strong evaluations. A major concern will be clarifying the political implications of Taylor's contention that there is a connection between identity and an orientation to the good, since this contention conditions arguments surveyed in later chapters, and it differentiates Taylor's standpoint among contemporary political philosophers. In particular, Taylor's concern with the good, rather than political liberalism's prioritising of 'the right', is related to his holistic liberalism. Also, we will briefly discuss some of the criticisms of Taylor's formulation of the relationship between identity and the good, such as that proposed by Hans Joas (2000). It will be argued that Taylor's conception of the self and human action form part of his endeavour to clarify the nature of freedom in modernity.

This discussion highlights Taylor's emphasis on how freedom involves capacities for articulation and moral actualisation. In particular, therefore, we examine Taylor's argument that liberalism's notion of negative liberty is deficient and his consequent disagreement with his former teacher Isaiah Berlin, who famously distinguished between negative liberty and positive liberty. Taylor's distinction between opportunity and concepts of liberty will also be covered in light of this. Taylor's account of positive liberty is important, because it discloses some of the critical weaknesses of the dominant interpretation of political liberalism. We show how certain connections can be drawn between Taylor's notion of freedom and core features of the contemporary politics of democratisation, like the demands for heightened participation. Furthermore, how positive liberty has been a central concern of critical social theory will be assessed, and we will briefly compare Taylor's conception with Jürgen Habermas' and Axel Honneth's respective communicative interpretations of freedom. This comparison will be returned to in later chapters, especially in relation to Taylor's account of the politics of recognition.

Chapter 3 explores Taylor's attempt to work out the implications of Romanticism's influence on modernity and the tension, in his opinion, between modernity's dominant emphasis on instrumental rationality and Romanticism's ideals, like expression, creativity and community. Taylor wants to show, we argue, the extent to which the strains of modern society derive from this tension and how Romanticism's ideals have influenced modern political movements. In particular, Taylor's own critical diagnoses of the 'malaise of modernity' is influenced by Romanticism, as is evident from his observations on the fragility of social bonds in the face of industrial and technological advancement, as well as in his comments on contemporary culture's potential loss of meaning and significance. These experiences of alienation are the other side, so to speak, of the modern ethic of authenticity, which has resulted in the widespread concern with self-realisation. Taylor is well known for his explication of the influence of Romanticism on Hegel's thought, but he has highlighted the importance of other authors even more directly connected to this tradition, especially Humboldt and Herder. He argues that they developed an expressivist theory of language, a holistic conception of liberal freedom, and were among the first to appreciate the importance of a community's political culture to modern freedoms. Significantly, modern nationalism was partly inspired by the Romantic understanding of popular sovereignty, with its idea of the nation as enabling a people to be authentic and giving expression to their culture. Taylor also acknowledges nationalism's negative dimensions and we evaluate his critique of misunderstandings of popular sovereignty and solidarity.

Chapter 3 will also include an overview of Taylor's claim that the debate between liberalism and communitarians has been at cross-purposes. If the expressivist conception of freedom is one major aspect of the influence of Romanticism on Taylor's political thought, then the other major aspect is the significance of the sense of community and the idea that a holistic orientation is compatible with a liberal commitment to individual rights and freedoms. In the context of these debates, Taylor is often regarded as a communitarian, but, as suggested previously, this is to misunderstand his holistic liberalism. In this chapter we assess whether Taylor's position is entirely satisfactory, and detail the kinds of counter-questions that have been addressed to his arguments, such as whether his critique of proceduralism is overstated. Specifically, we discuss three aspects of Taylor's political perspective that are indebted to his reading of Romanticism and discuss how they are indicative of the kinds of dilemmas that recur in his political thought: providing arguments for transformation and seeking to delimit the implications of change. First, although Rousseau is recognised as a major proponent of the idea of authenticity, Taylor develops an extended critique of Rousseau's notion of the general will. As later chapters demonstrate, Taylor repeatedly returns to the problem of radical mobilisation. Second, Taylor highlights the influence of expressivism on Hegel's thought, but he endorses Hegel's critique of the French Revolution's attempt to institute Absolute Freedom. Third, Taylor recognises that certain strands of contemporary philosophy have affinities with Romanticism; however, he is opposed to influential post-structuralist and postmodernist perspectives, viewing them as irresponsible and 'deviant' versions of the ethic of authenticity. Finally, attention will be drawn to how Taylor's writings have influenced authors concerned with political subjectivity.

Chapter 4, 'Democracy and Recognition', will examine the question of identity, which has been a consistent thread running through Taylor's work, and illustrates how meaning informs his interest in political culture. Taylor considers that formal political institutions have to be located in a broader horizon of understanding and that this background framework shapes the way that institutions operate, as well as the conditions of legitimacy. It was partly in these terms that Taylor criticised liberal proceduralism. This is one of the ways in which Taylor's political perspective can be differentiated among contemporaries, and it is somewhat similar to that of Alexis de Tocqueville's on democracy and democratisation. Tocqueville highlighted the broad background experiences of democratic – that is, free and equal – forms of social association and the general orientation provided by cultural meaning. Of course, Taylor's reworking of aspects of Tocqueville's diagnoses of modern society's potential for 'democratic despotism' and the paradoxes of individualism made these affinities explicit. What is of interest here is the parallels in their respective approaches to politics and democratisation and the way that this parallel illuminates our claim about Taylor's important contribution to understanding long-term processes of democratisation. The aim at this point is to note how it enables Taylor's holistic liberal perspective on democracy to address major political concerns in the period after the collapse of state socialism, like citizenship, civil society, human rights and the prospects for progressive social change.

Nevertheless, the major focus of this chapter will be Taylor's account of the politics of recognition and the broad debates that his essay on multiculturalism and recognition stimulated. Taylor can be seen as responding to the new politics of identity and the contestation over the implications of cultural diversity, especially in multicultural societies like Canada and Australia. We explore how Taylor brings his own theoretical framework to bear on these topics and develops an important account of recognition, emphasising the underpinnings of identity politics in the values of equal respect and equal dignity. While acknowledging its significance, the critical responses to Taylor's account of recognition and how the discussion of recognition has significantly expanded since the publication of his essay are discussed. For instance, Taylor's conception has been criticised for potentially entailing the negative features of communitarianism. Similarly, the parallels and differences between Axel Honneth's more elaborated account of recognition and Taylor's version is considered in this chapter too. Although Taylor's essay on multiculturalism and the politics of recognition originally appeared two decades ago, its contemporary relevance is reinforced by situating his arguments in relation to the current debates in Critical Social Theory, and through noting some of the substantive contemporary social developments to which the recognition framework has been applied. Finally, we will remark on Taylor's updating of his perspective on recognition and its connection to his later analysis of the tendencies for 'democratic exclusion and their remedies'. Taylor's response to the criticisms of his account of the politics of recognition and his own appreciation of the need to finesse his arguments about the liberal–communitarian controversy influenced his introduction of the category of social imaginaries, and his desire to offer a new interpretation of modernity's cultural underpinnings and the broad historical processes that shaped its political order.

Chapter 5 examines Taylor's concept of modern social imaginaries. Taylor's political thinking has been shaped by the need to come to terms with the changed ideological and political context that coalesced during the last decades of the twentieth century and the new millennium. For Taylor, this involves a reinterpretation of modernity in response to criticism of its key tenets, such as progress, freedom and rationality. Taylor attempts to develop a new appreciation of the cultural background to modernity's dominant institutional forms, especially liberal democracy and modern capitalism. He seeks to develop two theoretical perspectives that are regarded as offering important insights into the present. They are the perspective of multiple (or alternative) modernities, on the one hand, and the notion of social imaginaries, on the other. Both multiple modernities and social imaginaries have longer intellectual backgrounds, and developed in response to specific theoretical and political problems, like the dissolution of state socialist societies, anti-colonial struggles and religious fundamentalism. These background considerations are taken as criteria for assessing Taylor's recent proposals. We discuss how Taylor's analysis of the invoking of civil society by oppositional movements under state socialism and new social movements in the West prefigures his work on modern social imaginaries. It is suggested here that the evolution of Taylor's thought was strongly influenced by the recent experiences of the regressive as well as progressive features of identity politics, and the need to better understand the sources of the differences between them. Although it has been a major concern from the outset, his desire to revisit the question of the relationship between religion and the secular, above all, motivated the approach taken in his latest writings, including *A Secular Age*. Taylor argues that the modern social imaginary generates a notion of society as constituted as a moral order of mutual benefit and that this image informs individual practices. Taylor's position differs significantly from the contemporary radical political perspectives that are influenced by post-structuralism. We will explore these differences in the context of explicating Taylor's interpretation of the dominant modern social imaginary.

Chapter 5 will also analyse Taylor's interest in the constitution of modern civil society (Browne 2006). He traces this modern social imaginary's origins to the natural law tradition and explains how the image of a moral order of mutual benefit overturned the long-standing idea of society as organised according to a principle of hierarchy. We will examine, therefore, how Taylor's arguments stand at the intersection of many contemporary theoretical debates (e.g. liberal–republican, structure–action, modernity–postmodernity) and why his endeavour to navigate between various positions is both a strength and a weakness. This will involve a comparison of Taylor's interpretation of social imaginaries with leading alternative formulations, especially those of Cornelius Castoriadis and Claude Lefort. There are not only theoretical differences between these notions, but also diverging political considerations. Taylor makes a major contribution to our understanding of liberalism and democratisation, but his vision of liberal modernity is inadequate with respect to forms of inequality and subordination. Taylor overestimates the extent to which hierarchy has been overturned and we note that radical critics highlight neo-liberal capitalism's ideological distortion of the image of a moral order of mutual benefit.

Similarly, Taylor's adoption of elements of the framework of multiple modernities was partly motivated by a desire to move beyond an exclusive focus on European and North American modernity. This theoretical move is significant to the extent that it enables Taylor to highlight divergences from the dominant Western narrative of secularisation, but Taylor does not realise the full implications of this gesture towards a global perspective on modernity and that it is necessary to take into account the difficulties that the more recent critiques of the multiple modernities framework have disclosed. Finally, we draw attention to how Taylor's comparison of modern revolutions relates to his endeavour to define the place of religion in secular societies. According to Taylor, religion can serve as a way of articulating a sense of the common good and as a means of negotiating conflicts in secular societies, whereas the violent consequences of modern revolutions, such as the French Revolutionary Terror, evidences the risks of political action without the limits that is conveyed by a sense of transcendence. Needless to say, many secularists would find this a contentious claim, and the history of modern revolutions is open to alternative readings.

In Chapter 6, 'Living in a Secular Age', we turn to a detailed reading of Taylor's landmark study of religion and secularism. Although presenting a number of innovative ideas, *A Secular Age* is a large, cumbersome book, and we will in this chapter try to make sense of its major themes. Religion has become a major political topic in the new millennium, due to factors like religion's capacity for political mobilisation, spectacular violence, bioethical developments and secular regulation of personal adornment. *A Secular Age* has served as something of a focal point for recent theoretical debates over the character and relationship of religion and the secular. Taylor's latest writings give a particular inflection to some of the themes of his earlier work, such as the problem of meaning, the specific qualities of the modern self and the deployment of frameworks of understanding. In short, Taylor wants to provide an alternative to the dominant conceptions of the secular, and this involves the provision of a historical narrative of how the West arrived at a secular age. Taylor contests the typical notions of the secular, because they are based on assumptions about subtraction, like declining religious attendance, the exclusion of religion from the public domain and the notion of disenchantment. Taylor claims that these varieties of secularity fail to address the persisting demands for meaning and significance. For Taylor, a secular age is where religious belief and non-belief are both possible, yet where the former encounters greater difficulties. In his opinion, this amounts to a considerable historical shift; several centuries ago belief was basically inevitable. Taylor deploys the category of social imaginaries to show how this inevitability of belief derived from, and was reflected in, understandings of self and world.

But before analysing the contents of *A Secular Age*, it is important to situate its arguments in the larger context of both Taylor's career, and in debates about religion in the modern world. Some of the ideas presented in *A Secular Age* were first broached in previous works (see MSI; VRT; and CM), but here Taylor presents them as parts of a larger synthesis that seeks to understand our contemporary thinking about religion. As well as this, Taylor wants to examine why religion has persisted in spite of the forces of modernity. Taylor has been interested in questions of faith in modern conditions since the beginning of his career, and in his early work on Hegel, his interest in a series of what he calls 'reforms' is obvious. In his writings on Hegel, for example, Taylor looks at the impact on faith from the Enlightenment and Romantic Movement, which emphasised reason over faith and feeling over revelation, respectively. Furthermore, a reading of *A Secular Age* is greatly enhanced in light of key arguments he makes in *Sources of the Self*. In fact, key observations he brought forward in this earlier book, such as the affirmation of ordinary life, are given much more concrete grounding in *A Secular Age*. Also, as mentioned, the intellectual context in which *A Secular Age* is situated also needs to be appreciated for a fuller understanding of its key themes. In recent decades the theory of secularisation, the processes whereby religion is pushed into the private sphere by the secular state and the diminishing of belief, has been hotly contested.

Classical secularisation theory suggested that as societies undergo modernisation, they become less religious, revealed through 'the decline of popular involvement with the churches; the decline in scope and influence of religious institutions; and the decline in the popularity and impact of religious beliefs' (Bruce 1996: 26). Modernisation, in the form of mechanised production, higher levels of education, individualism, and a scientific worldview that provides alternative explanations for phenomenon once explained by religion, such as the origins of the universe and the place of human beings in nature, offers an alternative narrative (Chadwick 1975). However, with the resurgence of religion evident since 1979 (Kepel 1994), analysts have been interested in how religions have again become public (Casanova 1994), and in their impact on national political debates and geopolitics

(Huntington 1997). This resurgence in religion has been dubbed by some as a post-secular phase, in which secular states must recognise the religious sensibilities of their citizens as an important aspect of social inclusion (Habermas 2006). Taylor tries to unpack these issues, showing how the word 'secular' signifies three different conditions: the separation of church and state, the diminishing of religious belief, and the onset of an age of religious options, whereby individuals are free to choose what they believe in. As we hope to show in Chapter 6, Taylor traces the trajectory of how we came to live in such a situation.

Chapter 7 remains focused on *A Secular Age*, but with a change in emphasis. In this chapter we explore the various critical reactions that the book has generated. A great deal of secondary literature is emerging that analyses different aspects of the book, and so we will limit our discussion to a selection of these. Our focus, therefore, will be on responses from some of the world's leading intellectuals who have vast expertise in the issues that Taylor raises, including John Milbank, Robert Bellah, José Casanova and Ruth Abbey, among others. In critically unpacking *A Secular Age* we will focus on what these authors have said about major ideas that underpin Taylor's book, including modernity and the secularisation thesis, Taylor's historical methodology, and secularism. As we will see, critics contend that Taylor makes certain assumptions about modernity that are not always shared by other scholars, including his view that interpreting modernity as a radical rupture with the pre-modern past is detrimental to adequately understanding contemporary problems (Bellah 2010).

Critics have also claimed that Taylor's idea of the secular is too smooth and uniform. Is secularism the same everywhere, or are there local variations? Taylor suggests that today we live in a world of spiritual options, but is that the case in all societies, or only in the West? History and historiography are also contested issues vis-à-vis Taylor's arguments. Taylor admits to what he calls a stadial consciousness, that is, seeing history in stages. This underpins his description of specific periods of time as 'ages', such as the Age of Authenticity, the Age of Mobilisation and a Secular Age. For his critics, however, such a view of time and historical change is based on reconstructing history from a genealogical methodology, one which is akin to a history of ideas. This may make interesting reading, but his critics argue that it is a shaky foundation as the basis for theory, as such a use of history does not rely on detailed historical research using primary sources. Finally, as we indicated above, scholars are interested in the resurgence of religion at both the social and political levels since the late twentieth century. If this is indeed the case, critics of *A Secular Age* ask how Taylor can claim that we live in an age of religious options, and that non-belief is one of them, in a time when traditional religions seem to be popular again. In this vein, Taylor is charged with not providing sufficient social scientific data about the true state of religion in modern society. For all of these criticisms, Taylor's book continues to be read and discussed, and a copious secondary literature continues to develop in response to its central ideas. Assessing its many criticisms reveals the fruitful avenues for further research that his arguments have generated.

Chapter 8 brings us up to date with the work that Taylor has produced since publishing *A Secular Age*. As we will see, his recent work continues themes that he has contributed to throughout his career, including studies on religion, a report on the social and political state of affairs in Quebec, and new books on realism and language. Although we will need to limit our discussion to only some of these projects, we hope to show that Taylor's work continues to aid our understanding of the present political situation, both regionally and globally. After writing *A Secular Age* Taylor's interest in religion shifted slightly to a consideration of the issue of freedom of religion in pluralist societies. Here we can see an intersection of strands of thought that Taylor has been working on for some time, including secularism, multiculturalism, communitarianism and freedom. Taylor argues that freedom of religion is an important right, which democratic states should uphold and champion. On the other hand, this must be done while maintaining secularism, for it is secularism that provides the conditions for greater political harmony between competing beliefs. Secularism here should be understood as more than the separation of church and state – rather it should be viewed as the maintenance through politics of a variety of commitments in pluralistic societies.

Taylor's thinking on freedom of religion is influenced to some degree by his participation as co-chair for a report commissioned by the Quebec Government into the accommodation of migrants. The commissioning of this report was prompted by cases in the Canadian media of friction between migrants and native Quebecers, and the government set out to investigate these and reassess its policies on multiculturalism. Taylor and his co-author on the report, Gérard Bouchard, conclude that there is no immediate crisis in Quebec's multiculturalism, and that reports that this is so can be attributed largely to media sensationalism. They do, however, highlight a number of issues that Quebec should look into to enhance its successes with multiculturalism. These include continuing the policy of state neutrality towards religion, so that the state can provide the best conditions for preserving freedom of conscience without favouring one religion over another, as well as enhancing policies that encourage interculturalism over multiculturalism. Interculturalism encourages migrant groups to adopt the values of Quebec, and its language, while at the same time maintaining their own unique cultural traditions, providing a harmonious tapestry of cultures rather than cultures having to shed their identity to assimilate to the majority culture. We round off our discussion of Taylor's work after *A Secular Age* with an analysis of his book *The Language Animal* (2016). This publication draws on Taylor's distinction between designative and expressive language (see PA; HAL), and here we dwell on some of the political implications of his view that language since the Romantic Movement is better able to express the modern concern with the self, and for understanding contemporary pluralism and nationalism.

Attempting to make sense of Taylor's contribution to political thought (in the widest sense of the word 'political') over the course of his career presents some challenges. The primary one is the non-systematic nature of his approach. The scope and variety of his work has led to a variety of readings. Taylor is different things to different people. To some he is first and foremost a moral philosopher and an interpreter of Hegel, while others focus on his social theory. Others read Taylor as a critic of modernity who has reconstructed the importance of Romanticism for the modern self. For others Taylor is an analytical thinker with a deep interest in language, while a new generation of scholars are focusing on his work on religion. The authors of this book have drawn on their own specialisms in their treatment of Taylor's work, and by bringing these together we have, hopefully, gone some way at least towards offering a more holistic vision of Taylor's influence on contemporary thought and politics.

1

Charles Taylor: A Thinker for Our Times

Introduction

Charles Taylor is recognised as one of the world's leading intellectuals, contributing a series of landmark books and papers to a diverse range of topics, from analytical philosophy, phenomenology, modernity, multiculturalism, to communitarianism and religion. But Taylor has tried to be more than a thinker only, involving himself deeply in the politics of his native Canada, even running for public office. In this chapter we will uncover a little of who Taylor is, and what his life's work is concerned with. What we hope to show is that Taylor understands his philosophical work as underlying his practical efforts to shape public policy in both Canada and the world; and vice versa, that his political ideals are informed by his philosophical investigations into life in modern times. Also, as will be made clearer below, Taylor's work is closely linked and connected to the important historical changes and world affairs taking place in contemporary times. In this respect, Taylor's work has consistently revealed a strong sense of relevance to our current challenges, and he is able to help us better understand the disruptions and upheavals that have been the result of transformations and calamities in recent history, from recognising the importance of pluralism in modern society, through to the consequences of 9/11 on world politics. Therefore, one reason why readers are able turn to Taylor and find something beneficial in his work is because he is able to focus on a specific social issue, and provide a deep and detailed meditation on its origins and historical context. With these points in mind, let's explore in a little more detail who Taylor is and what he has achieved.

The Life and Works of Charles Taylor

Charles Margrave Taylor was born in Montreal, Canada, in 1931. He grew up as the Great Depression was spreading across the globe, and as a child he witnessed the economic and social pressures that the Depression exacted on the everyday lives of ordinary men and women. As a teenager he watched from afar as the Second World War was fought across Europe and the Pacific, and with his fellow Canadians heard the news about the explosion of the first atomic weapons that were used against Japan in 1945. The beginnings of the Cold War were major headlines by the time the young Taylor attended the prestigious Selwyn House School in Westmount, Quebec. Like many of his generation, these historical events made a keen impression on him as a youth, and were firmly in the back of his mind as he mapped out his future life and career while completing his secondary education at Trinity College in Port Hope, Ontario. His mother was a dress designer and his father was a partner in a steel factory, ensuring that home life was comfortable but also well-grounded in the concerns of financial practicalities. Politics was openly discussed in the Taylor household, and this especially centred on national debates about Quebec and its relationship to the rest of Canada, a theme which would reverberate throughout Taylor's work. Taylor and his older brother and sister were brought up Catholic, a faith which he would have a lifelong commitment to. Catholicism would also have a long-lasting impact on his work, especially for his thinking about how faith is sustained in modern times. These are reoccurring themes in his writings, and are core concerns of some of his major books. After leaving school Taylor continued his education at McGill University, studying a wide range of subjects, including history.

In the mid-1950s Taylor moved to Oxford University as a Rhodes Scholar. He undertook a BA in Philosophy, Politics and Economics. After this degree he completed a Masters, and then began his doctorate. In 1956 he met one of the icons of twentieth-century philosophy, Isaiah Berlin, who was to be his doctoral supervisor. Berlin, who died in 1997, held Taylor in high esteem as he watched his young student progress from an Oxford researcher to an internationally recognised philosopher in his own right. Berlin described Taylor as a teleologist: 'He truly believes, as so many in the history of thought have done and still do, that human beings, and perhaps the entire universe, have a basic purpose' (Berlin 1994: 1). Although Berlin was generous in his praise of Taylor, he was under no illusions about their philosophical views being at odds, especially when it came to the idea of meaning, highlighting that in contrast to Taylor, he believed that meaning is created by human beings acting on the world and interpreting it, rather than coming from a source outside society, such as God (Berlin 1994: 2). Berlin pointed out that Taylor's teleology was what attracted him not only to Christianity, but also to Hegelianism and

Marxism. As to Marx, Berlin felt that what Taylor had taken from him was the idea that social structures such as capitalism needed to be tamed so that individuals could flourish and have the freedom to seek the purpose of their lives. It was not possible for individuals to thrive or reach their full potential, Berlin writes when summing up Taylor's views on Marx, under the yoke of the social inequalities and alienating labour relations created by the capitalist mode of production, or any social system for that matter, which threatens the intrinsic worth of persons.

Elizabeth Anscombe was another of Taylor's teachers during his time at Oxford. Anscombe reinforced in Taylor an appreciation for the intellectual heritage of Catholicism, particularly for ethics and moral theory. Anscombe was a leading proponent of Wittgenstein's philosophy, and she had studied under him and translated much of his work. Her work with Wittgenstein helped her to develop a unique action theory based on intention. She also contributed to moral philosophy, arguing that virtue was superior to the ethical systems developed by Kant and the utilitarians, and that virtue ethics served as a much simpler alternative to these, and to the social contract theorists (Driver 2014). Both of these topics have continued to interest Taylor. He finished his doctoral dissertation under the guidance of Berlin, and graduated in 1961. His topic was a critical investigation into behaviourism. The main concerns in his dissertation, which was published in book form under the title *The Explanation of Behaviour* (EB, 1964), was to analyse the compatibility of research methods used in the natural sciences with the social sciences, and to examine the debate between behaviourist researchers and those from the humanist tradition about whether or not we can say that human behaviour shows purpose, and so elevate the human condition above the rest of nature. As Taylor writes when setting out his investigation: 'the behaviour of human beings and animals shows a purposiveness which is not found elsewhere in nature' (EB, 3). Against this view, behaviourism suggests that human action is not really dissimilar to that of any other natural organism. After analysing learning theories, arguments about action and intention, and a range of psychological perspectives, Taylor concludes that the notion that humans and the higher primates show greater purpose in their behaviour, particularly as they are able to engage in goal achieving activities, remains an open question (EB, 272). Although he has not reached a conclusive answer, Taylor suggests that his and similar research moves the question forward. However, he also suggests that behaviourism, if it cannot prove more conclusively its own arguments, may well be defective. Given the subsequent decline in behaviourism, particularly that associated with the work of B. F. Skinner, Taylor's views here are somewhat prescient.

The relevance of this first book is that it allowed Taylor to investigate ideas central to this philosophical project. First, that a desire to mimic the methods of the natural sciences has had a detrimental impact on humanism and the social sciences, and that hermeneutical approaches are much more rewarding avenues for understanding human social arrangements (Geertz 1994: 83). Second, he was able to work out some of the intricacies of human action, which would later be an important element in his writings about how individuals support notions of uniqueness and difference in society (see Chapter 2). But study was not the only thing that kept Taylor occupied while at Oxford. While there he married Alba Romer and the couple started a family, eventually having five daughters. Alba was a social worker and artist, and their mutual interests converged on a number of levels.

After his time as a student and Fellow at All Souls College in Oxford, Taylor and his family returned to Canada so that he could fill dual university posts in political science at McGill University, and in philosophy at the Université de Montréal. He would hold these positions until 1971. This was also the time he became involved in Canadian politics. This political involvement would have a lasting impact, and throughout his career he has continued to contribute to Canadian politics, being especially interested in the issue of Canadian unification and multiculturalism. His first political foray was in 1962 as a candidate for the New Democratic Party, a Leftist party which advocates for social justice and fair work relations, as well as environmentalism, gender equality and minorities. Taylor was seeking a ministerial position in Canada's House of Commons. Much of the political debate in Canada over the last few decades has revolved around Canadian unification. Although Canada is today a multicultural nation, historically two cultural groups have dominated the public sphere for much of modern Canada's history. These are the French speaking Québécois and the English speaking Canadians. Tensions between the French and English speaking populations, and the added pressures that have arisen with greater levels of multiculturalism has, as we will see below, been a focus of Taylor's work on culture and politics in Canada, and in society generally.

In his first political campaign, Taylor came third, which served to fire his enthusiasm for politics. In 1963 he ran in another election, coming very close to winning. Not deterred by these losses, he launched a third campaign in 1964, this time losing to a political newcomer who would go on to have a significant impact on the Canadian political scene, Pierre Trudeau. Trudeau, after securing the leadership of the left leaning Liberal Party, would become the prime minister of Canada, serving from 1968 to 1979, and again from 1980 to 1984. Trudeau died in 2000, but his son, Justin, also of the Liberal Party, was elected prime minister in 2015. After losing to Trudeau in 1964, Taylor took one last shot at a political career in the 1968 election, but failed to win. This marked the end of his career in party politics in elections, but as we shall see, his experience in politics has provided him with valuable insights that he has shared in his research on a range of political issues, as well as informing his views on everything from multiculturalism to religion. Taylor's political career took place during a decade of transformation, and across the border in the United States the 1960s saw an upsurge of social movements as youth and civic-minded citizens sought to address issues such as racial and gender inequality, social inequity and the war in Vietnam. In Canada the force of these social changes was also being felt. As Peter Wagner (2008: 62) has suggested, the social movements of the 1960s can be understood as part of a 'project of emancipation' under modernity. Those protesting and expressing themselves through new lifestyle options understood their actions as a process of overcoming the limits set on self-expression and autonomy by modern capitalism, and the conformity that it engendered. Such conformity, as Herbert Marcuse (1964) points out, renders social life banal and 'one dimensional'. These social movements had an impression on Taylor, and he would revisit debates about personal autonomy and expressivism often.

The cultural shifts taking place during the 1960s also gave rise to increased nationalism in many parts of the world, especially in developing countries that were trying to shake off the yoke of colonialism (Fanon 1967; Jameson 1988: 180; Veer 2001). Having been colonised by England and France, Canada was also affected by this wave of nationalism, especially in Quebec (RS, 3). As Taylor points out, the idea of separatism and sovereignty has always been an issue in Quebec, but during the 1960s there was a pervasive feeling that the province had come of age and was ready to accede from the rest of Canada and claim its independence. These issues provided the backdrop for much of the political debate of the 1960s in Canada, at the time that Taylor was running for office, and they have done so many times since. But Taylor has long advocated caution over Quebec claiming sovereignty, and he does so for a number of reasons. First, Taylor argues that Quebec should remain a part of Canada to protect the welfare state which Canada has developed. Independence could put both English Canada and Quebec in a situation where they would have to trade more aggressively with the United States, which might demand the dismantling of welfare provisions. Second, as Taylor often highlights, Canada's close proximity to its neighbour, the USA, means that it is constantly under pressure to imitate the superpower next door, in economic and other matters. Taylor is cautious, however, about Canada adopting American-style free market economic policies, largely because of the social consequences of such a direction. Splitting Canada into two blocks will weaken both economies, perhaps making them more susceptible to America's free market ideology. Finally, Taylor points out that northern Canada is the source of abundant natural resources, and Quebec's independence risks cutting itself off from the benefits of future resource booms (RS, 144–5). Taylor also reminds readers and those in government that the place of Canada's Aboriginal peoples, and the protection of their diverse cultures and languages, needs to be taken into account when considering unity and nationhood (RS, 148). These are all reasons, he suggests, for Canadian unity. On the other hand, Taylor comments that if unity is the way forward, as he advocates, then Quebec should maintain its unique identity. For this reason the continued policy of bilingualism should be encouraged, and both Quebec and Canada as a whole should maintain their generous social policies regardless of pressure from the United States or Britain to dismantle its welfare state (RS, 142–3).

After his political work, Taylor settled down to some solid academic writing. He produced a major study on Hegel, which was published in 1975. Why a book on Hegel? A part of the answer to this question was the intense interest in Marx during this time in academia, particularly in the work of Marx's early years and his writings on alienation and the influence of Hegel on his work. The French philosopher Louis Althusser published his landmark study of the young Marx in 1965 (see Althusser 2005), arguing that in the writings of Marx there was a split evident between his youthful work and the output of his mature years. Althusser also drew attention to the role of Hegel in Marx's philosophical critique of capitalism (Althusser 2005: 77–8).

Taylor's view was that Althusser had attempted to purge Marx of his Hegelianism in favour of scientism (H, 556). Nevertheless, scholars seized on these developments in Marxist thought to return to the idealism of the young Marx and his work on alienation. The New Left, which was a movement in academia that sought to apply the insights of the young Marx to culture, undertook a number of major studies which applied the insights of the young Marx to modern society and consumerism. At the Institute for Social Research in Frankfurt, Germany (the Frankfurt School), scholars such as Herbert Marcuse turned their attention to the impact of alienation in areas as diverse as work and consumption, continuing a tradition of research that included contributions from Erich Fromm (1963), who had in the mid-1950s written about the psychological impact of alienation in the context of capitalism.

Taylor's justification for writing his book on Hegel was that, in his view, Hegel remains relevant to our rationalised, industrial society, even if his theories of dialectics and *Geist* have been abandoned. Modern society, with its emphasis on individualism and autonomy, has its origins in the Enlightenment, Taylor reminds us, and 'Hegel's philosophy claims to be the fulfilment of Enlightenment thought' (H, 539). For Taylor, Hegel's work provided a synthesis of Enlightenment rationalism with the spirit of expressivism and the freedom of Romanticism, two strands that are central to modern life. However, this synthesis is not without tension, as industrial, rational social systems work towards smothering the autonomy of individuals, who must struggle against technological and bureaucratic subjugation to realise their full potential (H, 540). This struggle against the alienation created by modern social life, especially by industrial production, is most effectively examined by Marx in his critique of capitalism. Marx, however, owes his understanding of how class conflict reoccurs throughout history, in the form of historical materialism, to Hegel's theory of dialectics.

A draft of *Hegel* was read and approved by Isaiah Berlin, and the book put Taylor on the academic map in philosophy. As anyone who has perused the work of Hegel will appreciate, being able to interpret and write clearly about his ideas to a wide audience is no mean feat, and the book showed that Taylor was a serious philosopher who could make important contributions to philosophical debate. Furthermore, in *Hegel* Taylor was able to connect the philosopher's work to contemporary debates in society. His comments on May 1968 in *Hegel*, for example, include his view that much of what was going on in Paris at that time was a drive towards higher levels of autonomy that were not just instances of what Berlin (1986: 122) defines as negative freedom (where our actions are free from coercion or restriction from others), but as a drive towards expressivism and creativity, something which 'is of more than merely historical interest' (H, 29). To that end, the book foreshadowed a number of themes which would occupy Taylor for much of his career, including modernity, the self, religion, language and history. *Hegel* was also a book in which Taylor showed that he could write long, sustained works that had a solid impact on scholarship, and although he has written a number of essays and shorter works, his other large-scale volumes, including *Sources of the Self* and *A Secular Age*, have generated in their own right many intellectual avenues for scholars engaging with his ideas. *Hegel* was followed up by *Hegel and Modern Society* (1979), which was a much shorter volume summarising the key points from the larger book, particularly their application to modernity.

After publishing the big book on Hegel, Taylor was appointed to the Chichele Chair as Professor in Social and Political Theory at Oxford in 1976. This position had previously been held by his teacher, Berlin, and attaining the chair attested to Taylor's high standing in academia. By this stage Taylor was in his forties, and as many would see it, he had reached the pinnacle of academic life and also had had a political career of sorts. But he was not thinking about resting on his laurels. He held the job at Oxford until 1981, after which he held numerous posts at universities around the world. But it was back to his much loved Canada that he was drawn, and he took up his longest held university position at McGill. In 1983 Taylor was invited by Pope John Paul II to attend a seminar series at Castel Gandolfo in Rome. Taylor was accompanied by a small number of intellectuals, including Hans-Georg Gadamer, Emmanuel Lévinas and Catholic theologian Johann Baptist Metz (Weigel 2005: 467). Each member presented a paper that was the subject of conversation among the group, including the Pope, and participants were able to carry on these discussions over dinner. John Paul II wanted to be kept abreast of what the best minds in the world were working on, and to explore common ground between their thought and that of the Catholic Church. Receiving an invitation to such an event reveals Taylor's growing reputation at this time as a public intellectual, and someone seen as having much to contribute to questions about the state of play in modern civilisation.

It was also during the 1980s that Taylor turned his attention to an analysis of the self in modern society. His interest in the self is evident in his work on Hegel. The recognition of the importance of the self for modern individualism was a breakthrough made by the philosophers of the Romantic period, including Herder and Rousseau (Solomon 1990). Taylor began work on a major study of the modern self, tracing its development over history. Published as *Sources of the Self* (1989), this long and detailed book soon became required reading across the academic spectrum, influencing debate in the humanities and social sciences. We will return to the arguments in *Sources of the Self* in more detail in the pages that follow, but put briefly, Taylor's central argument in the book is that the modern self is something unique in human history. Debates about selfhood go back to Plato and St Augustine, Taylor writes, but it is in modern times that a vision of the self as an autonomous entity gains force. Taylor focuses on three key issues which he sees as scaffolds for the modern self. These are, first, our sense of inwardness, or the idea that we understand ourselves at all, and that we have inner lives that can be plumbed and understood. Second, the affirmation of ordinary life, whereby the Reformers stressed that the mundane day to day activities of laypeople are as important to spiritual development as is the life of monks or ascetics. In the book, Taylor's training in history is evident. For Taylor, social and philosophical debates cannot be addressed in a vacuum that ignores history and social and cultural contexts. Third, the expressivism that emerged in the Romantic era, which countered the Enlightenment's emphasis on reason and rationality, is an essential ingredient of the modern self. That we can express our desires and wishes, through our lifestyles or through art or literature, are key elements, in Taylor's estimation, about what it means to be modern. The Romantic poets show us the ideal of this, and throughout the book Taylor draws on his interest in literature, both novels and poetry, to illustrate the impact of the Romantic mindset on the modern identity. It is these three areas of concern, Taylor argues, that help us to understand the self in modern times, and how it contrasts with – even if it might continue to hold elements recognisable to – pre-modern subjectivities.

Another element of the modern self that Taylor highlights in his book is its narrative character (Smith 2010: 50). This means that moderns are able to tell stories about themselves and their place in the world. The modern self is able to articulate a vision of the life that it wants to lead, and to put that vision into action and act on the world. People can reflect on their successes and failures, and give meaning to their lives. In this way, human beings are shown to be self-interpreting, something that makes us unique compared to the rest of nature. This ability to narrate and self-interpret is made possible because of the expressivist turn that took place in the counter-Enlightenment during the Romantic era, and the literary and philosophical movement that underpinned it, all of which Taylor discussed in *Hegel*. By expressing themselves, moderns are able to show that their life has a purpose and end goal. By being able to reflect on their lives moderns have acquired what Taylor calls 'radical reflexivity' (SS, 130–1), which means that they can think about their lives in the first person, as an 'I', and in doing so the connection between the self and the external world is separated, so that the world becomes a sphere which the 'I' can work on and exploit. This allows the modern subject to be able to think about their place in the world more deeply, and make changes so that they can lead lives that are more fulfilling. Moreover, through radical reflexivity we 'become aware of our awareness, try to experience our experiencing, focus on the way the world is *for* us' (SS, 130, emphasis in original). However, there is a dark side to this process. The constant need to be seeking a more fulfilling life can lead to anxiety and a state of permanent expectancy for things to get better, which may not square with the pressures and obligations of modern life (Smith 2010: 52–3). This is a point which Taylor revisits in his book *The Ethics of Authenticity*. Furthermore, Taylor concludes that the modern self has lost its connection to the transcendent and the moral values which faith inculcates in the personality. If life is a quest for greater levels of authenticity, Taylor seems to be suggesting that this search should lead individuals to higher ideals beyond this life. This point has raised a number of criticisms, including the claim that Taylor's ideas here are a thinly disguised championing of Christianity and a call for a return to traditional forms of faith that pre-date modernity (Skinner 1994: 46–7).

If *Hegel* put Taylor on the map in university philosophy departments around the world, *Sources of the Self* made him a 'household name' among intellectuals. The depth, richness and originality of the book attracted a number of fellow-travellers and critics. Whether readers agreed or disagreed about the details of Taylor's thesis, the general point of his book could not be ignored, and it was relevant to scholars in a number of disciplines. By the time *Sources* was published Taylor was approaching sixty, and so although the book made him somewhat famous in intellectual circles, it was a success that came late in life. Also, not long after the book came out and Taylor was enjoying some notoriety, his life was marked by profound sadness. His wife Alba passed away in 1990. All of his children were by this time independent, but this was still a difficult time as he adjusted to life without Alba's presence and support. During this period he kept busy with responding to the many reviews and criticisms of *Sources*, and touring the world giving lectures and keynote addresses at various universities. By 1995, however, things were on the improve, and in that year he married Aube Billard, an art historian, and he was made a Companion of the Order of Canada, one of the nation's highest honours. This award is one of many that Taylor has received, in recognition of his work in Canada and internationally. Other honours include the award of Grand Officer of the National Order of Quebec (2000), the Templeton Prize (2007) and the Kluge Prize (2015). In 2016 he was the first recipient of the Berggruen Prize, and has received a string of other prizes and awards. He is also a member of a number of international learned societies.

In the 1990s Taylor began work on a number of projects which were underpinned by reoccurring themes in his writings, including modernity and religion. He contributed lectures and books that examined how individuals negotiate modern social life. These include *The Ethics of Authenticity* (1992), the essay 'The Politics of Recognition' which Taylor wrote for the edited volume *Multiculturalism: Examining the Politics of Recognition* (1994), *A Catholic Modernity?* (1999) and *Varieties of Religion Today: William James Revisited* (2002). We shall return to each of these works in later chapters, but it is worth noting here what motivated Taylor to embark on these projects. Both *Ethics* and *Multiculturalism* were published while postmodern theories where being hotly debated in the academy. Postmodernity, according to Peter Wagner, builds on an understanding of society becoming post-industrial. Post-industrialism took place when Western nations began to move from a capitalism based on heavy industry and production, to economies emphasising services and knowledge work (Wagner 2012: 11–12). This in turn led to social change in these countries as they adapted to a new way of organising capitalism, and as workers sought new jobs in services and knowledge industries, such as sales work or research. Postmodernity challenges the idea of grand narratives in history, such as Marxism or Christianity, instead promoting the idea that knowledge is localised to specific times and places, and relative to particular cultures (Lyotard 1984). Postmodernity also challenges the idea of a secure self, instead suggesting that the self is fragmentary and made up of a collage of experiences and beliefs that the individual pieces together over time and which can change with the times.

Overall, postmodernity challenges the idea that morals and ethical rules, and interpretations of reality, come from external authorities such as religious organisations or experts. Rather, subjects become their own moral legislators, and interpret the world themselves as best they can. No one idea about right or wrong takes precedence in postmodernism, which means the adjudication of ethical dilemmas becomes a dilemma in itself. The consequences that derive from all of this can be devastating for our ability to construct schemas and theories about the social world, as Alexander points out in his critique of the work of Richard Rorty and Lyotard: 'The conclusion Rorty draws from the nonexistence of universals is that foundational arguments – general theoretical ones, in the language of social science – are impossible to make' (Alexander 1995: 106). Without metanarratives or grand theories, intellectual work turns to discussions of 'difference' as it is experienced by particular social groups. This can lead to the abandonment, in the social sciences, of universal theorising about sociological categories such as race, class or gender.

Taylor's work, however, while acknowledging that postmodern theories have much to offer our understanding of the current predicament, contests a number of the conclusions that derive from them. For Taylor, grand theorising can still offer much in how we understand the present and how we got here, as the wide sweep he takes in his most detailed studies in *Sources of the Self* and *A Secular Age* reveal. Furthermore, an overemphasis on individualism and a reliance on instrumental reason, which stresses the use of technology and the marketplace, as promoted by both modernity and postmodernity, can give rise to an atomised society of social agents only concerned with their own affairs and withdrawing from social participation (EA, 2–10). Moral subjectivism is also a result of increased relativism: 'By this I mean the view that moral positions are not in any way grounded in reason or the nature of things but are ultimately just adopted by each of us because we find ourselves drawn to them' (EA, 18). Furthermore, Taylor contributed his essay to *Multiculturalism* at a time when the issue of social pluralism was being debated in his native Canada. The unification of Quebec and English Canada was in question once again, and English Canada's growing diversity was unsettling for many Québécois, who feared that their status might be reduced to that of a large minority (RS, 161–2).

In *A Catholic Modernity?* and *Varieties of Religion Today*, Taylor focuses on religion, one of his long-held interests, entering the debate about faith in secular modernity. Taylor gave his lecture on Catholicism and modernity in 1999, and his interest in religion was further galvanised by international events. The attacks on the World Trade Centre in New York on 11 September in 2001 drew the world's attention to the use of religious ideals and rhetoric by those antithetical to American world hegemony, or as a justification for violence. This was not the first time that religion had been cited as the motivation for political terrorism (Juergensmeyer 2000), but 9/11 brought the issue front and centre. For decades many analysts had been happy to assume that religion would be assigned to the private sphere of social life as the forces of industrialism and globalisation pushed it to the margins of society, a situation predicted by the classical statement of secularisation theory. But now religion was again centre stage in domestic politics and foreign policy. Although some theorists had already argued that religion was a powerful force in political events (Huntington 1991; Casanova 1994; Kepel 1994), and that a potential clash of civilisations was possible in the not too distant future (Huntington 1997), most scholars continued to hold to the secularisation thesis, and believed that religion was a minor influence on social change in late modernity. 9/11 abruptly changed that perception. After the attacks in New York, scholars began to examine religion in earnest to assess its power to motivate individuals and groups around a common view of reality and a common cause. As we shall see in later chapters of this book, religion's sudden reappearance in the public forum prompts a number of questions about secularisation and modernisation, one being the way in recent times religion has become more important in some societies, and in the private lives of many individuals, while public institutions remain secular (see Norris and Inglehart 2004; Bruce 2011). These issues became part of the intellectual fabric as Taylor began his work on religion in earnest. As interesting as *A Catholic Modernity?* and *Varieties of Religious Experience Today* are, however, they were only precursors to a much more sustained treatment of religion that Taylor was working on.

In 2007 Taylor published a work on religion and secularism that was to generate intense debate in intellectual circles. *A Secular Age* argues that modern society is not as secular as many would like to think. Taylor criticises the secularisation thesis as being a subtraction story, arguing that such theories only reveal what society would look like minus religion, rather than adequately explaining what is really going on. Rather, for Taylor, many Western societies today are beset by a number of religious and spiritual options. Taylor offers three interpretations of secularism. Secularism 1 is about the secularisation of public spaces. As Taylor points out, these 'have allegedly been emptied of God, or of any reference to ultimate reality' (SA, 2). Taylor has in mind here the kind of secularism that patrols a clear division between church and state. Secularism 2 is about the kind of vanishing of belief predicted by secularisation theory. This theory states that as societies become highly industrialised with educated populations, we see a 'falling off of religious belief and practice, in people turning away from God, and no longer going to Church' (SA, 2). But for Taylor this is a subtraction story, an argument that takes religion out of society and then tries to examine what is left, and he is not at all convinced that it is an adequate way of understanding our current predicament. This leads Taylor to his third version of secularism. Secularism 3, which Taylor writes is what many modern societies are facing today, is about the spread of avenues for belief, or unbelief, where faith 'is understood to be one option among others, and frequently not the easiest to embrace' (SA, 3). Taylor emphasises that each of these three versions of secularism stand alone, but they are also interconnected. What Taylor tries to assess, for much of the book, is how we have arrived at this situation.

We will go into more detail about Taylor's discussion of religion in *A Secular Age*, and what his respondents have had to say about his ideas, later in this book. Since the publication of *A Secular Age* Taylor has not been idle. In early 2007 he and fellow academic Gérard Bouchard were commissioned by the Government of Quebec to produce a comprehensive report about multiculturalism in the province, and how this reflected multiculturalism in the rest of Canada and in other societies. A motivation for commissioning the report was the Quebec Government's desire for higher levels of successful accommodation of migrants in the province. For the report Taylor and Bouchard held a number of meetings, and thirty-one days of public hearings around Quebec to garner as much public participation as they could. They heard testimony on issues ranging from religion and secularism, language use and its impact on French, religious dress such as the wearing of the headscarf, to employment issues and inequality, and education, among others. In the final report (see BF) the authors made a number of recommendations for how multiculturalism in Quebec could be made more successful. The report once again shows

Taylor's deeply held interest and concerns for Canada and its future, and, as we shall see later when discussing the report further, reveals his active involvement in Canadian social life through his interests in both philosophy and politics.

In his eighties, Taylor collected the Kluge Prize, and published two new books. The Kluge Prize was jointly awarded to Taylor and Jürgen Habermas in 2015. His two new books reprise philosophical debates which he contributed to in former years, and which he feels have continued relevance. In *Retrieving Realism* (2015), co-authored with Herbert Dreyfus, the authors examine questions of epistemology. The authors argue that Cartesian dualism left us with an impoverished understanding of reality because Descartes, in declaring *cogito, ergo sum*, separated the mind from the world around it, creating an unbridgeable chasm between the self and the external world, a problem which Taylor highlighted in some of his early writings, including in *Hegel* (H, 6). This creates limits in our attainment and understanding of knowledge. The authors argue here that we are embodied beings, and that we experience the world through embodiment. Existing in bodies contests the Cartesian idea that we are pure mind; rather we have a direct and tactile relationship with the world around us, and we experience it as social beings, interpreting reality with the aid of others and their understanding of the world. In *The Language Animal* (2016) Taylor returns to his long-held interest in language and its importance for the development of the self, and as the phenomenon that sets humans apart from the rest of the natural world. He stresses that language is inherently social – we learn language from others and it situates us within specific communities. These books will no doubt precipitate wide debate in the intellectual world, just as Taylor's previous works have done.

Conclusion

As we have seen above, Charles Taylor's work has been closely interconnected to his times and to his own personal biography. His interests in multiculturalism, the individual, modernity, religion and a host of other issues have been influenced by the struggles and conflicts that he witnessed around him, growing up in Canada with its unique history of biculturalism and emergent multiculturalism and its Christianity, particularly Catholicism in Quebec, through to the social pressures that he has seen people engaged in in the many countries where he has worked and studied, including the pressures of life under modern capitalism. Taylor has also lived through times of intellectual paradigm shifts, as Marxism and structuralism, post-structuralism and postmodernism have all dominated the intellectual scene at one time or another. But Taylor has maintained a cool detachment from these academic paradigms, which goes some way in explaining the perennial interest of his work, and its staying power. Rather than convert to any of these perspectives, Taylor has watched from a position of objective distance as these paradigms and theoretical perspectives are hotly debated, offering his own perspective on the issues that they raised while maintaining a focus on his own areas of interest. In the chapters to follow we shall examine in greater detail Taylor's perspectives on some of the topics outlined above.

2

Meaning, Identity and Freedom

Introduction

In this chapter, the general philosophical arguments and suppositions of Charles Taylor's thought will be explored. It will be argued that Taylor's political perspective is intimately bound up with his general philosophical approach and that it is possible to perceive significant continuities in his thought. Given that Taylor's philosophical work is extensive and that it has been elaborated through detailed reflection on the history of philosophy, as well as interventions in current philosophical debates, the current overview is quite selective and indicative. The chapter will focus on four key philosophical themes that inform Taylor's political thought. These are the concern with identity, the problem of meaning, the idea of moral ontology and the notion of effective freedom. Taylor regularly seeks to clarify the larger background to political perspectives and controversies. And, in so doing, he draws on the philosophical elaboration of these four themes. It will quickly become apparent just how much these four themes are interconnected. Taylor's theoretical orientation is one that is critical of delimited frames of reference, such as one finds in political models founded on individual choice. Taylor, rather, shows how political positions are enfolded in larger concerns. His philosophical works seek to illuminate 'inescapable frameworks' of interpretation and the 'horizons' of understanding in which things appear. These horizons and frameworks, Taylor argues, enable individuals to perceive their lives and the world they inhabit as meaningful and significant (SS).

Taylor's philosophical approach is primarily grounded in the tradition of hermeneutic phenomenology, hence the use of terms like 'horizons of understanding'. For hermeneutic phenomenology, understandings are framed by horizons of interpretation that extend beyond the particular meaning or perception that is most present or in the foreground, yet these wider horizons and tacit background understandings are considered to be the condition for making sense of what appears or is expressed. In particular, modern hermeneutics has emphasised how language and culture are constitutive of horizons of understandings. At the same time, one of the distinctive features of Taylor's thought is its engagement with questions that are typically associated with the analytical tradition of philosophy. Notably, Taylor has addressed the question of what is human agency and his substantial discussions of the history of thought excavate the origins of the analytic tradition and its different lineages (SS; PA).

Taylor considers that the analytical tradition intersects at certain junctures with, what he terms, the modern perspective of 'naturalist consciousness' (SS, 5; 22). This is a broad current of thought that is antithetical or sceptical towards the kind of moral and ontological claims that Taylor seeks to advance. It rather accepts the rationalist and empiricist restrictions on knowledge that characterises modern science, being wary, for instance, of value claims and the qualitative distinctions between value claims (SS; PA). Taylor appreciates the precision and rigour of analytical philosophy, but contests some major facets of its perspective. He particularly disputes the implications that have been drawn in political theory from naturalist consciousness. In short, naturalism results, in Taylor's opinion, in misunderstandings about the nature of politics and it generates instrumental views of social relations that are inconsistent with their real character and individuals' experience of them (SS; HAL; PHS; PA).

Taylor seeks to sustain the connection between political thought and the moral standpoint of practical reason. His philosophy is meant to accurately represent the characteristics of practice and it prioritises this depiction of practices over the problem of epistemological justification. Taylor's first major work, *The Explanation of Behaviour* (EB), was significantly influenced by Merleau-Ponty's phenomenology and Taylor's later work incorporates a phenomenological concern with the standpoint and orientation of subjects towards the world (EB). In his words, he attempts 'to understand how agents are understanding the world when they are acting in one way or another' (Taylor in Bohmann and Montera 2014: 5). Similarly, the assumption of philosophical hermeneutics that meanings are shaped by a background horizon is basic to Taylor's philosophy. It partly explains the significance that Taylor attributes to language, as well as to his interest in disclosing the wider horizons of meaning that are presupposed in adopting particular political and theoretical positions.

One further comment is useful for grasping Taylor's general philosophical approach. As we mentioned in the introduction to this book,

Nick Smith has commented 'that Taylor's mode of philosophizing is problem-oriented rather than system-oriented. That is to say, he will write on a particular topic in accordance with what he takes the subject-matter to demand, rather than in accordance with the exigencies of systematization' (Smith 2002: 9). For this reason, the four key themes that are overviewed in this chapter, that is, the concern with identity, the problem of meaning, the idea of moral ontology and the notion of effective freedom, should not be interpreted as the rigid components of a system. Taylor's approach is more discursive and dialogical, inviting readers to participate in an incredibly erudite conversation.

Identity

The discussion of Taylor's biography and particularly his interest in the politics of his native Canada has already demonstrated how he was predisposed to engage with the question of identity. The question of identity can be broadly defined as concerned with the problem of defining who one is and living in a way that is consistent with this sense of who one is. The identity in question may be that of the individual person or it may be that of a collective, such as that of a group or nation. In the latter case of collective identity, it is a matter of who we are and how do we wish to live. These two senses of identity significantly overlap. Taylor highlights how personal identity is shaped, but not fully determined in its distinctiveness, by the sources of the larger collectively shared identity, especially emphasising the role of language, customs and practices. At the same time, Taylor argues that modernity is an epoch that has foregrounded the sense of the personal identity of the 'self' (SS).

The question of identity is central to Taylor's thinking about politics. Its importance goes beyond that of an explicit theme to which he has devoted major works, especially his magisterial study of the 'making of modern identity': *Sources of the Self*, and his manifold discussions of themes like nationalism and Canadian identity (SS; RS; DC). More importantly still, the theme of identity has an organising function in Taylor's thought. Many of his arguments radiate from his interpretation of identity and refer back to his position on identity. In one sense, this is primarily because Taylor seeks to show that our identity, or who we are, conditions how we approach things in the world. That is, identity provides orientation to how we relate to what happens in the world and what we would like to happen. For Taylor, this works the other way around as well, that is, our practices sustain and constitute our identity.

One of the central aims of Taylor's thought is to detail the connection between identity and 'the good' (SS; Abbey 2000; Joas 2000; Smith 2002). The 'good' represents the things that we desire and value. The good is therefore present in our moral and ethical practices. The larger sense of the moral that Taylor takes as integral to identity contrasts with the more restricted conception of the moral that has taken hold in modern philosophical discussions. According to Taylor:

> This moral philosophy has tended to focus on what it is right to do rather than on what it is good to be, on defining the content of obligation rather than the nature of the good life; and it has no conceptual place left for a notion of the good as the object of our love or allegiance. (SS, 3)

Given Taylor's claims about this orientation towards the good, the identity of individuals and groups has significant implications for their politics. For instance, whether one defines one's identity as national or cosmopolitan would influence the position that one adopts on the project of the European Union. In Taylor's work, the notion of identity provides critical insights into the underpinning political commitments of individuals and collectives. What this means in a democracy, for example, is that the underlying sense of identity is involved in respecting the dignity and rights of every individual who is a member of the political community, and possibly extending this respect to those who are not citizens as well (M; BF). While this claim about how politics is related to identity may appear uncontroversial, as will be discussed later, there are influential strands of contemporary political theory that argue that such commitments do not require a strong conception of identity and they work with models of politics that abstract from identity. In fact, they sometimes consider that the valorising of identity is a hindrance, rather than a condition of the fair and just treatment of all members of the community and strangers as well.

Taylor has written extensively on the philosophy of Hegel (H; HMS). Based on his interpretations of subjectivity and Spirit (*Geist*), Hegel contended that identity is never just a matter of external definition and labelling (see Habermas 1974; Hegel 1977). Identity depends on the agency of subjectivity or Spirit, because it involves processes of creation and reproduction. A particular identity will always have a specific content and meaning, hence what it means to be Canadian is something that is open to interpretation and dispute. To be Canadian may involve membership and some minimal commitment to the nation state of Canada, but it may involve a stronger set of values, such as a commitment to equal liberty and an appreciation of cultural diversity. For this reason, the interpretation of Canadian identity is reinforced by the actions of individuals in accordance with these values (BF; RS). In this sense, a collective identity is a practical creation and something that is derived from the interpretations of identity that inform and inflect these practices.

In *Sources of the Self* Taylor explores the different ways in which identity has been interpreted in the history of Western culture, such as how identity has been conceived in the moral terms of doing good works or interpreted as being able to rationally regulate and control oneself (SS). What is most important for Taylor, to reiterate, is that identity is intrinsically connected to some orientation to the good and that identity incorporates moral considerations. It is necessary to emphasise this at the outset because Taylor contends that some of the most influential strands of contemporary thought are founded on inadequate notions of the individual subject. Notably, this estimation applies to those perspectives that work with the limited suppositions of individual rational choice and, alternatively, those more structuralist approaches that reduce the capacities of individuals to their position in a social structure. In short, Taylor believes that these perspectives can only amount to a partial conception of the individual subject and that they abstract from the significant facets of identity, being particularly deficient with respect to the complex features of self-interpretation and the sense of meaningfulness that makes up an identity.

Taylor argues that the attributes of identity include things like political commitments and religious affiliation. These give content and definition to the sense of the good that goes together with a particular identity. In making these connections between identity and the good, Taylor endeavours to clarify the relationship that one has to oneself, as well as to others. Indeed, Taylor emphasises that any identity is the product of the relations and interactions with others. He describes these others as the 'interlocutors' of the 'self', drawing attention to the importance of discussion and communication in the making and sustaining of identity (SS). Taylor wants to show that identity is something that is not just confirmed through communication but that it is actually clarified and even, to a large extent, constituted in the process of articulation or expression. For the moment, it is sufficient to note that whether and how articulation and expression are possible is a political matter. Taylor is by no means, as he himself acknowledges, the first theorist to underline the importance of this facet of identity to politics. Nevertheless, his approach to the intertwinement of identity and the good is one of the features that distinguish his work among contemporary political theory. Taylor's 'moral ontology' will be sketched in greater detail below.

Taylor's claim that an identity presupposes meaning and frameworks of understanding is evident in his account of the formation of the modern identity or the sources of the self (SS). Modern individuals' sense of self is the product, Taylor shows, of a historical lineage of conceptions of identity, particularly the philosophical and religious views of the subject or self. In *Sources of the Self*, Taylor 'attempts to define the modern identity in describing its genesis', focusing:

> on three major facets of this identity: first, modern inwardness, the sense of ourselves as beings with inner depths, and the connected notion that we are 'selves'; second, the affirmation of ordinary life which develops from the early modern period; third, the expressivist notion of nature as an inner moral source. (SS, x)

In *Sources of the Self* Taylor demonstrates that these different constituents of modern identity have had a significant bearing on modern political theory and practice, irrespective of whether 'inwardness', 'expression' and 'ordinary life' are properly recognised (SS). It does, however, make a significant difference, in Taylor's view, whether these sources of identity are recognised and subjected to reflection. The influence of these lineages of identity is evident in the modern models of the political subject as a rational and self-possessing agent, and the notions of freedom that will be discussed shortly. It should be clear by now that Taylor's interpretation of identity is thoroughly grounded in his accounts of meaning and morality. For instance, he places considerable emphasis on the narration of identity. Narration serves to bind together the past, the present and the future; it likewise connects the individual's biography with that of the larger collective history, such as that of a nation, community or city. Most importantly, for Taylor, narration constitutes a moral source and, therefore, a way of articulating morality (SS).

It is worthwhile noting some of the contemporary social and political developments that have reinforced Taylor's engagement with identity. These will be subsequently shown to be significant to the elaboration of his political theory. One of the major developments in capitalist nation states has been the increasing diversity of the social make-up of communities, particularly owing to migration patterns and more general social changes that have altered identities, including difference in the life experience of generations. The patterns of migration have contributed to the emergence of multiculturalism. Similarly, the past half century has witnessed the development of so-called 'identity politics', which is sometimes contrasted with the politics of class relations, with its focus on matters of material distribution. The feminist movement is regularly classified as a major strand of identity politics, as reflected in the feminist slogan that the 'personal is political'. The contemporary politics of 'first nation people' have likewise been seen as framed by concerns about the recognition of distinct identities and cultural difference. All of these political expressions of identity have received considerable articulation in Canada and other Western societies. More broadly, in social theory, Taylor's interlocutor Jürgen Habermas has proposed that the major conflicts of capitalist society are increasingly taking the form of crises of identity, owing to the erosion of the conditions for the communicative reproduction of social identities, institutions and cultural traditions (Habermas 1976; 1987a).

The centrality of identity to Taylor's thought is clearly connected to these various developments concerned with the struggles over the recognition of social and political identities (see Chapter 3; M). Likewise, identity is a theme that derives from the distinctive internal priorities of Taylor's philosophical perspective. The combination of these two considerations has come to structure much of Taylor's work on politics. Broadly stated, Taylor seeks to understand the implications of diversity and to offer accounts of how different identities can relate to one another in a mutually affirming manner. Taylor wants to show how the deep commitments that are associated, in his view, with identity can be compatible with plurality or diversity. Further, Taylor believes that it is possible to articulate a common identity, with shared interests, under these conditions as well.

Meaning

Meaning is an integral concern of Taylor's thought. In a trivial sense, meaning is a consideration that is present in all forms of human understanding, inquiry and knowledge. Taylor's interest in meaning is much deeper and takes the form of a philosophical anthropology. Philosophical anthropology is concerned with the nature of the human being and it aims to clarify the universally shared capabilities of human subjects (Taylor 1988). Meaning, Taylor argues, is something that is bound up with the human condition. He embraces the philosopher Maurice Merleau-Ponty's statement that humans are condemned to meaning (SS; Merleau-Ponty 1962). In particular, Taylor argues that humans are 'self-interpreting animals' (SS). This implies that humans live through meaning and always stand in some relation to meaning. The notions of frameworks and horizons, which were discussed at the beginning of this chapter, are key elements of Taylor's explication of this human propensity for self-interpretation. According to Taylor:

> Frameworks provide the background, explicit or implicit, for our moral judgements, intuitions or reactions . . . To articulate a framework is to explicate what makes sense of our moral responses. That is, when we try to spell out what it is that we presuppose when we judge that a certain form of life is truly worthwhile, or place our dignity in a certain achievement or status, or define our moral obligations in a certain manner, we find ourselves articulating inter alia what I have been calling here 'frameworks'. (SS, 26)

The contention that humans are self-interpreting animals may, again, appear relatively uncontroversial. However, Taylor claims that many currents of modern thought exhibit a forgetfulness concerning meaning. In short, they do not consider the meaningfulness or significance of what they claim. As we will see, Taylor deploys variations of this argument in many contexts and he does not limit its critical application to modern philosophical positivism. Positivism does not so much forget meaning and significance as embrace the distinction between facts and value, as well as assimilate the human sciences to the methodology of the natural sciences. Taylor believes that this positivist position is contradictory and insufficient, because it has to draw its justification from an interpretation of the value of the distinction between facts and values. In so doing, positivism neglects key features of the human sciences, like the role of interpretation, which is already present in human interaction and is intrinsic to its investigation. Likewise, the philosophical tradition from which positivism derives, Taylor argues, depends on a limited view of the role of language in the constitution of meaning. In fact, Taylor claims that modern reductionist conceptions of knowledge actually depend on a larger framework of meaning and that this dependency generally remains either latent or unrecognised. Taylor makes similar claims in relation to several influential perspectives in contemporary political theory, such as those of rational choice theory and liberal procedural theories of justice, which might be considered to involve somewhat similar reductions of meaning to the dictates of method or procedure (PA; see Chapter 4). Now, the parallels between these political perspectives and naturalistic scientific consciousness are not coincidental, as Taylor argues that the reduction of meaning originates from the same historical movements in thought.

One finds another variant of this argument in Taylor's approach to secularity (SA). He argues that it is not sufficient to explain secularism in terms of the empirical reduction in the amount of church attendance or the modern institutional separation of church and state. This is not to say that these tendencies are unimportant, but, rather, secularism needs to be understood in terms of *meaning* and therefore the 'framework' of understanding and interpretation. Specifically secularism is related to the emergence of the 'this-worldly' immanent frame in modernity (SA; see Chapter 6). Taylor's contributions to the political discussions of religion and secularity hinge a great deal on these assumptions about meaning and the implications that it holds. Taylor believes that 'subtraction' narratives of a secular age are insufficient. In his opinion, it is necessary for there to be a response to the demand or quest for meaning.

The most significant version of the contrast that Taylor draws between more restrictive notions of consciousness and more expansive horizons of meaning is probably that between two traditions in Western thought of theorising language. This contrast is particularly important because the position on language is a kind of switching point between the reductionist conceptions of meaning and more expansive understandings. Without going into the historical and technical details of the distinction between the two approaches to language that will be discussed later, it is sufficient to note here that the more reductionist perspective regards language as primarily serving the purpose of designation, that is, to name, categorise, classify and pick out an object or referent, whereas the opposite standpoint emphasises the creative and constitutive quality of language (LA; PA; see Chapter 8). That is, the latter standpoint, which Taylor associates with the critique of the rationalist and empiricist conceptions that limit language to designation, is concerned with how language constructs a world of meaning and is integral to the entire formation of culture. For reasons that should already be apparent, Taylor endorses this more expansive view of language and meaning. He argues that language is bound up with the entire life-form and culture; language especially enables the expression of identity, the articulation of values, and forms of poetic creation. It follows, in Taylor's opinion, that language should be understood holistically, rather than as an aggregation of individual perspectives.

The expansive view of language as a form of creative expression was initially articulated by authors associated with Romanticism and Taylor's concern with the broad implications of the Romantic tradition will be outlined in the next chapter. Language is an important link between meaning and identity. Taylor considers that the processes of articulation is formative of identity, since one makes and consolidates one's identity in the very process of articulation and in relation to interpretation that is expressed (SS). The Romantic tradition not only anticipates this position but its view of subjectivity has significantly shaped modern consciousness and its interpretation of human freedom. Further, Taylor's later works on modern social imaginaries represents an attempt to clarify horizons of understanding and the corresponding practices (MSI).

Taylor's characterisation of meaning is by no means distant from his political theory. In fact, the conceptions of meaning and language are critical to his distinctive political perspective and the normative position that it is meant to express. The different ways in which this is the case will become apparent over the course of this book, but a couple of key dimensions of how the problem of meaning configures Taylor's politics is worth noting at this point. First, Taylor's approach to politics and related concerns, particularly those of morality and ethics, generally involves explicating the broad background context. As has already been noted, Taylor wants to show the larger meaning that lies behind and informs political concerns. In this sense, political concerns are subject to hermeneutic interpretation of the horizon of meaning that situates and locates them. This is the opposite of a narrow and instrumentalist approach to politics. Second, language and meaning is something that is never simply for a single individual and nor can it be the outcome of an addition of solitary individuals, as may be proposed by atomistic conceptions. Rather, language is something that is always collectively shared. This points towards Taylor's concern with community or the common way of life. For instance, he states this in the following terms: 'The language I speak, the web I can never fully dominate and oversee, can never be just *my* language, it always *our* language' (SS, 99).

In a number of works, Taylor discusses how language creates a speech community and it is integral to the formation of a sense of a shared and common way of living together. The normative commitments that follow from this perspective have regularly seen Taylor viewed as a communitarian, but it is more consistent with his own self-understanding to define Taylor' political position as that of a 'holistic liberal' (PA). Nevertheless, it is important to appreciate the shared and cooperative character of language. That is, the sense in which Taylor considers that language is a collective enterprise, whereby we are with one another, is to recall Hegel's view of intersubjectivity (see Honneth 2014). Taylor's statement about the mutuality of conversation clearly brings out this position and how, in his view, it is through linguistic communication that we transcend the isolated standpoint of the single individual.

> What the conversation opener does is to make it a matter for us: we are now attending to it together. It is important to see that this attending-together is not reducible to an aggregation of attending-separately . . . A conversation is not the coordination of actions of different individuals, but a common action in the strong, irreducible sense: it is *our* action. It is of a kind with – to take a more obvious example – the dance of a group or a couple, or the action of two men sawing a log. Opening a conversation is inaugurating a common action. (PA, 189)

Language may be a way in which we overcome our isolated perspective, but, in reality, there is never such a truly isolated perspective once there is language. The standpoint that takes the single individual consciousness as the foundation of knowledge and meaning, Taylor argues, is rather a product of a particular interpretative framing associated with a strand of modern thought (SS; PA). At the same time, by placing so much importance upon language, Taylor invites a specific criticism in response. Karl Smith argues, for instance, that 'Taylor's theory of the narratively constructed self does not adequately account for the unsayable dimensions of the individual subject' (Smith 2010: 50). Finally, from his first works in philosophy, Taylor has provided technical accounts of perception and behaviour. These interpretations of perception and action are strongly inflected by phenomenological considerations and they attempt to clarify individuals' lived experience. In many respects, Taylor's aim is to show how meaning is present in our experience of the world.

Moral Ontology

The centrality of the interconnection between identity and 'the good' to Taylor's entire theoretical and political project has already been highlighted. To fully appreciate Taylor's conception of this interconnection, however, it is necessary to sketch some of the key features of his 'moral ontology'. The notion of a moral ontology is admittedly complex and difficult, since it addresses questions concerning what lies behind and underpins individuals' moral commitments and understandings of morality. There is another equally fundamental reason for emphasising the importance of Taylor's moral ontology and its relevance to the justification of his various arguments. That is, that it is not difficult to contend that there is a large amount of evidence of contemporary individuals' relative indifference to moral considerations. This probably suggests that individuals are mainly pragmatic and self-interested with respect to the good. Perhaps even that there is a certain reluctance on their part to engage strongly with moral considerations, either because they do not have a developed moral outlook or simply that they want to avoid the potential conflicts that may ensue from opposed moral standpoints. At the level of an empirical description, Taylor agrees with elements of this account of contemporary individuals, although it is accepted in a somewhat qualified manner that will be clarified later. But, at a deeper level, Taylor's moral ontology is precisely meant to show that this assessment is wrong and misleading.

Taylor wants to demonstrate with his moral ontology that it is impossible for individuals to be truly indifferent and disengaged from morality. One of the formats of Taylor's response to claims about the self-interested and pragmatic character of individuals has already been identified. Taylor argues that such a view represents only a particular strand of thinking about morality that has developed historically in Western society and that it has its roots in specific interpretations of the self. In short, this utilitarian and instrumental approach to morality works, in Taylor's opinion, with rather narrow parameters. It draws on a notion of gaining 'control through disengagement' (SS, 160). Taylor develops this point in a way that clarifies how this notion enabled a 'mechanistic' view of the world to take hold. It explains why he considers that approaching morality from such a standpoint involves a certain misunderstanding of the core problem of practical reason or moral action.

> Disengagement is always correlative of an 'objectification' . . . Objectifying a given domain involves depriving it of its normative force for us. If we take a domain of being in which hitherto the way things are has set norms or standards for us, and we take a new stance to it as neutral, I will speak of our objectifying it. (SS, 160)

The major dimension of Taylor's response to claims concerning the relative indifference and disengagement of individuals finds its justification in his moral ontology. Taylor wants to argue that moral orientations are part of our make-up as human beings. In other words, Taylor's moral ontology is an extension of his philosophical anthropology, one that highlights the integrity of moral orientations with identity and human agency (SS; PA). These ontological contentions differ from more limited justifications of morality, such as those based on the factual presence of morality within particular cultures or the functional role of the moral in maintaining social order and enabling social integration. In overviewing the details of Taylor's moral ontology, it is important to keep in mind the claims that have been outlined with respect to his interpretation of meaning. Specifically, the importance that Taylor attributes to the practical stance that individuals adopt towards the world and the background understanding or horizon of meaning. Taylor believes that this is the means by which he can elucidate moral practices, rather than simply present a particular theory of morality and its justification. 'By its very nature', Taylor suggests,

> practical reason can only function within the context of some implicit grasp of the good, be it that mediated by a practice to which this good is internal or by practices which contribute to it as cause and constituent, or by contact with paradigm models, in life or story or however. (Taylor 1994: 35)

Taylor is particularly well known for the thesis that human agency and identity involve strong evaluations (SS). The concept of strong evaluations implies a comparison and Taylor originally drew on Harry Frankfurt's distinction between 'first' and 'second order' desires. The first order desires are the basic and rudimentary desires that humans share with other animals, like those of the desire for food, shelter or the avoidance of danger. There can be little dispute that humans are oriented towards the satisfaction of these first order desires. Yet, humans have an additional capacity to evaluate their desires and to assess how they relate themselves to these first order desires, as well as their modes of satisfying them. In particular, humans engage in processes of evaluation in establishing preferences between desires and determining their relative importance. This means that 'second order' desires are desires about desires (see Abbey 2000; Smith 2002).

Taylor emphasises the qualitative character of these features of human agency and valuing. Strong evaluations imply a greater depth of commitment and, significantly in Taylor's view, articulation (SS). Hence, he suggests that an individual understands herself or himself on the basis of the articulation of values and the reflexivity that articulation enables about moral orientations. For Taylor, weaker evaluations are basically interchangeable preferences that have less bearing on the identity of the individual subject. For instance, one may prefer gelato to a custard tart, or vanilla gelato on Monday and chocolate gelato on Tuesday. These are all desires or appetites, but satisfying one over the other does not reflect a deeper engagement or 'strong evaluation'. Of course, it is possible to enact such a desire on the basis of a strong evaluation, such as where one perhaps chooses gelato because of the less exploitative labour conditions that may hypothetically be involved. Strong evaluations are desires that are ranked as more worthy and that may elicit, according to Taylor, a sense of admiration or contempt (SS; PHS; HAL). Put differently, one could suggest that there is more of the self or an identity at stake in a strong evaluation and, consequently, that manifest differences in identity follow from an individual's acting either in accordance with the strong evaluation or not. The point, for Taylor, is that strong evaluation generally involves more explicit reflection and strength of conviction than more weakly evaluated desires. The strong evaluation is, effectively, more strongly founded:

> our understanding essentially incorporates our seeing ourselves against a background of what I have called 'strong evaluation'. I mean by that a background of distinctions between things which are recognised as of categoric or unconditioned or higher importance or worth, and things which lack this or are of lesser value. (HAL, 3)

Taylor's moral ontology has so far pointed to the basic attributes of humans and their propensity to engage in strong evaluations. If humans did not have these qualities then social life would, on this view, be fundamentally and radically different. Unlike the emphasis of a good deal of contemporary moral and political philosophy on justification, Taylor is primarily concerned with how we experience and enact morality. He argues that we feel the moral in an especially compelling manner. The position that Taylor develops is, however, 'anti-subjectivist' in a particular sense. Taylor argues that moral orientations are experienced as something that does not simply emanate from our own subjectivity; rather, the moral is something that we feel an obligation towards and that it is appropriate to act in accordance with. Strong evaluations, Taylor claims, are 'normative for desire. That is, they are seen as goods which we ought to desire, even if we do not' (PHS, 120). In fact, Taylor claims that the moral is truly experienced in an embodied manner. Yet, the moral is connected to strong values that go beyond ourselves and that are present in the culture. The 'good' or the moral is not in opposition to our subjectivity, but it cannot be collapsed into it. The 'good' possesses a sense of externality. In Taylor's opinion, we have a sense of being 'moved' by the good.

This contention concerning the qualitative character of the moral ontology can be read in different ways and, to our mind, Taylor never entirely resolves them. One sense is that the moral is experienced as something that imposes itself on us, but is nevertheless dependent on our volition as subjects. The other meaning is the moral is an ontological given and that it is properly anti-subjective (see Smith 2010). Needless to say, considerably different implications, especially for politics, follow from these alternatives. For instance, it has implications for how one reads Taylor's position on topics like the nature of community and secularity. Taylor may believe that what is more important than the epistemological status of this distinction is the clarification of the human experience of how the sense of moral being there is constitutive of morality. Nevertheless, there is possibly more at stake here than Taylor admits and much of the controversy concerning the implications of his work turns on it. Without going into the critical debates, Taylor never states that religious orientations are more likely to meet his criteria of strong evaluations and, in principle, there is no need to suggest it; however, it is clear that many critical commentators have read his work this way (see Skinner 1994).

All of this raises the further question of whether Taylor is really proposing a traditional ontology or does he really mean something else by the term ontology. One can see how this may have considerable bearing on adjudicating on the implications of his moral ontology. To this end, Steven White (2000) is largely right to claim that Taylor shifts between strong and weak versions of ontology. In White's terms, strong ontologies are about the nature of being itself, the way the world is and human nature itself, whereas weak ontologies are concerned with the 'stickiness of subjectivity', based on its embodiment, and conditions of everyday life. 'Weak ontologies allow us to think and feel the world differently than others do, whereas strong ontologies stress common fate' (Redhead 2002: 175). Now, without going into the exact merits of White's distinction between strong and weak ontologies, it does point to the different ways in which Taylor's philosophy can be read and how the claims about moral ontology seem to alternate in his work (see White 1997; 2000).

What we can say for sure is that Taylor's position on the good is opposed to 'deontological' theories of justice and morality. Deontological theories make universalistic claims on the basis of an abstraction from particular contexts and the ethical practices that apply in those circumstances. Deontological theories formulate principles of justice that are meant to apply in all times and places. Kant's notion of the categorical imperative, that is, that of acting according to a rule that we would will to be a universal norm is probably the most important source of deontological moral theories. In a qualified manner, Habermas' discourse theory of justice is deontological in its presentation of the discourse principle: 'Just those action norms are valid to which all possibly affected could agree as participants in rational discourse' (Habermas 1996: 107).

There are a number of commentators who have questioned whether Taylor sets up a false binary between his claims about moral practices and those of the demands of theoretical justification (see Smith 2002). Why should we not want to meet demands for justification and is not the process of justification a condition of the claim that our moral conceptions are ones worthy of universal assent? Taylor contends that the process of justification should not be equated with the fulfilment of procedures, since procedures are external to the problem of the moral and the way that individuals relate to it. Rather, Taylor proposes that the problem of justification is a hermeneutic one of understanding and interpretation. He argues that the validity of convictions should derive from the acceptance of the 'best account' (PA). In the context of this debate, Taylor's approach has the decided advantage of better connecting with the moral experience of individuals. For instance, it is not difficult to perceive how the best account can match with narrative understandings of identity. Nick Smith makes the implications of Taylor's departure from deontological and procedural approaches to morality clear in a decisive manner that deserves to be quoted extensively. Smith's critical commentary reflects the alternative intentions of Habermas' discourse theory of justice:

> At first sight, it does not seem that Taylor's model is well-suited for understanding the moral use of practical reason. It is not set up to test the universalizability of norms. It does not of itself incorporate a mechanism for including the point of view of all others, a mechanism which seems to be necessary if the outcome of practical reason is to reflect the general and not just an individual's or a group's interest. And it is not geared towards establishing the impartiality of norms, a feature we expect of justice. If we want our model of practical reason to show how claims to impartiality can be justified, if we want it to supply a rationally grounded means of testing the 'moral' status of normative claims – with all that implies for their obligatory force – we will have to look elsewhere. Taylor's model simply does not seriously address the issue of the rational foundation of morality construed this way. (Smith 2002: 109)

Freedom

The notion of freedom is a recurrent theme in Taylor's work. The interpretation of freedom that Taylor develops informs almost every aspect of his thought. It should be apparent already that some assumptions concerning freedom are present in Taylor's positions on identity, meaning and morality. It will equally become clear that these three organising categories contribute to the distinctive qualities of Taylor's notion of freedom. Since the implications of Taylor's notion of freedom will be explored in detail at various junctures over the course of this volume, the current discussion will be limited to setting the scene, so to speak, for these latter analyses and it will explicate some of the details of Taylor's substantial critique of the concept of negative liberty. In some ways, this critique exemplifies, in short, many of the political arguments that Taylor advances, especially those relating to his interventions into contemporary theoretical debates. Taylor's conception of freedom is broader than that of the notion of freedom as self-determination, which implies independent decisions and choices. Rather, Taylor's conception involves, in addition, the idea that freedom implies the realisation of particular values and life-commitments, as well as the freedom of self-expression and creative agency (see Honneth 1995b)

It is not by chance that Taylor initially developed the distinction between strong and weak evaluations in a paper on 'What is human agency?' (HAL). One's conception of agency will have significant implications for the interpretation of freedom. Taylor's work can be seen to be exploring the complexity of the relationship between agency and freedom. Indeed, it will be shown that Taylor seeks to correct the misunderstanding of alternative theories of freedom, particularly the crude liberal version of negative liberty. The reasons why misunderstandings concerning freedom have gained traction is partly to do with the history of twentieth-century politics and the disastrous consequences of some of the collective projects associated with nationalism and socialism. On the one hand, the threat of totalitarianism formed the counterpoint for the consolidation and elaboration of the liberal notion of freedom as that of negative liberty, that is, freedom 'from external interference by others, be these governments, corporations or private persons' (PHS, 211). On the other hand, the increasing significance in liberal democracies of the law and courts in determining the rights of individuals and the scope of agency has not only influenced the development of procedural theories of freedom and justice, but it has contributed, in Taylor's opinion, to a delimited conception of the enactment of freedom and the corresponding notion of the subject. Taylor does not actually deny the importance for freedom of such developments in liberal democracies as the legal institutionalising of rights (see Dworkin 1977). Rather, he contests how these developments are regularly understood, or misunderstood. In short, Taylor places greater emphasis on social practices in his accounts of freedom and this is related to his views on identity, meaning and morality.

The historical perspective of Taylor's work constitutes a major component of his explorations of freedom. Broadly stated, Taylor contends that freedom is one of the pre-eminent ideals of modernity. Modernity has, to varying degrees, institutionalised freedom. For this reason, Taylor considers that there is some justification to the liberal vision of progress and, indeed, it would be possible to argue that the different phases of Taylor's work has each involved some interrogation of the nexus between freedom and modernity. Interestingly, Taylor's position on the nexus between freedom and modernity remains roughly the same across these phases, but there are clearly various refinements in his conceptualisation of modernity, such as in connection with the elaboration of the notion of social imaginaries and the engagement with the politics of recognition (MSI; M). Taylor's endorsement of the modernist vision of freedom is not unequivocal. He proposes positions on the limitations to the realisation of freedom and highlighted the deleterious consequences of certain attempts to realise or enact freedom. The fact that Taylor takes quite evaluative positions on the historical realisations of freedom and projects for the radical expansion of freedom is a distinguishing feature of his political thought. It is something that will be returned to in later chapters. The content of his evaluations constitute a point of contrast with the work of other authors on the modern social imaginary, particularly that of Cornelius Castoriadis and Claude Lefort (Castoriadis 1987; 1991; 1997a; Lefort 1986; 1988).

Taylor wants to develop a notion of freedom that overcomes the juxtaposition of the individual and collective. As we have seen, Taylor believes that this is one of the major implications of the modern appreciation of language. Further, Taylor's view of freedom is connected to the nexus between identity and the good. It implies that if you are unable to realise the good to which you subscribe then you are not completely free, since you cannot actualise your identity. The implication of this position is a notion of freedom that is oriented toward self-actualisation. In some respects, the good has been principally defined in modernity in terms of freedom and this contention is something that Taylor's account of the modern social imaginary of a moral order of mutual benefit seeks to detail (MSI). His book *Modern Social Imaginaries* traces the social institutionalising of norms of mutual autonomy and the consolidation of a particular interpretation of freedom as a horizon of understanding that shapes modern individuals' practices.

Taylor's teacher Isaiah Berlin is famous for his distinction between negative liberty and positive liberty (Berlin 1986). Negative liberty essentially refers to the freedom of individuals from interference by the state and other authorities. It signifies a space for independent actions by individuals. The notion of negative liberty reflects the historical view of liberalism and its conception of the precedence of private individuals relative to the state and society. Berlin described this interpretation of individual independence as negative freedom because it does not entail some positive description of freedom, that is, it does not define some positive content as the objective and meaning of freedom. Rather, the notion of negative liberty leaves the exercise of freedom entirely up to the individuals and its main point is to place restrictions on the potential 'obstacles' to individual choice and action. In a general sense, negative liberty was important to the development of the independence of civil society from the state. Its point was to place restrictions on the state and other authorities, hence it can be seen to be connected with the liberal freedoms of conscience and freedom of assembly. Taylor is nevertheless dissatisfied with the notion of negative liberty.

In the paper that he wrote on 'what's wrong with negative liberty', Taylor gives the following answer to his question (PHS). First of all, it is not clear whether the notion of negative liberty actually represents or refers to freedom. Rather, the notion of negative liberty, as freedom from interference, refers to a potential for freedom. Negative liberty, Taylor argues, is an 'opportunity concept', it is not necessarily an 'exercise concept', hence it is not clear that freedom can or will be realised on the basis of 'negative liberty'. On Berlin's definition, positive liberty, by contrast, is an 'exercise concept', it concerns the actual enacting of freedom and the substantive conditions that enable the realisation of freedom (Berlin 1969; see Browne 2017a). For instance, the ability to participate as a citizen probably depends on having access to sufficient material resources to enable involvement. Significantly, Taylor's conception of agency informs the contrast that he draws between these characteristics of negative and positive liberty. According to Taylor, the absence of interference extends in notions of negative liberty to not making claims about what agents may want or desire (PHS). In other words, negative liberty is less concerned with how individuals will exercise their freedom; it accepts the liberal view that it is up to these individuals to determine. Taylor argues that positive liberty, as an exercise concept, by contrast, 'requires that we discriminate among motivations. If we are free in the exercise of certain capacities, then we are not free, or less free, when these capacities are in some way unfulfilled or blocked' (PHS, 215).

Taylor's notion of freedom takes into account whether individuals are able to actualise their values. On this view, individuals are not free if there are internal, as well as external, obstacles to their being sufficiently self-determining to be able to actualise these values. As we will see, Taylor's debates with strands of political liberalism extend and refine this assessment of the insubstantial character of negative liberty. Taylor's second major line of criticism is related to the points made above about the conclusions that have been drawn about freedom from the negative and oppressive dimensions of twentieth-century history. Berlin's opposition to interpretations of positive liberty in collective terms informs his alternate conception of negative liberty (Berlin 1969). Berlin highlighted the dangers of collectivist visions of freedom and the potentials for undermining freedom in the attempt to establish the positive condition for its realisation. In particular, there is the danger of subordinating the individual and particular to the collective or general interest. Taylor does not dispute the oppressive renderings of freedom in modernity, but he believes that Berlin's argument is a misinterpretation of the concept of positive liberty. He argues that positive liberty has 'no necessary connection with the view that freedom consists purely and simply in the collective control over the common life, and that there is no freedom worth the name outside a context of collective control' (PHS, 212).

Conclusion

It is undoubtedly the case that in focusing on four core dimensions of Taylor's general philosophy some of his theory's nuances have been neglected. Even so, the four themes represent general suppositions that are present in Taylor's discussion of other topics and problematics. This implication of the four themes should be readily discernible in the later chapters' discussions, although the precise articulation of the questions of identity, meaning, moral ontology and effective freedom may not always be transparent. Before proceeding, it may be worthwhile noting three broad criticisms of Taylor's theory that are relevant to its overall assessment. First, prior to Taylor's later works on a secular age and a Catholic modernity, several critics suggested that Taylor's concern with meaning and morality are conditioned by theological considerations that are not always explicit (Mulhall 2004; Skinner 1994). Second, there is no disputing Taylor's engagement with political differences and their meaningful expression, but it is less clear whether his approach is able to deal with certain orders of political conflict. It has already been noted, following Nick Smith, that Taylor may underestimate the salience of procedures to resolving antagonisms and ascertaining the general interest (Smith 2002). Third, Taylor endorses the alleviation of injustice and the transformation of oppressive social relations, yet it may be the case that Taylor's approach's emphasises lead to certain oversights and to, what Anthony Appiah describes as, a fairly accommodating view of existing collective identities (see Appiah 1994: 156).

These three lines of criticism are by no means straightforward and it may turn out that they are not completely valid objections. However, they raise important questions about the priorities of Taylor's political theory and the implications of its general philosophical underpinnings.

In relation to the latter, it has been shown that Taylor's philosophy explores questions that are basically unavoidable, because they are bound up with the human condition and the nature of social relations. He proposes a moral ontology that seeks to articulate how individuals are oriented towards the 'good' and a philosophical anthropology that centres on the problem of meaning. Although these constitute complex theoretical questions, Taylor attempts to clarify how the relationship between the identity of individuals and the good is realised in behaviour and practices. In this way, Taylor develops an account of agency that is based on the idea of 'strong evaluations' and an interpretation of freedom that is concerned with the positive liberty of actualising one's identity and the collective context that makes this possible. The latter considerations have a significant bearing upon Taylor's political standpoint of holistic liberalism. Similarly, various forms of linguistic experience are central to the explication of his theory, especially those of the shared identification that derives from conversation over matters of common interest and the self-understanding that is produced through interaction with significant interlocutors. This dialogical conception of identity is particularly important because a good deal of Taylor's political theorising is concerned with issues arising from the interaction of diverse communities in modernity and the need to engage with the modern pluralistic self (SS).

3

Romanticism and Modernity

Introduction

One of the distinguishing features of Charles Taylor's philosophy is the degree to which it has been shaped by its engagement with Romanticism. Taylor has refined some of the intentions typically associated with Romanticism, but he has, nevertheless, sought to clarify and to build upon its legacy. Romanticism was a movement that extended well beyond the domain of philosophy and political theory; its proponents include poets and artists, like Shelley, Wordsworth, Keats and Caspar David Friedrich. For Taylor, Romanticism constitutes a strand of thought that runs counter to the rationalist and scientific outlook that took hold with the Enlightenment. Romanticism likewise rejected the rational and intellectual value system of neo-classicism in aesthetics, with its privileging of the formal over the affective. Nevertheless, even to define Romanticism is a complicated and indefinite process. The major themes that Taylor identifies with Romanticism were associated with broad currents of eighteenth and nineteenth-century thought. In particular, the notion of nature as an inner moral source has, Taylor argues, wider adherents (SS). Likewise the Romanticist notion of expressivism has been incorporated into modern culture in a very general and diffuse manner. It is a core component of modern conceptions of subjectivity and freedom. Taylor argues that Rousseau and Hegel were significant contributors to the expressivist strand of thought. This is the case, even though Rousseau properly preceded the Romantic Movement and Hegel's commitment to reason diverged from the Romantic challenge to the sovereignty of reason and rationality (H; HMS; SS; PA; EA).

Taylor's explication of the significance of Romanticism has many important implications for his work on modernity, but two core elements are worth highlighting at the outset. First, Taylor contends that Romanticism and the ideals that are directly linked to Romanticism and its worldview considerably shaped modernity. Some of the grounds for this contention have already been introduced, particularly with respect to Taylor's account of the making of modern identity and the importance that Taylor attributes to articulation, with its antecedents in Romanticism's core notion of expression (SS). For the moment it is sufficient to note that expression involves the transmission of what is inner outwards or, as Taylor suggests, it concerns manifestation, whether it be the facial expression of a feeling or the poetic creation of the creative imagination (SS). Taylor's exploration of the Romantic outlook and its broad implications contests the view of Romanticism as an influence that was subsequently surpassed and overtaken in modernity. In this respect, Taylor builds on the work of his former teacher Isaiah Berlin and his underlining of the constitutive significance of expressivism as a current of thought (Berlin 1998). Second, Taylor illuminates the significance of Romanticism to modernity in another way. He argues that the values and standpoint of Romanticism stand in tension with the dominant tendency of modernity, which is that of instrumental rationality. Johann P. Arnason's conceptualisation of modernity as a field of tensions can be drawn on to characterise this central thread of Taylor's social and political theory (Arnason 1991).

Although Taylor's work reveals an enormous fascination with Romanticism, his overall position on Romanticism is difficult to classify. Taylor is clearly heavily indebted to Romanticism. This will be shown to be the case especially with respect to his interpretation of language and his conceptualisations of freedom. Taylor identifies with Romanticism's concern with meaningfulness and the fullness of being or experience. At the same time, he is aware of Romanticism's limitations and the extent to which it was conditioned by its time and place. It is not by chance that Taylor published a major study of Hegel and a related work on Hegel's interpretation of modern society (H; HMS). On Taylor's reading, Hegel attempted to synthesise Romanticism's expressivism with modern reason. There is another reason why Taylor's engagement with Romanticism is salient to his political thought. Romanticism can tell us a great deal, according to Taylor, about the types of critical politics that develops in modernity. Romanticism has informed the mentality of attempts by individuals and social movements to overcome alienation and divisions, including those of the major ideological movements of political nationalism and socialism. Romanticism is one of the major sources of the interpretations that modern individuals have of how they want to live and their aspirations to freedom.

Romanticism and Expressivism

The Romantic Movement contributed to some of the major transformations in thought that would constitute the general horizon of meaning in modernity. Taylor argues that Romanticism significantly informs modern individuals' interpretation of themselves (SS). In short, notions derived from Romanticism have substantially influenced the expectations that modern individuals have about the meaning and purpose of their lives. Similarly, the Romantic Movement contributed to the crystallising of the major form of modern collective identification. That is, some of the ideas associated with the Romantic Movement provided part of the justification for nationalism and the impetus for the creation of nations. Romanticism drew attention to the distinctiveness of national cultures and to how the freedom of a people or nation depends on capacities and opportunities to express themselves. For this reason, the interpretation of language that was put forward by figures associated with Romanticism, especially Johannes Herder, was important to the deepening of the meaning of the notion of self-determination and the association that the modern concept of freedom has with the idea of authenticity (EA; SS).

Taylor considers that the 'expressivist turn' is a major effect of Romanticism and that it is connected to the view of 'nature as a source' of morality and meaning (SS; EA). As will be explained in greater detail later, this view implies that to be divorced from what is natural in oneself is to be limited and not fully free. Further, the expressivist view suggests that freedom involves the realisation or expression of one's potential. That is, that one is constrained and oppressed if one does not have the opportunity to express oneself and to realise this potential. This dimension of the Romantic view of freedom was in certain respects compatible with John Stuart Mill's conception of liberalism. Taylor points to Mill's 'robust' standard in *On Liberty* of 'a person whose desires and impulses are his own – are the expression of his own nature, as it has been developed and modified by his own culture' (Mill as quoted in SS, 258). It is worth noting that this interpretation of freedom is critical to the position that Taylor adopts in the contemporary debate between liberalism and communitarianism that will be examined in the next chapter. Taylor aims to contest what he considers to be this debate's false antitheses and to show how it is possible to adopt a complementary position; one that reconciles elements of liberalism and communitarianism (PA).

There is a further dimension of the expressivist turn that makes it significant to the modern conception of freedom. That is, that the individual's potential that is realised, or given expression, is understood to be open-ended and, in some respect, self-defining or self-authorising. This contrasts with the ancient Greek or, specifically, Aristotelian understanding of the realisation of the teleological purpose in nature. In other words, the Aristotelian view is that of the fixed realisation of what is natural, whereas the modern view, which partly derives from Romanticism, is one where it is open to the subject to create and define its potential. The expressivist conception of the manifesting of potential means that freedom and identity are not fixed and limited to fulfilling an inherent telos, or unfolding development. Rather, the opposite is supposed to be the case. Taylor argues that this major change in thought and the self-understanding of modern individuals is connected to a shift in the interpretation of the world as a whole or the nature of being. That is, the prior interpretation is one based on everything in the world having a relatively fixed position, and hence that their inherent telos was to realise this essential quality, whether it be that of an animal species, a human infant or the gender of a man or woman. Taylor associates this view of the world with the notion of a 'great chain of being' (SS; EA; MSI; SA). Further, this understanding of the world served to justify pre-modern forms of social hierarchy. Taylor repeatedly points to how the change in the background understanding of the world is integral to the full development of modern democracy and the process of democratisation.

Even though the Romantic Movement endorsed community, its commitment to expressivism consolidated and inflected the modern emphasis on the individual. Romanticism did not just emphasise the differences between individuals and the uniqueness of each individual. Based on its expressivist vision, Romanticism gave these qualities an additional attribute; one that modern individuals have, to varying degrees, embraced. According to Taylor, the Romantic Movement put forward the value of originality (SS). It was not sufficient for individual expression to conform to type; rather one's expression should be original. The true identity was not an imitation or mimesis, rather it was to be truly original. That is, it suggested that each of us has an obligation to 'live up to our originality' (SS, 173).

This notion of the originality of the expression of identity naturally takes its bearings from the modern understanding of artistic creation. Romanticism assumed that the work of art of whatever kind, whether it be poetry, music or painting, was an expression of its creator. The work of art was a concrete manifestation of subjectivity, as is shown in William Wordsworth's epic poem *The Prelude* (1850). Over time this notion of creative self-expression has been diffused to many of the areas of the deployment of the self in modernity, such as in relation to fashion and even to areas seen by many critical theorists as contrary to originality, such as consumption. Like its rupture with the notion of teleology, Romanticism's conception of expression resulted in a break with earlier aesthetics. The Romantic notion of originality drew heavily on a conception of the powers of the 'creative imagination' (SS). According to Romanticists, the creative imagination gave rise to novel and original forms, rather than the lesser forms that derive from repetition and reproduction. One finds examples of this view of the creative imagination in works of Romantic poetry and it was explicitly stated in Samuel Taylor Coleridge's contrast between the imagination that creates something new and the mere 'fancy' that is limited to repetition (SS; Coleridge 1954). Taylor sketches some implications of this position on the power of the creative imagination:

> The creative imagination is the power which we have to attribute to ourselves, once we see art as expression and no longer simply as mimesis. Manifesting reality involves the creation of new forms which give articulation to an inchoate vision, not simply the reproduction of forms already there. This is why the Romantic period developed its particular concept of the symbol. The symbol, unlike allegory, provides the form of language in which something, otherwise beyond our reach, can become visible. (SS, 179)

There are various other ways in which the expressivist view is present in modern culture. One need only think of how romantic fiction regularly concerns overcoming the socially imposed barriers to one's 'natural' feelings. The expressivist outlook has continued to be elaborated upon; as well as subject to extensive criticism, particularly from perspectives that contest its view of symbolic forms, whether it be of art, language or aspects of culture more generally, as primarily manifestations of subjectivity (Foucault 1970). In certain respects, Taylor accepts the validity of this criticism, but for the most part he considers that the disengaged position of the critique of expressivism misses some of the reasons for the identification of modern subjects with it. In short, expressivism is connected to their experience of meaning and sense of freedom. The objectifying critique of expressivism neglects or denies the philosophical anthropological basis of expression. For instance, Taylor claims that: 'We experience our essentially human emotions not primarily in describing but in expressing them' (SS, 98). Taylor acknowledges that Romanticism's valuing of emotional expression has been institutionalised more in the private sphere than in the public realms of modern capitalist society, such as those of work, administration and politics (EA; M). That is, emotional expression is accepted as a dominant tendency in the private sphere and a basis for organising intimate relations, whereas the public realms of modern societies are primarily conditioned by instrumental reason.

These tensions in modernity will be explored further in the next section, but it is worth commenting on how the expressivist outlook has been socially and politically consequential in the contemporary period. The priorities of expressivist interpretations of freedom and identity have influenced the restructuring of intimate relations and tendencies of the democratising of the private sphere, such as with respect to the interaction of partners and the concern with affect and feelings (see Giddens 1992; Beck and Beck-Gernsheim 2002; Honneth 2014). In a more general sense, the expressivist outlook can be seen to be central to what Luc Boltanski and Eve Chiapello (2005) describe as the artistic critique of capitalism. Capitalism has been contested, they argue, in expressivist terms by the artistic critique, with its emphases upon individual self-fulfilment and the overcoming of alienation. In their view, the artistic critique differs from the 'social critique' of capitalism, which is primarily concerned with the abolition or alleviation of material injustice and inequality. Similarly, Anthony Giddens has contrasted the relatively recent emergence of progressive 'life politics', which is concerned primarily with 'self-actualisation' and lifestyle, in the sense of the way of living, with the longer standing political tradition of 'emancipatory politics', which is more concerned with rectifying material inequalities, rather than the conditions for the self-realisation of subjectivity (Giddens 1992; 1994).

Before turning to the field of tensions between rationality and Romanticism, it should be pointed out again that these contemporary exemplars evidence the traces of the 'expressivist turn' rather than represent direct expressions of the intentions of the Romantic Movement. These differences will become evident from the discussion of the Romantic images of community in the next sections. Indeed, many of the contemporary socio-political translations of expressivism are more commonly seen as promoting individualism and undermining some of the connotations of community, such as that of community's constraining and restricting of individual freedom. Taylor clearly contests some of the individualising tendencies that are associated with contemporary expressivist practices, or, rather, he believes that these practices and understandings represent misinterpretations of expressivism's implications. In his opinion, they reflect how contemporary individuals' self-understanding of freedom has been contaminated by atomistic conceptions and their narrow definition of the good (SS; EA). Taylor's work can be seen as retrieving aspects of Romanticism's expressivist vision of unity against such interpretations or misunderstandings. As we will see in more detail, he highlights how the notion of expression implies a community of shared and reciprocal understandings.

Modernity and Romanticism as a Field of Tensions

Taylor's account of the tension between Romanticism and the 'objectifying' tendencies of scientific thought, technological development and capitalist work organisation and exchange is critical to his assessment of the sources of political discontent within modernity. Taylor details how Romanticism put forward a critique of these objectifying tendencies of the emerging modern industrial civilisation (SS; MSI). Romanticism represented a critique of the detachment of modernity from the nature in humanity and the increasing fragmentation of social relations in the modern world. It contrasted this fragmentation with the organic unity of premodern community. Although it constitutes a critique of modernity, Romanticism particularly consolidated the view of 'nature as a source' that Taylor considers one of the formative components of the modern conception of the self (SS). The notion of nature of source was, on Taylor's analysis, propounded by Rousseau in particular. Rousseau contended that it was necessary to listen to nature as the 'voice within' us (SS, 357). Romanticism would have a major influence upon modernist notions of freedom as authenticity. That is, of freedom as living in a manner consistent with one's own 'nature' and authentic self (EA).

Romanticism, broadly defined, added the notions of self-actualisation and self-expression to modern political philosophy's primary notion of freedom as that of self-determination. In this way, Romanticism points towards a much richer and more extensive conception of freedom, because not only do the notions of self-expression and self-actualisation entail additional attributes of how the individual subject is involved in the realisation of freedom, but also that the domains of enacting freedom are potentially far broader and apply to wider domains of social life (see Honneth 2014). It is important to underline the importance of this extension, since it is one of the ways in which modern understandings of freedom and, therefore, what counts as freedom differs from that of classical or ancient notions of politics (see Arendt 1958; Castoriadis 1997a; Browne 2014b). In a certain sense, the ancient understanding was one that restricted freedom – in the sense of equal liberty – to the political sphere, with a division between it and the private sphere. Taylor is, arguably, more focused on the notion of identity that derives from Romanticism and he was originally less concerned with the institutional expansion of freedom into these broader domains of social life. Taylor does, however, discuss this broadening in his explications of Hegel's notion of 'ethical life' and it is implied by what he describes as the new valuing of the 'ordinary' in modernity (SS; HMS). Nevertheless, it is really only later with the category of social imaginaries, in our opinion, that Taylor fully engages with these broader social spheres in terms of freedom (MSI). In some respects, this may explain why the political implications of gender relations remains arguably a blind spot in Taylor's work.

It is Romanticism, Taylor argues, that consolidated the modern critique of the alienation that derives from the divorce of the subject from itself. Rousseau had initially made a critique of the separation of man from nature and of the imposition of false social relations upon him (Rousseau 1968). Society, Rousseau claimed, made the individual subject to social opinion and the effects of calculation that are part of social relations (SS; Rousseau 1968). Rousseau was probably the major initiator of the notion of freedom as authenticity and he likewise, naturally, contributed to the critique of the counter-condition of inauthenticity. Broadly, Rousseau argued that the calculative mentality of life in an unequal society, in which individuals were concerned with self-advantage, undermined authenticity and inculcated instrumental orientations, as well as insincere social relations. While Taylor is rightly critical of interpretations of Rousseau as a kind of 'primitivist', he considers that Rousseau inaugurated a major line of questioning of notions of progress and reason (HMS; MSI). Romanticism saw the alienating and fragmenting character of social relations in modern society as a counterpart to the disconnection from nature. In some cases, the Romantic

Movement pointed to the medieval community as an organic form of unity, as well as to earlier forms of social association. These constituted an alternative to the modern condition and its rupturing of social bonds. At the same time, even when the backward looking format of these Romantic critiques were rejected, the problem of reconciliation has been recognised as a major dilemma of modernity and this is clearly evident in the political thought of theorists like Hegel and Marx, who sought to overcome the divisions or diremptions of modern society (see Habermas 1987b; Hegel 1967; Marx and Engels 1977; see Lefort 1986).

Taylor highlights how the Romantic Movement took the work of art as a model for this sense of unity. In the work of art, according to such an interpretation, the particular details contribute to the whole. Similarly, the meaning of the whole is expressed by the details of the work, and, for this reason, one could say that a work of art represents a type of organic unity. One can go further with the artistic analogy and contend that the unity that takes shape in the work of art is not based on the rational and instrumental connection between elements and dimensions. It is a connection based instead on meaning, imagination and symbolic expression. The important point is that the latter unity of meaning cannot be reduced to the quantifiable and logical. It cannot be reduced to something that is quantified, since this would kill, so to speak, that which is constitutive of it. As we have seen already, Taylor reiterates variants of this argument in a number of contexts, but it more broadly fits with the notion of modernity as constituted by the tensions between the perspectives on the world of Romanticism and instrumental rationality. Taylor appreciates that these two views can come together, but he considers that they are founded on different principles and presumptions. The discussion of Herder's view of language that follows will make this difference clearer and the contrasting orientations to reality is evident in Taylor's outline of the different conceptions of 'the language animal' (LA; PA).

Taylor's argument is that instrumental reason is so important to the modern worldview that it has to satisfy the conditions of meaning. It now represents a major interpretation of human purpose and therefore constitutes, or potentially constitutes, a framework within which modern subjects understand themselves and recognise the purposes of their activities. This is one of the implications overlooked by defenders of instrumental rationality and its limited sense of purpose, such as that of maximising utility or efficiency. According to

Taylor, the relatively circumscribed interpretation of *the good* that goes with instrumental reason is one of the reasons why the modern self-understanding is somewhat fragile and prone to crisis (SS; PA). It does not address the full gamut of human experience and it does not of its own accord facilitate genuine trust and mutuality in human relations, rather it tends to prioritise self-interest and the detachment of the individual from the community. In other words, it disrupts some of the conditions of confidence in meaning and social solidarity.

Max Weber provided the most famous diagnosis of modern rationalisation leading to a loss of meaning, owing particularly to instrumental or purposive rationality's focus on the means rather than the ends that it serves (Weber 1958). Weber saw modern rationality culminating in potentially irreconcilable conflicts between different spheres of value, like that between the aesthetic and the rational, or hedonistic forms of living and ascetic lifestyles (Weber 1958). Taylor's interpretation of a secular age, in particular, is in large part in dialogue with Weber's disenchantment thesis and the conclusions that Weber drew from it, such as that modern individuals have no alternative but to live with the implications of the disenchanted view of the world and its denial of the kind of holistic interpretations of the meaning of existence that had been provided by religion and metaphysical thought (Weber 1958; SA; see Chapters 6 and 7).

The loss of meaning in modernity is something that, in Taylor's view, was grasped by the Romantic Movement at an earlier phase in the historical development of institutions like the capitalist factory system and urban metropolis. The underlying assumptions of the Romantic Movement's critical perspective were, however, quite different to those of Weber, even though Weber derived the term disenchantment (*Entzauberung*) from Goethe, who had an early connection to the Romantic Movement and the *Sturm and Drang* that intersected with it (Weber 1958; 1995). *Sturm and Drang*, meaning loosely storm and fury, contributed to the 'expressivist turn' that was previously overviewed. In particular, the *Sturm and Drang* aesthetic placed considerable significance on emotions and the somewhat fraught expression of emotional states. Like Romanticism more generally, the *Sturm and Drang* movement contested the emphasis on reason of classicism and neo-classicism. As we have seen, Taylor is critical of the objectifying and disengaged character of some rationalist strands of modern thought and instrumental reason. Similarly, he believes that the deficiency of such modes of thought with respect to meaning can never be fully overcome from within the perspective of instrumental reason. In Taylor's opinion, the modern commitment to instrumental reason results in a deep-seated and recurrent crisis of meaning:

> The dispute between spiritual outlooks is deeply embedded in the inner conflicts of advanced industrial, capitalist societies. Instrumental reason plays such a large role in their institution and practices that whatever shakes our confidence in it as a spiritual stance also causes deep malaise in contemporary advanced societies. There is a circular causal relation between the other crises and difficulties of capitalism and this spiritual malaise . . . (SS, 384–5)

Given the diversity of the figures that Taylor associates with Romanticism, it is difficult to define a particular politics that is Romantic. This is especially the case if one looks at later movements inspired by Romanticism, or elements of the Romantic Movement. Romanticism can be seen, on the one hand, as a source of radical politics, including the neo-Marxist philosophy of praxis and later ecological critiques of capitalism. On the other hand, Romanticism can be regarded as inspiring elements of conservative thought. In particular it was a major stimulant of modern nationalist movements and it is certainly the case that some strands of Romanticism were backward looking, with a view of the past as superior to the present in terms of the harmony and unity with nature. In this respect, Romanticism was concerned with the losses as much as the gains of modernity and modernisation. In fact, the nationalist strand of Romanticism was consolidated in opposition to the importation of rationalism and the reorganisation of the social order on the basis of rationality in parts of Europe.

Taylor certainly rejects aspects of the retrogressive perspective of some of the Romantics. He recognises the limitations of Romantic oppositions to reason. In this regard, Taylor's arguments are, nonetheless, quite different from those of Weber and incorporate elements of the Romantic outlook, such as is evident in their stronger commitment to holism and expressivism. It is therefore not surprising that Taylor is sympathetic to Hegel and, as will be discussed in greater detail, he reads Hegel as attempting to realise in a rational form the expressivist intentions of Romanticism (HMS; H). In short, Hegel's philosophy represents both a diagnosis of the tensions within modernity and an attempt to overcome the divisions and antinomies of modernity. That is, Hegel's notion of subjectivity synthesises the intentions of expressivism and reason (H; HMS). In Taylor's opinion, Hegel particularly appreciated a line of political thought that can be traced to expressivism and its critique of the abstract relationship of reason to subjectivity. Hegel perceives that this critique informs political movements committed to overcoming the distorted political and social institution of freedom in modernity (Hegel 1967; 1977). Before turning to some of the themes of Taylor's engagement with the philosophy of Hegel, it is necessary to reflect on his concern with the work of Herder and the particular influence of Herder's philosophy on Taylor's thought.

Herder, Language, Community

During the twentieth century there developed in philosophy, the humanities and social sciences an increasing appreciation of the importance of language. Taylor argues that figures associated with the Romantic Movement, like Herder and Humboldt, were major precursors and antecedents of this so-called 'linguistic turn' (Rorty 1967). In Taylor's opinion, Herder pioneered an 'expressivist' interpretation of language and he commenced the critique of the 'designative' conception of language that would be subsequently refined by twentieth-century philosophers like Wittgenstein (PA). Wittgenstein argued that language entails an entire form of life and that it is wrong to treat language as simply serving the designation of objects and things (Wittgenstein 1953). In other words, language is not merely an adjunct of consciousness; nor does it simply relate to things in the objectifying manner of an instrument or tool. Rather, the use of language depends on practices of understanding. These practices draw on wider forms of meaning and, in this sense, language analysis reveals specific capabilities used by individuals in the use of language, and different to those involved in conscious perception (Wittgenstein 1953; PA). In one sense, this appears like a fairly straightforward point of difference between language use and the consciousness of objective reality, but Taylor believes that a major tradition of language analysis treats language as if it were an extension of the cognitive perception of things (PA; LA).

Taylor's interest is in the expressivist view of language that initiates a concern with meaning rather than simply designation. The designative conception considers language to be primarily a matter of how a word, or sign or sound, refers to things and entities. Taylor argues that such a view is committed to an objective standpoint and that it abstracts from the normative and subjective qualities of language and the practices of communication. In Taylor's opinion, the designative conception cannot deal with the complexity of language and the multi-faceted forms of meaning inherent in language. For instance, he notes that there is a reasonably straightforward approximation between the statement: 'do not smoke' in English and its French equivalent (SS). However, if one wants to translate more complex formulations, with their implicit and explicit allusions, then it is a much more difficult and imprecise process of conveying the understandings that are involved. One has to evoke the view of the world, so to speak, that is contained in language in this case, because one immediately encounters thicker layers of meaning. In Taylor's opinion, the philosophers of language associated with the Romantic Movement, especially Herder and Humboldt, recognised these qualities, and this led them to make important connections between language and culture. In particular, this gave rise to an appreciation of language as constitutive of a world of meaning and experience, rather than simply a means of referring to things and events in the world. According to Taylor,

> The revolutionary idea implicit in Herder was that the development of new modes of expression enables us to have new feelings, more powerful or more refined, and certainly more self-aware. In being able to express our feelings, we give them a reflective dimension that transform them. The language animal can feel not only anger but indignation, not only love but admiration. (PA, 98)

Taylor perceives Herder to be a 'hinge' in the history of interpretations of language (PA). Herder opened the way for the alternative tradition to that of the designative conception of language that derives from the empirical and analytical philosophical tradition of thought. Locke and Condillac particularly shaped the designative conception. It is Condillac's interpretation of the origins of language that Herder contested and Herder's alternative led to a radically different interpretation of language. Herder's fundamental critique was that Condillac's interpretation of the origins of language presupposed precisely what it was meant to explain (PA). Condillac tried to explain the origins of language by way of an exemplary story; a story of how individuals in a desert could assign meaning to gestures, cries and signals. The basic problem of the constitution of language was defined in terms of designation, that is, this sign means this and that sign means that, so that this refers to that. It would clearly be a mistake to deny that language performs such a function. Rather, Herder argued that Condillac's starting point was the wrong one. That is, Herder argues that it is only someone who possesses a language that can assign meanings to signs and gesture. In short, Condillac 'ignores the background understanding necessary for language' (PA, 95).

Herder further argued that language is not created in a piecemeal fashion. It is not a product of the combination of one individual term with another term, and then that the addition of terms and words produces a language. Language is something that exists as a whole or totality. It is very important to Taylor's perspective that Herder initiates a holistic approach to language. Condillac did, to be sure, have some intuition of this with the view that there is an instituted language (PA). In Taylor's opinion, this position did not go far enough, since it is only possible to institute a language on the basis of the possession of a language. One of the reasons why this is the case is the shared character of meaning. Herder appreciated this in approaching language from the perspective of a speaker and hearer. This standpoint is quite different from that of the perspective of an individual external observer. The observer standpoint only really engages in a limited mode of communication and it omits what is essential to meaning and understanding: that it is something that is shared in common. According to Taylor, the designative conception of language cannot adequately convey the subjective expression and the moral component that is inherent in the relationship to another in communicating (see Chapter 8 for further discussion of Taylor's views on language).

It should be clear from the discussion in the preceding chapter that Taylor's reflections on Romanticism's conception of language intersects with some of the key dimensions of his political perspective. In particular, Taylor's position as that of a 'holistic liberal' derives much of its justification from this interpretation of language. Put differently, were the designative conception of language correct then the contrary, 'atomistic' liberal position would be more convincing. Taylor's argument is that appreciating this holistic quality of language enables the 'atomistic' view of liberal individualism to be contested. Most importantly, it upends the suppositions of the priority of the individual relative to society that underpins the atomistic notion of liberal individualism and its related conception of negative liberty, that is, the freedom from interference.

Herder showed that it would not be sufficient to simply focus on designation, although one should not ignore it. Taylor argues that the designative conception nevertheless continues into the present and it is the basis of views about how animals can learn to equate the sound of a word and thing or how a computer can make similar equations – Taylor was admittedly discussing this at an earlier phase of computer technology. Rather than providing a justification of the designative conception, these examples reveal their limitations in his opinion. In a nutshell, he argues that these conceptions neither convey subjective expression nor the moral standpoints involved in taking up a relation to another in communicating.

Hegel and the Politics of Modern Revolution

Taylor is well known for his reading of Hegel's philosophy of Spirit in terms of the notion of expressivism (H). Taylor argues that Hegel's philosophy incorporated into this category some of the assumptions of Romanticism. The development of Spirit is conditioned by expression and its denial. That is, the negation of contradictions is conditioned by the alienation of Spirit and the future reconciliation. Whether Hegel holds to nature as externalised in Spirit in the manner that Taylor proposes is an open question (see Smith 2002). Be that as it may, Hegel's philosophy constitutes a major version of the synthesis of modern rationalism and Romantic expressivism. In other words, Hegel's philosophy attempts to overcome divisions and tensions in modernity. It is partly for this reason, as well, that Hegel provides one of the major analyses of social and political alienation. In particular, Hegel offers an interpretation of the political dilemmas and consequences of the French Revolution's attempt to overcome alienation and to realise Absolute Freedom. Taylor's political writings are considerably influenced by this interpretation of the descent of the French Revolution into the period of the Terror (HMS: MSI; SA). Indeed, Taylor will basically provide a variation of this interpretation in his account of the constraints on the institutional realisation of the modern social imaginary and the potential consequences of the immanent frame in modernity (MSI; SA).

It is not only the expressivist dimensions of Hegel's conceptions of Spirit and subjectivity that connect his work with the themes of Romanticism. Taylor strongly emphasises Hegel's conceptualisation of Spirit in collective terms and Hegel's commitment, more generally, to the perspective of the whole. It means, in Taylor's view, that Hegel gives a certain priority to the community. Indeed, Taylor describes Hegel's implied criticism of the 'atomistic' approach or 'prejudice' in modern thought in probably stronger terms than Hegel does himself

(HMS, 87). The 'atomistic' conception in political thought takes individual consciousness and action as the foundation and objective of the political order. For Hegel and Taylor, it involves an unjustified abstraction of the individual from community and it is founded on an epistemology that is exclusively centred on individual consciousness and action. Taylor notes, of course, that Hegel's notion of collective subjectivity is met with scepticism by those committed to an ontology and epistemology that is restricted to that of the individual. Further, Taylor acknowledges that Hegel's understanding of collective subjectivity is mistakenly presumed to be representative of the type of thinking that inspired such views of collective agency and integral nationalism as that of National Socialism (SS). Taylor naturally endeavours to dispel such misconceptions concerning Hegel's philosophy and its political implications. Rather, he argues that Hegel's philosophy is important precisely because of its challenge to individualism and simple versions of holism:

> Hegel is important today because we recurrently feel the need for a critique of the illusions and distortions of perspective which spring from the atomistic, utilitarian, instrumental conception of man and nature, while at the same time puncturing the Romantic counter-illusion they continually generate. It is because Hegel is constantly engaged in doing just this, and with an exceptional depth and penetration of insight, that he has something to say to us even though his own ontology of the necessary unfolding of reason may seem as illusory to us as some of the doctrines he attacks. (HMS, 72)

At the same time, it is undoubtedly true that the historical experience of the twentieth century, with its exemplars of destructive collective mobilisation, including nationalism, fascism and communism, did influence a shift towards more individualistic political theories and this means towards liberalism in particular (see Wagner 2008). Taylor will seek to develop a position that can mediate between the collective and individual. Indeed, the mediating process is integral to how he conceptualises the modern social imaginary, which will be overviewed in a later chapter (MSI). Hegel similarly sought to develop a complex form of mediation and this is apparent from his accounts of the struggle for recognition (Hegel 1977; 1979; 1986). Hegel's theory of recognition is a major informant of Taylor's position on identity politics and multiculturalism (M). Hegel underlined the extent to which individual identity is conditional on collective membership and, there is, in this sense, a strong social or communitarian dimension to his thought. Hegel argued that modern freedom was grounded in 'ethical life' (*Stittlickheit*). Taylor draws attention to this important, yet difficult, concept, noting its origination from the term *Sitten*, which could be translated as 'custom' and its contrast with more abstract and formal notions of morality, like that of Kant, which stand in abstract relation to existing practices and subjective experience (HMS, 83).

> *Sittlichkeit* refers to the moral obligations I have to an ongoing community of which I am part. These obligations are based on established norms and uses, and that is why the etymological root in *Sitten* is important for Hegel's use. The crucial characteristic of *Sittlichkeit* is that it enjoins us to bring about what already is. This is a paradoxical way of putting it, but in fact the common life which is the basis of my sittlich obligation is already there in existence. It is in virtue of its being an ongoing affair that I have these obligations; and my fulfilment of these obligations is what sustains it and keeps it in being. Hence in *Sittlichkeit* there is no gap between what ought to be and what is, between *Sollen* and *Sein*. (HMS, 83)

Although there are important differences, it is not entirely implausible to contend that Taylor's political theory is directed towards the affirmation of a version of ethical life. It is important to keep in mind the metaphysical meaning and implications of Hegel's terms, such as existence and reality. The latter can encompass, for instance, the potential that the existing reality contains and Taylor emphasises how Hegel attributed particular significance to the processes of 'realization' or actualising (H; HMS). Hegel's conception of reality can then be interpreted as a reworking of the Romanticist vision of expression and as indicative, as Taylor suggests, of the broader concern at the time with 'expressive unity'. Hegel's 'doctrine of *Sittlichkeit*', Taylor writes, 'is that morality reaches its completion in a community' (HMS, 84).

Hegel therefore argued that the rational state should embody the identity of the collective and that of the individual that is constituted by its membership of the collective (H; HMS; Hegel 1967). In other words, the rational state would be a genuine reconciliation between the universal and the particular. This position can be read, on the one hand, as a conservative endorsement of the existing state, since it embodies the rational and the universal. On the other hand, Hegel's contention can be turned critically against the state and the existing social order, since it establishes a standard that the existing reality may not fully actualise. This standard of rationality and universality then becomes an objective of transformation and indeed makes change necessary, since the state would then currently exist in contradiction with its principles. This was, in fact, basically the programme of the Young Hegelians and particularly that of the young Karl Marx, as his critical theory very much commenced from contesting the false 'universality' of the state owing to its separation from the actual material conditions of the reproduction of social life and the state's embodying particular class interests, such as was reflected in the delimitation of citizenship to male property owners and the bureaucratic organs of the state apparatus functioning in the service of their own ends.

It is worth noting that a case could be made that Taylor's contrast between the Romantic Movement's expressivism and rationalist philosophy's disengaged concern with the logic of quantification and designation is misleading. Although it is not necessarily inconsistent with Taylor's explication, Manfred Frank has shown just how much the Romantic philosophers were concerned with the most traditional problems of philosophy (Frank 2004). In particular, the Romantic philosophers were, like Kant, seeking to define the characteristics and limits of reason. In other words, it could be argued that they were more an extension of the discussion of logic, rather than a perspective that is divorced from these discussions. In some respects, Taylor's explication conveys this connection, but it would be possible to read his own ambivalent relationship to the analytical tradition of philosophy as inflecting his account of the division between Romanticism and the philosophical rationalism of the analytical tradition of philosophy. It is possible to argue that Taylor's account may suggest that the Romantics did not just have a different orientation but that they deprecated the problem of basic logic and rationality. According to Frank, the Romantic philosophers were actually much closer to Kant and sought to reformulate the conditions of knowledge and the corresponding conception of subjectivity. Romantic philosophers, like Friedrich Schlegel and Novalis (Friedrich von Hardenberg), presented interpretations of consciousness or, to follow Kant, the 'I' that thinks and perceives (Frank 2004).

Taylor certainly agrees with the claim that the Romantic philosophers sought to reformulate the notions of consciousness and reason. His interpretation nevertheless accentuates the contrast between the Romantic Movement more generally, including its poets and artists, and philosophical orientations that define reason in terms of quantification, instrumental rationality and the conception of language as primarily a matter of designation. At the same time, Taylor admits that the anti-rationalist stands of Romanticism are untenable. This reinforces the importance of Hegel's work and its synthesis of reason and expressivism. Hegel recognised that modernity was an epoch that had to generate its own foundations and justification. In this sense, modernity aims at the realisation of freedom. These characteristics of modernity generate a condition that Hegel's evaluation of the French Revolution partly turns upon. That is, that freedom has to define for itself its own limitations; in the same way that Kant had described the Enlightenment as the use of one's own reason. Hegel, however, developed a critique of the dangers and risks of the modernist aspiration of Absolute Freedom and its intended abolition of forms of alienation.

One line of this mode of political thought can be traced to Romanticism and the impact upon Romanticism of Rousseau's conceptions of the politics of authenticity and alienation (EA). Rousseau's position could properly be called the politics of 'disalienation', according to Taylor, since the intention of this political standpoint is to transcend alienation. Rousseau's political philosophy sought to overcome divisions and separations, so that in a democracy the will of the individual and that of the 'general will' of all should coincide. For Rousseau, one should obey only the laws that one has formulated oneself. Taylor notes that the 'only way to reconcile this with life in society is by the universal and total participation which is the formula of the general will' (HMS, 106). In a similar vein, the French Revolution, partly under the influence of Rousseau's philosophy, initiated festivals that aimed to overcome the division between the performer and the spectator. By this means, the restraints upon freedom are supposed to be overcome. Modern democracy would be more direct and participatory than that of liberal representative democracy, as Rousseau considered that representation was inconsistent with the 'general will'.

Likewise, romanticism, in its many variants, was an account of a particular value system and critique of the divorce or separation from these values. These values are generally those that have already been encountered, like that of nature as source and the organic unity of the community, but the Romantic critique was especially directed at the institutional separation of individuals from their capacity for expression (SS). Marx's later theory of alienation is possibly the most influential iteration of this position (Marx 1977). Marx argued that under the conditions of capitalist production the labourer is alienated in four senses: from its own activity in the process of labouring, from the product of its labour (which is appropriated by the owner of capital and exchanged on the market), from the cooperative character of social relations, and from the 'species-being' (*Gattungsgewesen*) of humanity as a universal and many-sided producer (Marx 1977). Marx was, however, a modernist in his view that the abolition of alienation presupposed the future historical transcendence of capitalism. The creative expression of the human capacity for labour, Marx argued, required the free association of producers and the transcendence of the limiting features of the division of labour.

Rousseau and Marx's conceptions of emancipation are indicative of the view that forms of alienation are contrary to the modernist vision of freedom and the autonomous constitution of society. Taylor considers that the opposition to alienation is one of the major mobilising tendencies in modernity, but he adapts Hegel's argument about the dangerous implications of the attempts to transcend divisions. In particular, Taylor refers to Hegel's critique of the drive for 'Absolute Freedom' in the Jacobin period of the French Revolution. Hegel contended that the Terror derived from dilemmas internal to the ideal of Absolute Freedom, specifically the aim of founding freedom solely on itself. It entailed, Hegel argued, the rejection of external authority and institutional differentiation, since these compromised the 'unconditional freedom of the rational will to make the world according to its dictates'. In Hegel's opinion, Absolute Freedom 'gives no basis for a new articulated structure of society' (HMS, 79). Hegel's critique of Absolute Freedom basically prefigures Taylor's later assessment of the French Revolution (H; HMS; MSI; SA). It could be argued that Taylor even takes the descent of the French Revolution into the Terror and the derivation of this historical development from the politics of disalienation as paradigmatic of the dangers inherent in the unrestrained attempt to realise modern ideals of freedom and equality (see Browne 2009).

Taylor perceives that the ethic of authenticity and romanticism's expressivist ideals have become formative components of modern culture and, as a consequence, they have become open to different modes of actualisation. In some respects, expressivism and the ethic of authenticity have become aspects of the horizons of meaning that are not always fully recognised as sources of modern individuals' thought and practices. On the basis of these contentions, Taylor argues that deconstructive and postmodernist theories, such as those of Foucault and Derrida actually represent 'deviant' versions of the ethic of authenticity and amoral reinterpretations of the Romanticist notion of creation (EA). It might be asserted that Taylor is partly right, to the extent that theorists like Foucault and Derrida were deeply influenced by Nietzsche's philosophy. But this may mean that Taylor's assessment is mistaken, because it underestimates the discontinuity that deconstruction and postmodernist theories have with the ethic of authenticity and romanticism. At least, this is the position that reflects the self-understanding of postmodernism and poststructuralism. Taylor is, however, pointing to deeper sources and continuities, or even reiterations, that may not be fully appreciated by these perspectives. In fact, Taylor admits that there is a tension between the expectation of originality in the ethic of authenticity, with its implied 'opposition to the rules of society and even potentially to what we recognise as morality', and the assumption that there is a dialogical dimension to self-definitions and that linguistic creativity gives rise to a background horizon of socially shared meaning (EA, 66).

The postmodern and deconstructionists' deviance, Taylor argues, 'takes the form of forgetting about one set of demands on authenticity while focusing exclusively on another' (EA, 66). In short, according to Taylor, they stress 'the constructive, creative nature of our expressive languages', 'while altogether forgetting' that linguistic creativity requires 'an openness to horizons of significance (for otherwise the creation loses the background that can save it from insignificance)'. Of course, these claims about the oversight and deficiencies of postmodernism and deconstruction are most compelling when core dimensions of Taylor's philosophy are accepted, like its orientation to meaning, moral ontology and philosophical anthropology. Taylor's critique alludes to the limitations of postmodernism and deconstruction with respect to historical explanation, including in relation to that of their own standpoint. At the same time, it is clear that Foucault, for instance, had a much more ambivalent, and certainly at times critical, view of philosophical anthropology (Foucault 1970).

Be that as it may, Taylor's reference to the romantic sources of aspects of these theoretical perspectives discloses the significance of aesthetic considerations to them. The other side of this orientation to the aesthetic is the postmodernist and deconstructionist rejection or underestimation of the importance of moral and normative considerations – although a case could be made that over time these considerations did gain increasing importance in the work of theorists like

Foucault, Derrida, Lyotard and Agamben. Taylor is certainly alluding to the normative deficit of these theories in his comment about their forgetting the 'horizons of significance'. He later makes a similar point about the misunderstandings concerning the politics of recognition that result from postmodernist and deconstructionist theories' normative deficiencies. Taylor argues that, rather than engaging with the complex normative and ethical considerations present in according recognition and attempting to achieve greater justice on the basis of it, these theoretical perspectives have been invoked to justify demands for unconditionally positive responses to claims for recognition

> In fact, subjectivist, half-baked neo-Nietzschean theories are quite often invoked in this debate. Deriving frequently from Foucault or Derrida, they claim that all judgments of worth are based on standards that are ultimately imposed by and further entrench structures of power. It should be clear why these theories proliferate here. A favourable judgment on demand is nonsense, unless some such theories are valid. Moreover, the giving of such a judgment on demand is act of breathtaking condescension. No one can really mean it as a genuine act of respect. It is more in the nature of a pretend act of respect given on the insistence and of its supposed beneficiary. Objectively, such an act involves contempt for the latter's intelligence. The proponents of neo-Nietzschean theories hope to escape this whole nexus of hypocrisy by turning the entire issue into one of power and counterpower. Then the question is no more one of respect, but of taking sides, of solidarity. But this is hardly a satisfactory solution, because in taking sides they miss the driving force of this kind of politics, which is precisely the search for recognition and respect. (M, 70).

It is worth noting that Taylor is referring here to positions influenced by Derrida and Foucault, rather than the actual statements of these theorists. Nevertheless, the problem is that elements of these theoretical perspectives leave open the possibility of the derivation of such problematic normative positions and that, as will be discussed in the next chapter, the politics of recognition depends on a proper appreciation of its moral underpinnings (M).

Conclusion

Taylor's arguments concerning the politics of 'disalienation' and the fraudulent versions of the ethic of authenticity demonstrate that he does not uncritically embrace Romanticism. Taylor does, however, consider that the modern ideal of autonomy has been significantly informed by the Romantic values of expression and authenticity. The latter values have not only been crystallised in theories and practices of individual fulfilment and the private sphere of personal relations, in particular, but they have also influenced modern forms of collective identification, especially nationalism. Nationalist movements have appealed to notions of the authentic expression of a people and their way of life as a basis of a right to self-determination. In particular, nationalist movements have been influenced by the expressivist interpretations of language that were propounded by theorists like Herder and Humboldt. Taylor accepts these theorists' argument that language is a collective phenomenon; he emphasises how their work demonstrates that the linguistic expression of meaning goes beyond the designation of things. Significantly, Taylor's political perspective of 'holistic liberalism' draws considerable justification from this interpretation of language, and, as will be discussed later, he has recently sought to build upon this conception of the 'language animal'.

Taylor's vision of the constitutive tension between the Romantic Movement's interpretation of expressivism and the predominance of instrumental reason in modernity likewise underlies his political perspective and it subsequently inflects his accounts of democratic culture. He argues that the Romantic Movement's notions of creation and originality influenced the movement away from the ideas of fixed forms and teleology. These ideas were inherited from classical philosophy and images of a 'great chain of being'. Taylor believes, as will be explained in more detail in the next chapters, that this changed orientation towards the world is integral to democracy in modernity, as well as to the general enhancement of individual freedom.

At the same time, the opening to new understandings that this shift in the background horizon of meaning created would eventually enable, what Taylor describes, as morally problematic and 'deviant' versions of the ethic of authenticity and subjective expression. Taylor has likewise sought to contest the contaminating of expressivist understanding of freedom by individualism. Despite its questionable metaphysics, Taylor argues that Hegel's philosophy represented an attempted reconciliation of Romanticism's expressivism and reason. Indeed, Taylor's political thought can be seen as oriented towards the domain that Hegel described as that of 'ethical life' (*Sittlichkeit*). Hegel's writings are a major source of theories of recognition. For this reason, the next chapter's discussions of Taylor's accounts of democracy and recognition are a further engagement with many of the themes covered in this chapter. The explorations of democracy and recognition represent attempts on Taylor's part to articulate the contemporary manifestations of themes associated with romanticism and modernity.

4

Democracy and Recognition

Charles Taylor's approach to politics is dialogical or even conversational. This does not mean that Taylor has no serious political disagreements, but it does give some indication of the values that he embraces. In particular, Taylor considers that there is no way around coming to terms with pluralism and diversity in complex societies. The problem is how to do this in a genuinely democratic manner. In Taylor's opinion, political discussions are often stuck between two unsatisfactory alternative positions. On the one hand, in political theory the predominant interpretation of liberalism arguably treats pluralism and diversity, especially substantial cultural difference, as mainly a hindrance to democracy and pretends to resolve the question of 'difference' by effectively denying it. On the other hand, there is a diverse range of groups in liberal democratic societies that have advanced legitimate claims for recognition, such as with reference to ethnicity and sexual identity. However, on Taylor's view, many of these groups and the theoretical perspectives that are related to them either misunderstand or misrepresent the conditions of their political practice and how their demands for recognition are connected to liberal democracy. Taylor's approach to these alternatives is along the lines of his interventions into other controversies. He explicates the larger historical background to the dispute and the horizon of understanding that shapes the political context. On this basis, Taylor seeks to reveal false juxtapositions and the possibilities for developing new interrelationships of political positions.

This is precisely how Taylor claims to approach the debate between liberalism and communitarianism. He claims that this debate has been at cross-purposes and conditioned by a certain confusion concerning ontological and 'advocacy issues'. 'Advocacy issues concern the moral stand or policy one adopts' (PA, 182). Taylor argues that there is an alternative position that neither side in the debate has properly considered. Namely, that of the holistic liberalism that has its main antecedents in the work of figures associated with the Romantic Movement, like Humboldt (PA; EA). Taylor's claim that a strong sense of social solidarity can underpin the freedom of the individual is certainly appealing. Yet, it is equally the case that his political position is regularly viewed as much more proximate to the communitarian standpoint. In short, influential versions of contemporary liberalism disavow the commitment to the 'good' that Taylor endorses and they are more strictly individualist in their approach. It would not be too difficult to conclude that for these versions of liberalism Taylor's notion of holistic liberalism is actually communitarian. Liberalism's prioritising of individual rights, on this view, subordinates the types of considerations that Taylor associates with holism, such as the primary commitment to the notion of collective good and the salience of the wider cultural background.

One of Taylor's central arguments is that modern democracy needs to be understood in terms of historically crystallised forms of meaning and the broad transformation of society that extended across a variety of domains and institution. Taylor's explanation of the process of the consolidation of the modern social imaginary will be examined in the next chapter, but a central development in the constitution of modernity is highlighted in basically all of his discussions of democracy and other major dimensions of modernity, like nationalism and citizenship (PA; EA; DC). Taylor argues that the dissolution of key components of premodern social hierarchy is integral to the formation of modern democratic social orders and the implementing of liberal values, like those of equal liberty and universal respect for the dignity of individuals. Taylor contends that a variety of interconnected changes, but especially that of the 'ethic of authenticity', challenged the prior assumption that identity was 'largely fixed by one's social position'. That is, it had been assumed that one's position in the rank order of society, whether, for instance, as a feudal lord, knight, priest, serf and so on, was definitive of identity. One of the reasons why this was the case is apparent from Burckhardt's claim that in the Middle Ages: 'Man was conscious of himself only as member of a race, people, party, family or corporation – only through some general category' (Burckhardt 1958: 143).

In Taylor's opinion, the movement away from the hierarchical understanding of fixed positions and its allocation of value required a fundamental change in individuals' interpretation of their identity. This shift involved processes that went beyond those of the realisation of liberal values and its corresponding models of individual subjectivity.

> The background that explained what people recognized as important to themselves was to a great extent determined by their place in society, and whatever roles or activities attached to this position. The birth of a democratic society doesn't by itself do away with this phenomenon, because people can still define themselves by their social roles. What does decisively undermine this socially derived identification, however, is the ideal of authenticity itself. (PA, 229)

Taylor argues that one of the things that define modern democracy is the social imaginary of 'bottom up' control (Taylor 2009). The idea of 'bottom up' control represents a major historical innovation and it is likewise a part of a broad cultural transformation. Taylor's interest lies primarily in explicating the 'political culture' of democracy and its historical forms. It is an approach that has particular affinities with that of Alexis de Tocqueville. In fact, Taylor's assessment of the current tendencies of modern democracy is, in part, a reworking of Tocqueville's interpretation of democratic culture and Tocqueville's diagnosis of the potentials inherent in modernity that can undermine democracy (Tocqueville 2003; 1955).

Before considering Taylor's arguments concerning the potentials and limitations of modern democratic culture, his significant intervention in the liberalism–communitarianism debate will be overviewed. Taylor attempts to show the narrow framing of the currently dominant versions of political liberalism. He argues that these versions of liberalism are inadequate with respect to political demands and major controversies. Taylor expands on the implications of this critique of atomistic and procedural liberalism in his account of multiculturalism and the politics of recognition (M). The concept of recognition has become a major topic in social and political theory. In particular, it generated debates over the preconditions of social justice and the basis of social critique. These debates point to some weaknesses and deficiencies in Taylor's formulation of the category of recognition. In short, the subsequent discussions imply that Taylor may overlook some politically important implications of the shift to recognition.

The Liberalism–Communitarianism Debate

The renewal of normative political philosophy has been one of the major intellectual tendencies of recent decades. This renewal has resulted in the growing influence of political liberalism and the work of John Rawls is the most important contributor to this revival (Rawls 1971; 2005; see Browne 2014a). It is not surprising therefore that the communitarian critique of liberalism took the form of challenging a number of the suppositions of Rawls' theory of justice. Rawls proposed a conception of justice based on the hypothetical state of individuals making decisions about justice in an 'original position' under a veil ignorance concerning their position in society. In part, the veil of ignorance is meant to counteract the kind of preferences that may ensue from knowing your socio-economic situation, such as whether you are actually rich or poor, and similar considerations, like your relative talent. Rawls' theory of justice is classically liberal in its first principle that 'each person is to have an equal right to the most extensive basic liberty compatible with a similar liberty for others' (Rawls 1971: 60). Rawls further proposed the 'difference principle', that is, that no policy could be supported that made the poorest group or 'least advantaged' in the community worse off. According to Rawls, 'Social and economic inequalities are to be arranged so that they are both (a) to the greatest benefit of the least advantaged and (b) attached to offices and positions open to all under conditions of fair equality of opportunity' (Rawls 1971: 83).

Rawls' notion of justice aims to satisfy the condition of procedural fairness. It entails an inherent commitment to impartiality or neutrality concerning the 'good'. Indeed, Rawls wants to limit the notion of justice to that of the 'right', rather than the good (Rawls 1971). Rawls proposes a 'deontological' theory that leaves it up to the individual to decide on the morally right thing to do, rather than a teleological theory that is framed by the sense of the good that a society is oriented towards. Now, for reasons that should be apparent from the preceding discussion, the basic details of Rawls' theory of justice contrast with the philosophical foundations of Taylor's theory – with its commitment to the notion of the good and moral ontology. Taylor's various criticisms of procedural theories and 'atomistic' liberalism have already been encountered. Similarly, Taylor's arguments concerning the holistic character of language and his claim that a conversation instantiates an 'us' relationship can be seen to converge with aspects of the communitarian perspective. Taylor's arguments, in this regard, could be drawn upon as underlying justifications for communitarianism (PA).

The most detailed communitarian response to Rawls is probably that of Michael Sandel. Sandel (1982) questioned the design of Rawls' theory of justice and made a number of claims that are typical of the communitarian criticisms. In some respects, Sandel reiterates many long-standing criticisms of liberalism. Notably, Sandel criticised what he termed Rawls' 'unencumbered' notion of the self (Sandel 1982). Sandel argues that liberalism is mistaken in its treatment of the individual as independent of those elements that are constitutive, in his opinion, of the self, such as social bonds and beliefs. Rawls' construction reiterates aspects of this flaw of liberalism, with its unencumbering of the self in the original position of social status, talent and similar under the veil of ignorance. In particular, the occlusion in the original position of individuals' notion of the good leads, according to Sandel, to a conception that gives precedence to the individual's act of choosing over substantive ends (Sandel 1982). The alternative moral position is one in which the conception of the good informs individual choices, such as with respect to substantive values, like peace or environmental protection.

It is worth noting that deontological and procedural theories, like those of Rawls and Kant, do generally imply constraints on choices, in the sense that individuals, to the extent that they are rational, cannot make choices that contradict the basic principles or the categorical imperative (Rawls 1971; Kant 1964). The strengths of the liberal perspective, more generally, are reasonably well known. It represents a set of principles and ideals that facilitate individual freedom, like the rule of law, equal treatment, freedom of conscience, the right to assembly, freedom of movement, free public discussion. Taylor, as we will see, agrees with these liberal principles, ideals and institution. Taylor's argument is rather that the implication of deontological theory and the notion of liberal neutrality concerning cultural difference are actually misleading. He claims that the major principles and values of the liberal tradition derive from the Christian tradition (M, 62). In his opinion, it is important to keep this in mind in considering cultural difference from a liberal perspective and it is certainly relevant to comprehending why the acceptance of liberal principles may not be as straightforward as contemporary political liberalism tends to presume (M).

Given this perspective on the genealogy of liberalism, it is not surprising then that Taylor agrees with the communitarian argument that Rawls' theory of justice actually presupposes a basic conception of the good and that its 'viability', to use Taylor's terms, is conditional on taking the corresponding conception of identity and community into account. Taylor's 'thesis' is that the 'only alternative to discussing them is relying on an implicit and unexamined view of' community and identity (PA, 186). In this sense, it is actually possible to argue that Rawls' theory reflects the sense of the good that is held in politically liberal societies, most specifically the USA and possibly the UK (PA). The problem then, however, is precisely that Rawls' theory of justice may have very limited application outside these two national contexts. Taylor points to how Canada has a different conception of the good, which is manifest, he argues, in a variety of ways, such as with respect to a more socialised arrangement of the health system than that of the USA (PA, 203).

Taylor recalls an additional communitarian argument. It is one that is closely associated with the civic republican tradition and a variant of this argument has sometimes been used to explain modern nationalism. In the context of Rawls' theory of justice, it takes the form of the claim that Rawls' conception of justice, including such basic details as the respect for the principle of equal treatment and the 'difference principle', depend on the existence of a strong sense of solidarity (PA, 187). In short, solidarity is required in order to value other individuals in a way that leads to a preparedness to enact the principles of equal treatment and to make sacrifices for the 'least advantaged'. In the communitarian view, liberalism is wrong to presume either that such principles are simply accepted by individuals as given without taking into account the social context or that the institution of such principles as a legal right is sufficient. Taylor argues that the appreciation of the significance of solidarity was a major insight of ancient republican political theory. It would be taken up by its early modern successors, like Machiavelli, Montesquieu and Tocqueville. According to Taylor, the republican tradition used the term 'patriotism' as an equivalent for the modern idea of solidarity. Patriotism referred to identification with others in a particular common enterprise and it is 'somewhere between friendship or family feeling, on the one side, and altruistic dedication on the other' (PA, 188).

The underlying sense of solidarity of the republican conception of patriotism differentiates it from that of contemporary patriotic liberalism. The republican notion of patriotism is based on an appreciation of a shared common heritage and the creation of enduring bonds. Taylor acknowledges that a patriotic liberalism may claim to uphold the notion of a common heritage and strong bonds, but that the individualistic perspective of liberalism leads to a 'collective instrumental action' conception of public or collective goods (PA, 191). It is quite different from properly convergent goods. The collective instrumental conception is not the same as the republican conception of a shared collective good, since the latter derives from a sense of the community as a 'we' and the collective good is not reducible to a matter of the pursuit of self-interests. One reason why there is a difference between collective instrumental interests and convergent goods is the creation of distinctive properties through the engagement of the community, including at the level of an individual's experience (see PA, 191–2). Taylor has attempted to illustrate how some goods are 'irreducibly' social (PA).

The republican tradition further claimed that the participatory involvement of citizens was a good in itself. It made the political process legitimate and responsive to the demands of citizens, as well as serving to socialise citizens into the values of the community and consolidating their commitment to them. The republican notion of freedom differs substantially from that of liberalism's conception of negative liberty. Taylor notes that this difference is partly due to the republican tradition conceiving of freedom as associated with a form of political community that is the opposite of despotism. In this view, the abolition of despotism is an achievement of the community as a whole. It cannot be the accomplishment of an individual alone. Republican notions of freedom are based on the idea of self-rule, rather than the liberal notion of freedom from interference. Taylor makes this contrast in comparing the different conceptions of solidarity:

> This patriotic liberal regime differs from the traditional republican model. We have imagined that the values enshrined in the historically endorsed institution are purely those of the rule of right, incorporating something like the rule of law, individual rights, and principles of fairness and equal treatment. What this leaves out is the central good of the civic-humanist tradition: participatory self-rule. (PA, 199)

The republican conception of 'self-rule' is one of 'meaningful freedom' and it has broad significance. Taylor points to how its sense of active participation is contrary to the logic of despotism. The despotic regime replaces the actions of individuals with those of the external agency of the state or bureaucracy (PA). It may define the needs of individuals for them. Liberalism is, of course, opposed to despotism, but its vision of self-rule tends to be limited to the rule of law and individual rights. In this regard, the contrast Taylor is making is similar to that drawn earlier between negative liberty being an opportunity concept and positive liberty being an exercise concept. If Taylor's distinction is correct then liberalism is depicting some of the preconditions of 'self-rule' but not necessarily the actuality of freedom. As will be discussed later, Taylor develops the implications of this assessment in his adaptation of Tocqueville's diagnosis of the potential for 'soft despotism' in formally liberal democratic societies (Tocqueville 2003).

In the context of the debate between liberalism and communitarianism, Taylor draws two major conclusions about contemporary politics from his reflections on early modern republican understandings of political culture. First, he argues that without the aspiration of self-rule and opportunities to enact it there is likely to be an increasing disenchantment and dissatisfaction with the political order and political processes. In Taylor's opinion, the liberal position of negative liberty is insufficient to meet these demands for self-rule, because it requires a higher level of participatory involvement. For the civic republican tradition, participation is the precondition of democracy. Second, it is necessary to ask the question that procedural liberalism abstains from posing, that is, the question of what are the goods to which the community is committed. This question presumably entails the ensuing question of how should the community be organised to meet these goods. For Taylor, these questions are by no means incompatible with liberalism; they can be readily addressed from the standpoint of holistic liberalism. In his view, it is simply a mistake of procedural and atomistic versions of liberalism to consider that these questions are incommensurate with the principles of liberalism.

These two considerations are particularly relevant to Taylor's discussion of the politics of recognition and the next section will provide some indication of how they are manifested in contemporary liberal democratic societies. Before turning to the theme of recognition, it may be worthwhile noting the liberal position on these considerations and in relation to the arguments of Taylor's intervention into the debate with communitarianism more generally.

First, as we saw, contemporary liberalism opposes the notion of collective good on the grounds that it may lead to an impinging on the freedom of the individual. 'Each person' Rawls claims, 'possesses an inviolability founded on justice that even the welfare of society as a whole cannot override. For this reason justice denies that the loss of freedom for some is made right by a greater good shared by others' (Rawls 1971: 3–4). Second, liberalism contends that it is a matter of the balance between the rights that enable participation and the form in which it is expressed. In this sense, it is the notion of procedures that produces valid and justified outcomes, such as that outcomes are in the interest of all or that take into account the effects on the least advantaged in a community. Third, the notion that there is a communitarian background to liberalism may be of historical interest, but it does not alter the liberal commitment to individual autonomy. Liberalism originated as a philosophy that supports the individual relative to the prejudices of the community and sectarian beliefs. Without evaluating these liberal responses, they could be taken to suggest that Taylor would need to develop a more nuanced interpretation of the relationship between a holistic orientation at the level of meaning and a commitment to liberal values.

The Politics of Recognition in Multicultural Societies

Like his participation in the liberal–communitarian debate, Taylor's essay on 'Multiculturalism: Examining the Politics of Recognition' enhanced his profile in discussions in political theory. It demonstrated to a broad audience Taylor's considerable ability to bring philosophical conceptions to bear on contemporary political issues and his approach of elucidating the broader background context of understanding that informs political positions and the stakes of political controversies. Taylor was not the only philosopher and political theorist concerned with elaborating the notion of recognition at the time, which has its original source in Hegel's accounts of the struggle for recognition (Hegel 1977; 1986). Axel Honneth was engaged in systematising the theory of the struggle for recognition and Nancy Fraser would almost immediately become a significant interlocutor (Honneth 1995a; Fraser 1995). Fraser argued that the politics of recognition should complement or supplement, rather than replace or displace, the established progressive politics of redistribution. The ensuing debates over recognition have served to clarify the specificity of Taylor's conception, as well as its implications and limitations. In the case of Taylor's contribution, the category of recognition is an extension of the general themes and framework of his philosophical theory. In Taylor's opinion, recognition is a normative expectation that has developed in modern societies; one that groups and movements have come to increasingly mobilise around (M).

It is not surprising that Taylor's account of the politics of recognition appears to reiterate a tension that runs through his political theory. The politics of recognition can be understood as attempting to fully realise liberalism's ideal of equal liberty, whilst demonstrating, in Taylor's opinion, that the principles and ideals of liberalism have to be interpreted in ways that rectify their current deficient understanding and institution. In this sense, it is possible to claim that Taylor is arguing for a superior interpretation or a 'better account', to use his term, of liberalism and its institution, such as with respect to citizenship rights or the institution of the public sphere. Drawing on Michael Walzer's distinction between two different understandings of liberalism in Taylor's work, Habermas points to a second strain of Taylor's argument concerning the politics of recognition and its sequels (Walzer 1994; Habermas 1994). 'On closer examination, however,' Habermas states, 'Taylor's reading attacks the principles themselves and calls into question the individualistic core of the modern conception of freedom' (Habermas 1994: 109).

Broadly stated, Taylor's argument is that recognition has become important in modern societies because of the influence of the ethic of authenticity (M; EA). That is, the ethic of authenticity reinforces the need for the distinctive identity of each individual to be recognised. As we have seen, Taylor traces this conception of authenticity to Romanticism's notion of expression and, in particular, to the interpretation of subjectivity that Rousseau propounded, with its commitment to the inner voice and the demand for living in a way that is true to one's identity. Despite drawing attention to the historical significance of Rousseau's arguments concerning authenticity and how they have shaped understandings of the modern self and politics, Taylor is somewhat critical of its implied view of an intrinsic good that is inherent in humans (SA). Taylor compares it with earlier theological notions and the more general tendency of Western political thought. These, he argues, incorporate assumptions about the 'fallen' character of human beings and the negative potentials of human subjectivity (Taylor 2009; SS; EA). In Taylor's opinion, these political and theological conceptions are more realistic in their appreciation of the necessity for internalised constraints upon human freedom and in their view of the improbability of a complete integrity of individual desires and the general will of society.

Leaving aside the questions of the validity of Taylor's assessment and the extent to which alternate theological and political positions are conditioned by frameworks of understanding that are open to dispute, it is certainly the case that Rousseau's conception is part of a broader cultural diffusion of the ethic of authenticity (EA). The ethic of authenticity has created expectations that are ingrained in modern subjects; and it has influenced how individuals and groups experience their identities. Of major significance, the non-recognition or misrecognition of an identity has come to be considered a source of individual and collective suffering and oppression. This suffering is certainly experienced psychologically or in the 'self-relation' that individuals have to their identities, but it is not limited to these dimensions. Indeed, the effects of misrecognition are manifested in material conditions, institutions and social structures. It is therefore important to emphasise that recognition is something that emanates from the other. Recognition is very much a relational category; hence it refers to a condition of interdependency and how the perspective of the other is formative of identity. Now, this is why misrecognition or denied recognition is damaging for individuals and groups:

> The thesis is that our identity is partly shaped by recognition or its absence, often by the misrecognition of others, and so a person or group of people can suffer real damage, real distortion, if the people or society around them mirror back to them a confirming or demeaning or contemptible picture of themselves. Nonrecognition or misrecognition can inflict harm, can be a form of oppression, imprisoning someone in a false, distorted, and reduced mode of being. (M, 25)

Taylor points to how such 'withholding' of recognition is seen as a form of oppression, by feminism, race relations and multiculturalist politics, in general (M). As a consequence of their misrecognition or denied recognition, these groups experience themselves as being of lesser value than other members or groups of a community or the nation state to which they belong. In a sense, this experience is consistent with the actual subordinate position of particular groups and communities, since the practical translation of the withholding of recognition is manifest in such things as the exclusion of groups, such those relating to ethnicity or sexual orientation, from the full rights of citizenship and other legal entitlements, the lesser remuneration for work and the devaluing of skills, as in the case of women's labour in traditionally 'feminised' occupational spheres, and the lack of opportunities for expression in the public sphere and the mass media. Further, the lack of recognition implies that the group is likely to be subject to certain misunderstandings about their identity. Taylor refers to Frantz Fanon's famous argument that the social relations of colonialism results in the colonised misrecognising their own identity on account of the dialectic of recognition that is operative in these contexts (M, 65; Fanon 1967; 1986). The colonised, Fanon claimed, had internalised the coloniser's projection about them and therefore recognised, or properly misrecognised, themselves from the perspective of the other.

Significantly, the claims for recognition that groups in contemporary liberal democratic societies are making generally relate to the group and its qualities. That is, they want to be recognised for their 'difference' and not just their 'sameness' with other groups and individuals. For this reason, the politics of recognition concerns not just the general endowment of individuals with equal rights and the treatment of all according to the modern principle of universal dignity. These represent basic principles of liberalism. Rather, the politics of identity and difference concerns the appreciation or recognition of cultural diversity or multiculturalism (M).

Taylor argues that historically the politics of difference 'grew organically out of the politics of universal human dignity' (M, 39). In this sense, Taylor seeks to show that the antagonism to liberalism that sometimes characterises the politics of difference is founded on a misunderstanding. On the one hand, the politics of difference is able to draw on the consolidation of the rights of all to equal dignity. On the other hand, there are versions of liberalism and their conceptions of justice that cannot meet, in Taylor's opinion, these claims for recognition. Taylor considers that this criticism applies to the liberal conceptions of major contemporary figures like those of Rawls and Dworkin (M). These versions of liberalism argue that liberalism involves a commitment to procedures that satisfy the conditions of fairness and the equal treatment of all, but that it abstains from 'substantive' commitments to a particular vision of the 'good life' or 'collective goals' (M, 56–7). The concern with procedures partly reflects the significance of 'judicial reasoning' in the USA, especially in relation to political institutions and the bill of rights. In Taylor's opinion, these versions of liberalism's commitment to procedures over 'substantive' interpretations of the good life or collective goals are primarily based on presumptions about individual autonomy, on the one hand, and logical consistency, on the other:

> The reason that the polity as such can espouse no substantive view, cannot, for instance, allow that one of the goals of legislation should be to make people virtuous in one or another meaning of that term, is that this would involve a violation of its procedural norm. For, given the

> diversity of modern societies, it would unfailingly be the case that some people and not others would be committed to the favoured conception of virtue. (M, 57)

The key point for this procedural version of liberalism is that it is up to the individual to be self-determining. For this position, the principle of universal dignity is neutral with respect to matters of cultural difference and the good. It simply does not privilege specific interpretations of substantive goals over others. Taylor refers to the claim of the Quebec nationalists for the survival of the distinctive 'French Canadian' culture of Quebec as a substantive goal that would not be endorsed by this version of liberalism (M). Consequently, procedural liberalism is likely to leave substantial demands for recognition unsatisfied. This does not mean that Taylor argues that any and every claim for recognition warrants endorsement. Indeed, he explicitly argues the opposite (M). Nevertheless, Taylor claims that procedural liberalism is unable to resolve the actual problem that is at issue in cases like Quebec and that there are other strands of liberalism that are committed to collective goals or substantive definitions of the good. Taylor argues that the versions of liberalism that are 'suspicious of collective goals' and that 'insists on the uniform application of the rules', thereby defining rights without exception, are 'inhospitable' to difference 'because it can't accommodate what the members of distinct societies really aspire to, which is survival' (M, 60–1).

Taylor does not explain in detail how claims for recognition should be assessed, but presumably it should be done in a manner consistent with his moral ontology and the dialogical process of evaluating and accepting the 'best account'. In some respects, this position is fairly realistic and grounded in existing practices, yet it is worth recalling the potential deficiencies that were highlighted through the comparison with Habermas' procedural discourse theory of justice, with its commitment to universalistic standards of justice and its attempt to reach a rationally founded agreement between different points of view (Habermas 1996). Habermas considers that Taylor's opposition between collective goals and individual rights is mistaken and it derives from the somewhat misleading depiction of a particular interpretation of liberalism (Habermas 1994).

Taylor's conceptualisation of the politics of recognition clarifies some of the implications of his contribution to the liberalism–communitarianism debate. In particular, Taylor considers that while liberalism is correct to presume that some basic individual rights are inviolable, there are some collective goals, like that of cultural survival in particular, that can claim a certain qualified priority over the rights of the individual. It is worthwhile quoting Taylor's sketch of this position, since he recognises that considerable judgement needs to be exercised in privileging a particular collective goal over the equal, or 'uniform', treatment of individuals (M, 61).

> One has to distinguish the fundamental liberties, those that should never be infringed and therefore ought to be unassailably entrenched, on the one hand, from privileges and immunities that are important, but that can be revoked or restricted for reasons of public policy – although one would need a strong reason to do this – on the other. . . . A society with strong collective goals can be liberal, on this view, provided it is also capable of respecting diversity, especially when dealing with those who do not share its common goals, and provided it can offer adequate safeguards for fundamental rights. There will undoubtedly be tensions and difficulties in pursuing these objectives together, but such a pursuit is not impossible, and the problems are not in principle greater than those encountered by any liberal society that has to combine, for example, liberty and equality, or prosperity and justice. (M, 59–60)

The notion that the denial of recognition is damaging to identity is not just based on the political demands of contemporary movements and groups for justice. It is based on theories of identity and general social understandings of how an identity is constituted through the interactive relationship that one has with the 'other', that is, depending on the situation and phase of individual development, the partner and partners in social interaction. In certain respects, according to Taylor, the interpretation of recognition as integral to identity has been consolidated most of all in the domain of intimate relations (M). Indeed, Taylor seems to presume that the view that one's sense of self is contingent on the other's recognition is now quite widespread, rather than a perspective associated with contemporary theories of intersubjectivity, like those of Honneth and Habermas. Although this conception of recognition is present in Hegel's dialectical accounts of the struggle for recognition, it is the work of George Herbert Mead that constitutes the most important conception of mutual recognition. Mead shows how an individual's consciousness and sense of identity are constituted through the process of learning to perceive oneself by adopting the standpoint of the other (Mead 1934). The process, he argues, is one that is anchored in the communicative structure of social interaction and that is initially experienced in early infancy in the form of behavioural gestures. In particular, it involves adopting the perspective of the self as the 'me' rather than the 'I' (Mead 1934; see Honneth 1995a; Habermas 1992; Browne 2010).

Taylor does not really explore Mead's key claim about taking the standpoint of the other in detail. Taylor refers to the more popular notion of the 'significant other', rather than Mead's categories of the immediately present 'concrete other' and the more abstract view of society as a whole which is present in the later phase of adopting the standpoint of the 'generalised other' (Mead 1934). Mead does, however, speak of 'significant symbols' that have a collectively shared and agreed upon meaning (Mead 1934; Joas 2000). Taylor's account of the actual social dynamics of recognition is then less elaborated than that of the major theorists of intersubjective recognition that have been influenced by Mead, such as Honneth and Habermas. As we have seen, Taylor does emphasise how the use of language involves the intersubjective perspective of the 'us' (PA). Moreover, Taylor distinctively explicates the connection that recognition has to the new sense of equality and mutuality that was proposed by Rousseau and subsequently by Hegel in his account of the dialectic of lordship and bondage (Rousseau 1968; Hegel 1977).

These two perspectives in political philosophy undoubtedly had a significant influence upon Mead's thought (see Joas 1985; 1998; Browne 2010). Rousseau contended that the 'general will' of a democratic polity involve the equal participation of all and that this entailed a sense of the fusion of the individual and the collective. Similarly, Hegel's interpretation of the dialectic of lordship and bondage emphasised the significance of the recognition of interdependency and the creation of a self-consciousness of the shared perspective of the 'we' (Hegel 1977). Hegel's dialectical theory argued that autonomy was conditional on the other's recognition of its interaction partner's autonomy and that autonomy was empty and insubstantial without this recognition. Hegel likewise proposed that the struggle for recognition culminated in a more advanced synthesis of perspectives and an awareness of mutuality. In Taylor's opinion,

> The struggle for recognition can find only one satisfactory solution, and that is a regime of reciprocal recognition among equals. Hegel follows Rousseau in finding this regime in a society with a common purpose, one in which there is a 'we' that is an 'I', and an 'I that is a 'we'. (M, 30; see Hegel 1977: 110)

The notion of the struggle for recognition is clearly contrary to the atomistic perspective of liberal individualism. It implies that individual autonomy derives from processes of socialisation and social interaction (see Habermas 1992; Browne 2017b). Habermas has convincingly argued that Mead's theory results in a conception of individuation through socialisation (Habermas 1992). The concept of recognition can likewise enable the development of conceptions of intersubjective freedom and social freedom (see Honneth 2014; Browne 2010). It is therefore worth underlining that there is a considerable amount at stake for the tradition of Critical Theory in the interpretations of the struggle for recognition and intersubjectivity. In particular, the notion of recognition is associated with the conceptions of democracy that have been proposed in recent critical theory and their corresponding models of justice. These considerations will be returned to later in the discussion of criticisms advanced of Taylor's version of recognition from within the Critical Theory tradition.

The second explanation Taylor proposes for the increasing appreciation of the need for recognition is one that we have already encountered in terms of his interpretation of the emergence of a modern democratic social order. That is, Taylor proposes a historical explanation of a fundamental change in the cultural interpretation of the social order and, although this is not elaborated by him at length, a corresponding alteration in the social structure. The shift to a more democratic and less hierarchical social order results in a distinction between the categorical position that a person occupies in the social order and the actual unique identity of the individual person. As noted at the beginning of this chapter, individuals were previously identified by the position that they occupied in the social structure and they were principally recognised by others in these terms. In other words, the collective membership or group affiliation defined identity; that is, it was by way of their group affiliation and collective membership that individuals understood each other. The ethic of authenticity partly changes this conception, as does the liberal attribution of equal dignity to all individuals. This shift created a new element of uncertainty and the need for explicit recognition. Put differently, the movement away from identities that were fixed by the hierarchical social order and group membership created the possibility of non-recognition, and hence of the potential insignificance of the individual or group.

> What has come about with the modern age is not the need for recognition but the conditions in which the attempt to be recognised can fail. That is why the need is now acknowledged for the first time. In premodern times, people didn't speak of 'identity' and 'recognition' – not because people didn't have (what we call) identities, or because these didn't depend on recognition, but rather because these were then too unproblematic to be thematized as such. (M, 35)

The theme of recognition has become important to contemporary discussions of justice and democracy. In particular, it has been the topic of an extended debate between Axel Honneth and Nancy Fraser (Fraser and Honneth 2003). The connections between recognition and other aspects of social life have likewise been explored, such as in relation to social movements and labour (Smith and Deranty 2012). For this reason, there is now a better sense of the relative strengths of the category of recognition and its possible limitations. Notably, it has become apparent how different implications ensue from how recognition is theorised, for instance whether it is seen primarily as a form of political conflict or as a means of social integration, or, rather, how these two facets of recognition and the dynamics of its enactment are combined in a synthetic conceptualisation of recognition (see Browne 2017a; Deranty and Renault 2007).

In any event, these discussions of recognition have advanced well beyond the point of Taylor's contribution to this theme and it would be fair to suggest that Taylor turned to the category of social imaginary instead. The notion of social imaginary, in his conception, at least, has evident intersections with the key notions of his extant theory, such as those of frameworks, background and horizon, and its interpretation of the nexus between language and practice. It could be argued that Taylor's theory is more trans-subjective than intersubjective in its approach to meaning, referring to diffuse cultural backgrounds and individual subject's self-interpretation (see Smith 2010). The subsequent discussions of recognition have been largely shaped by the work of Honneth and Fraser, the debate between these two theorists, and the various attempts in light of their work to explicate and apply the category of recognition. In particular, the consolidation of the theory of recognition constitutes one of the major strands of Critical Social Theory today. Taylor's writings on this theme still form an influential point of reference, even though it is possible to recognise some of underlying differences in the respective approaches and particularly in the emphases given to struggle, conflict and domination (see Browne 2017a). Similarly, Taylor's turn to the notion of social imaginary is no doubt partly influenced by the centrality of the question of the secular in his subsequent work and the category of social imaginary is consistent with his concern with the long-term historical and cultural changes that facilitated the emergence of demands for recognition and that arguably continue to influence the determination of recognition, that is, the forms, distribution and meaning of recognition.

As noted with respect to the theories influenced by G. H. Mead, Taylor does not have the same depth of concern with the forms of intersubjective mediation and the dynamics of social interaction as some of the other major theorists of recognition. His approach to social action focuses more, as we have seen, on the hermeneutic interpretation of meaning and the orientation to the good, rather than the transactional exchange and the dialectics of control that are present in social relations of recognition (see Browne 2017a). Taylor is, of course, aware of these dynamics, but he does not develop a theory of the 'grammar of social conflicts' in the manner of Honneth's theory of the struggle for recognition (Honneth 1995a). Honneth's subsequent conceptualisation of social freedom certainly exhibits important parallels with Taylor's interpretation of recognition, something that is not surprising given its grounding in Hegel's philosophy, and it has similar difficulties in reconciling its conception of democratic ethical life with an appreciation of the dynamics of social conflict and heteronomy (Honneth 2013; 2014; see Browne 2017a).

Taylor's arguments concerning recognition have been subject to a variety of criticisms (see Gutmann 2004). For the moment, we will concentrate on those directly associated with the debates over recognition, since some of the other issues have already been canvassed in the discussion of liberal assessments of Taylor's position in its debate with communitarianism. Taylor's interpretation of recognition is probably most proximate to that of Honneth. This is particularly because Honneth defines justice in terms of self-realisation and the good life (Honneth 2003b). In fact, it is not difficult to perceive that some of the criticisms that Nancy Fraser makes of the recognition approach to justice apply more to Taylor's account than to Honneth's theory. Fraser argues that recognition is primarily a matter of culture and that injustices pertain to the institutionalised social status of groups and individuals. The latter reflects the level of recognition or misrecognition, such as with respect to gender identity. In Fraser's opinion, redistribution is basically concerned with the allocation of material goods and is largely about economic distribution, such as concerning remuneration and trade relations (Fraser 1995).

Honneth's conception of recognition is meant to explain both the cultural and material dimensions of social relations, whereas Taylor's interpretation of recognition does appear to be more distinctly concerned with cultural identities and their political implications (Honneth 1995a; M). Taylor's account of the politics of recognition does not really consider the economic or material features of the politics of recognition – perhaps this is something that he considers so obvious that it can be taken for granted. Even so, the broad line of Taylor's thought is one that contends that the instrumental approaches to justice that prevail in conceptions of distributive justice are ultimately insufficient and that the questions of morality and justice should be addressed from the wider ethical perspective of the *good*. In other words, any determination of a fair material distribution emanates from the culturally constituted values of a community and that corresponding ethical practices are required to bring about a fair distribution. Moreover, there are dimensions of the politics of recognition, such as those to do with the appreciation of the ways of life of particular cultures, that are of a considerably different form to that of matters of distributive justice and these dimensions of recognition need to be addressed as matters of values, meanings and respect for cultural difference. Taylor's lifelong experience of the situation of French-speaking Canadians had probably reinforced this distinction for him. However, Fraser's general point, in this instance, is that the political expression of such a view has led to the movement away from the politics of redistribution (Fraser 1995; 2003a). And, irrespective of whether Fraser is correct, it is true that the themes of Taylor's work have intersected with the emergence of identity politics, such as in its focus on identity and its emphasis on freedom as self-realisation.

Fraser's critical contention that Honneth's conception is focused primarily on identity appears applicable to Taylor's interpretation of recognition. This is true, even though Honneth's theory is far more developed in terms of the psychological theories of individual development. Honneth draws extensively on the work of D. W. Winnicott as well as Mead (Honneth 1995a). Taylor's discussion of the nexus between recognition and identity is more general and somewhat less nuanced. Hence, Taylor makes similar claims to Honneth about the damaging effects of denied recognition; however, Taylor lacks a sufficiently detailed psychological account to make specific, rather than general, claims about the pathological consequences of denied recognition or disrespect. Honneth, by contrast, distinguishes between different forms of disrespect and their consequences: a loss of self-confidence, he argues, is related to the psycho-social development of the individual in the family, whereas a loss of self-respect derives from a failure to receive equal treatment on the basis of the institutionalised recognition provided by the legal rights (Honneth 1995a; 2007). Although Honneth's explication of the forms of suffering ensuing from misrecognition or disrespect is more differentiated than Taylor's, these brief remarks about self-confidence and self-respect demonstrate the basic integrity that there is between the different spheres of recognition and identity.

Honneth, interestingly, has a highly positive view of Taylor's approach in general. He considers that Taylor attempts to formulate a broad philosophical anthropological critique of the distortions present in the overall cultural form, or, to use a different term, civilisation (Honneth 2009). At the same time, Honneth criticises Taylor for making a distinction between different historical phases of politics in order to explain how the politics of recognition has come to gain prominence (Honneth 2001). Honneth argues that this distinction is misleading, because recognition has always been at stake in political struggles. Material distribution, he argues, is a form of recognition and bound up with the overall dynamics of recognition (Honneth 2003a). The political dynamics that Taylor considers in the context of recognition tend to be those related to the public sphere, that is, whether claims for recognition are given expression in the public sphere and lead to a response by the state or are precluded from the public sphere. Honneth (2003b) much more strenuously underlines the pre-political, as well as political, social grounding of struggles for recognition and the social experiences of disrespect and contempt that are inherent in denied recognition.

Fraser's position is that recognition is primarily about culture and that there is a need to sustain a commitment to justice as redistribution (2003a; 2003b). The politics of recognition and those of redistribution are connected, but they are not the same, in her opinion. Fraser introduced a distinction, which though disputed, bears upon the need for differentiation between the types of recognition that are connected to identity politics. Fraser distinguished between affirmative and transformative demands for the recognition of identity and the remedies that correspond to them (Fraser 1995). The latter, transformative demands for recognition, involves the deconstruction, and not simply the affirmation, of an identity, such as with respect to the gender construction of femininity. It may be possible to extract from Fraser's contentions a more general assessment of Taylor's approach to the politics of recognition, since it is true that much of his work addresses the cultural context of politics, even if it is intended to enhance material redistribution. Fraser's position, though, relies upon questionable distinctions, such as that of the distinction between material redistribution and cultural recognition (see Young 2008). Fraser's further implication is that Taylor's position, like many communitarian perspectives more generally, does not permit sufficient scope for transformation, because it is based on a framework that fixes identity in its affirmation of recognition, such as what it means to be a women or a member of an ethnic minority. This criticism of Taylor's reinforcing existing identities relative to the changing of them in a way that is necessary for justice is certainly inconsistent, as Christopher Zurn notes, with Taylor's commitment to the hermeneutic notion of a 'fusion of horizon' (Zurn 2003). The 'fusion of horizon' involves the adaptation and altering of an identity in the process of coming to an understanding. Taylor sketches these processes of modifying and transforming understandings, values and identities in the following terms:

> We learn to move in a broader horizon, within which what we have formerly taken for granted as the background to valuation can be situated as one possibility alongside the different background of the formerly unfamiliar culture. The 'fusion of horizons' operates through our developing new vocabularies of comparison, by means of which we can articulate these contrasts. So that if and when we ultimately find substantive support for our initial presumption, it is on the basis of an understanding of what constitutes worth that we couldn't possibly have had at the beginning. We have reached the judgment partly through transforming our standards. (M, 67)

At the same time, Taylor's deployment of the notion of the fusion of horizons is open to question. He proposes a general sense of cultural recognition that finds some of its justification in the fusion of horizons. Taylor's claim that human cultures that are enduring are bound to possess something worthy of admiration and are therefore likely to be learned from hardly seems a strong basis for constructing justice (M). It could even be interpreted as potentially diverting attention away from the injustices of particular cultures. Habermas (1994) claims that Taylor's view supports a collective right that limits the potential for individuals' critical independence. Habermas' argument is not a straightforward restatement of the liberal position, rather it is based on his theory of intersubjective communication and its conception of rationality, that is, the ability to accept or reject 'validity claims' or statements based on reasons (Habermas 1984). Taylor could argue that appreciating aspects of human cultures does not preclude the possibility of critique, whether from a position internal or external to the culture. Nevertheless, these criticisms seem to imply that Taylor's claim about cultural recognition should not be understood so much as a normative prescription, but rather that it should be interpreted in the weaker sense of an orienting presupposition of social interaction. That is, that it is only possible to enact recognition on the basis of having some expectation of worth and according a certain dignity to what is encountered in another culture. This does not mean that one then has to uphold the value of the continuing 'survival' of the particular culture.

Paradoxes of Democracy

Taylor approaches the theme of democracy in a way that is consistent with his overall approach to politics. However, there are two contrasting facets of his writings on democracy. First, Taylor, like de Tocqueville, presents a critical assessment of the tendencies that undermine democracy in the present. These tendencies are, to some extent, consistent with the overall development of modern capitalist society, such as that of the dominance of instrumental rationality and the growth of the ethos of individualism. Taylor wants to specify how these tendencies that contribute to the decline of democracy can be reversed. The consolidating of democracy is primarily a matter of political culture in his opinion, rather than the establishment of some exact political procedure or institutional resolution. Second, Taylor wants to explicate and challenge some of the contradictions or paradoxes of democracy. In particular, he wants to show how democratic principles can be applied in a way that is 'undemocratic' or leads to forms of 'democratic exclusion' (DC). In some respects, this concern is close to the position that Taylor develops on procedural liberalism. He argues, as we saw, that procedural liberalism applies the rules of equal treatment in a uniform manner that is 'inhospitable' to difference (M).

In a general sense, Taylor considers that the failings of modern democracy, such as parts of the population's widespread sense of indifference and alienation from politics, the apparent inability of political processes to address major issues and concerns, and the predominance of sectional and private interests over the general and public interests, can only be rectified through more effective modes of participation. Taylor contends that political liberalism's commitment to 'negative freedom', that is, the freedom of the individual from interference and the right to pursue private interests, is unable to generate the commitment to the collective good that is required by a democratic polity (PA). Further, there are powerful tendencies in modernity that can lead, in Taylor's opinion, to the reduction of democracy to simply a set of political procedures and, to reiterate the claims made earlier in the chapter, these procedures can produce outcomes that appear formally justified but that can be devoid of substantive values. In fact, contemporary procedural liberalism does not so much challenge the broad tendencies of atomisation and individualisation as accept them as their implicit points of reference.

Taylor (EA) deplores a number of recent developments like the growth of consumerism, the acceptance of the pursuit of strategic self-interest as a basis for social organisation and as a normative ideal, and the narcissistic self that is informed by therapeutic discourses which emphasise the priority of self-gratification, as constituting distorted images of the ethic of authenticity. Yet, Taylor equally considers such developments to be explicable in terms of the misunderstandings of atomistic liberalism and the vicissitudes of capitalist society. In his opinion, the expansion of instrumentally oriented institutions, especially the bureaucratic state, capitalist corporations and technology, has compounded the displacement of moral conceptions of the good by subjective definitions of interests and gratifications. The consequences of atomism and instrumentalism are, he argues, a widespread sense of fragmentation and powerlessness, both of which weaken democracy and its preconditions. Despite sharing, then, Tocqueville's emphasis on the importance of civic associations, Taylor seeks to revise Tocqueville's diagnosis of how modern democracy is undermined by tendencies towards the 'soft despotism' of 'tutelary power'. In short, he believes that it is fragmentation, 'a people increasingly less capable of forming a common purpose and carrying it out', that represents the real danger to contemporary democracy (M, 112).

In large part, this diagnosis specifies the conditions for reversing the tendencies that undermine and limit democracy. Taylor follows Tocqueville in drawing attention to the importance of the 'decentralization of power' and he suggests that a cultural shift is necessary in order to 're-enframe technology' (M). The core problem today is, nonetheless, that of regenerating the democratic ethos. Taylor alludes to three elements of this task. The first is the prerequisite of effective forms of public participation and social cooperation; the second is the appreciation of the dialogical character of practices and their establishment of shared or common meanings; and the third is the generative power to produce outcomes that overcome binds and to instantiate processes of democratisation. This last dimension points to the affinity of creative practices and autonomy, since autonomy has, in effect, to presuppose itself in order to be truly actualised. The exercise of autonomy can disclose previously unrecognised potentials and, to this extent, there is a certain degree of reciprocity between it and creative practices. Taylor contrasts this capacity for regeneration with the experience of fragmentation:

> A fading political identity makes it harder to mobilize effectively, and a sense of helplessness breeds alienation. There is a potential vicious circle here, but we can see how it could be a virtuous circle. Successful common action can bring a sense of empowerment and also strengthen identification with the political community. (EA, 118)

The paradox of democracy that Taylor addresses is that it is broadly the same processes, in his opinion, that enable democracy to be truly effective that can generate forms of 'democratic exclusion'. In Taylor's view, democracy is a political form that depends on an acceptance of the legitimacy of the point of view of partners and opponents in interaction, and, indeed, of their right to exercise power. Further, the underlying sense of solidarity and trust that this involves is more likely to be achieved where there is a strongly shared cultural identity. Taylor believes that it is a common mistake to attribute the social exclusion that derives from social solidarity entirely to nationalism. No doubt, nationalism is a major source and justification of social exclusion, but Taylor argues that exclusion is connected to the meaning of democracy, especially the notion of popular sovereignty and the idea of 'the *government* of all the people'. The '*government* of all the people' is the other side of 'what makes democracy inclusive', that is, 'that it is the government of *all* the people' (DC, 124).

In a democracy, the involvement of all is valued and a condition of legitimacy. In this, it contrasts with other forms of political organisation, for instance in the case of empires there was not the same expectation of universal inclusion in political processes. Rather, there was typically a considerable disjunction between political centres and the periphery; hence there was not the level of interpenetration that characterises a democracy. Democracy is founded, at least in principle, on a new sense of 'collective agency' and democratic legitimation involves consultation and citizens' deliberation (DC). These demands of democracy can facilitate forms of democratic exclusion, because democracy can be interpreted in a way that suggests that those groups and individuals that appear not to satisfy the conditions of democratic involvement potentially undermine popular sovereignty. Now, this assessment of groups and individuals may be based on assumptions about their religious affiliation, as well as those concerning racial or cultural difference. The most extreme form of this 'dark side of democracy', to use the title of Michael Mann's book that Taylor's analysis appears to echo, is that of ethnic cleansing (Mann 2005). However, Taylor notes that there are a variety of forms of exclusion, for instance there can be the democratic exclusion of simple oversight and neglect, such as where ethnic groups and minorities are treated as spectators rather than participants in the public discussions about them (DC).

Modern democracy produces not only the exclusion of those who are not part of a community and lack citizenship, but the new form of 'internal exclusion', that is, the exclusion of part of the population and citizenry (DC; see Browne 2015). In one sense, this is the other side of the modern extension of the rights of citizenship to categories of persons that were formally excluded from them, whether they be women or other categories of formerly 'excluded' persons based on ethnicity, like the non-ethnically German guest workers and their children in Germany, which were formerly excluded from citizenship. The problem of internal exclusion is related to the lack of the substantive means to realise their membership of the community, such as owing to poorer material conditions on account of the nature of employment – or unemployment – or the absence of representation in the public sphere. It should not be surprising from the preceding analysis that Taylor considers that the liberal positions of procedural justice and neutrality regarding matters of cultural difference are inadequate responses to forms of democratic exclusion. In one sense, the remedy for democratic exclusion is democratic inclusion, but when simply stated in this way such a remedy overlooks the existing source of resistance to inclusion and the fact that the genuine accommodating of difference would lead to changes in political culture and possibly political organisation. Taylor, rightly or wrongly, points to federal measures in relation to contexts like Scotland and Catalonia as instances of the types of institutional measure that may be required to address democratic exclusion (DC).

Taylor's view may be realistic, but it could be considered rather inconclusive and a restatement of the problem of democratic exclusion. In one sense, this is precisely Taylor's intention, that is, he seeks to clarify and raise awareness of the problem of democratic exclusion. He is undoubtedly right to assume that democratic exclusion can only be addressed through public understanding, inclusive citizenship and commensurate policies. By contrast, the predominant liberal approaches acknowledge the problem of exclusion but compound it somewhat, in his opinion. This is, first, because they lack the means for broaching the sources of exclusion, and, second, they veil the fact that versions of liberalism emerge from particular cultural backgrounds. Taylor's proposal for addressing democratic exclusion is more in line with the hermeneutic notion of the fusion of horizons. It represents an alternative to the assertion of fixed identities and it is a means of enabling shifts in meaning. Taylor summarises this position in a way that reiterates many of the details covered in the discussion of recognition and the debate between liberalism and communitarianism:

> My argument here has been that a full understanding of the dilemma of democratic exclusion shows that there is no alternative to what I have called sharing identity space. This means negotiating a commonly acceptable, even compromised political identity between the different personal or group identities which want to/have to live in the polity. Some things will, of course, have to be nonnegotiable, that is, the basic principles of republican constitutions – democracy itself and human rights, among them. But this firmness has to be accompanied by a recognition that these principles can be realized in a number of different ways and can never be applied neutrally without some confronting of the substantive religious-ethnic-cultural differences in societies. (DC, 144)

Conclusion

Taylor has made a major contribution to contemporary political debates. He mobilised important dimensions of his overall philosophy in these contexts, for instance his conceptions of identity and meaning underpin his position on the limitations of procedural and atomistic liberalism. Taylor's proposed alternative to the 'cross-purposes' of the liberalism and communitarianism debate is not only appealing because of its apparent mediation of positions, but also because holistic liberalism incorporates additional elements derived from the expressivist conception of freedom. Yet, for many contemporary liberals, Taylor's position is more communitarian in its conception of the good and the precedence that it gives under certain conditions to the values of the collective relative to the individual. Similarly, Taylor argues that a strong sense of solidarity, or what the civic republican tradition termed 'patriotism', is the precondition for realising the values espoused by liberalism, including such basic ones as the principle of equal treatment. In this regard, Taylor's perspective involves complex considerations about groups and culture that are somewhat bracketed by liberal individualism and its presuppositions, such as those concerning the basis of justice in individual choice.

There is a certain ambiguity in Taylor's position on liberalism. These tensions are apparent in his contribution to the debates over the politics of recognition. On the one hand, he shows how liberalism's notions of rights and equal dignity underpin claims for recognition by groups and individuals. On the other hand, he points to the failures of liberal political theory and liberal institutions to meet legitimate demands for recognition. Of course, Taylor's position is open to challenge, since it could be argued that he reiterates similar dilemmas. He does not propose a procedure or mechanism for the mediation of major conflicts and differences. Rather, he argues that these conflicts have to be worked out in practice. And this standpoint reflects his acceptance of the hermeneutic notion of the fusion of horizons. The fusion of horizons involves processes of mutual appreciation and the transformation of identities. Taylor highlights the cultural background to the growing expectations of recognition and he draws specific attention to the roots that the politics of recognition have in the ethic of authenticity (M). Despite the significance of these arguments, Taylor's proposal might be regarded as exemplifying the flaws identified by Nancy Fraser in the theory and politics of recognition. Fraser claims that the recognition conception of justice is more concerned with cultural identity than material circumstances and redistribution.

Taylor's approach to the politics of recognition belongs to the liberal tradition in another sense. As Abbey notes, his 'work on the politics of recognition can be seen as continuing the traditional liberal concern with how a society can peacefully accommodate significant and enduring differences among its population with minimal recourse to coercion' (Abbey 2000: 148). One could argue that Taylor's explication of the conundrum of democratic exclusion is motivated by similar concerns. He believes that it is necessary to acknowledge the sources of democratic exclusion that derive from popular sovereignty. It has been suggested in the preceding analysis that Taylor's 'remedies' could be viewed as a restatement of the problem, but, in a sense, this is precisely his intention and there can be little doubt that there is considerable need to come to terms with this major issue of contemporary liberal democratic polities. Taylor's perspective on politics underlines the salience of the background horizons of meaning and the importance of the historical formation of cultural understandings and institutions. These considerations are subsequently consolidated in his works on modern social imaginaries that are examined in the next chapter.

5

Modern Social Imaginaries

Introduction

Charles Taylor's work on modern social imaginaries seeks to sketch the distinctive features of the horizon of meaning and 'self-understanding' of modern society (Taylor 2002; MSI; SA). Taylor's interpretation of the modern social imaginary is, then, a continuation and extension of his preceding discussions of modernity, although a number of formerly subordinate and relatively peripheral themes acquire much greater prominence. In particular, the explication of social imaginaries and their historical transformations is integral to Taylor's major later endeavour of developing a theory of a secular age, and which is meant to constitute an alternative to established theories of secularisation. At the same time, the notion of social imaginaries is probably the most important later refinement in Taylor's theory, since it consolidates the relationship between different components of his work, such as the linkages between the interpretation of social practices and the defence of 'holistic liberalism'. Taylor draws many of these components together around the category of social imaginary. The notion of social imaginary enables Taylor to explore the political forms of modern society, to borrow from the title of Claude Lefort's book, and to offer a more complex framework for understanding political culture and the long-term processes of the historical sedimentation of meaning in social relations, particularly in terms of the consolidation of meanings that enable diverse social practices and that serve as a matrix that conditions political alternatives and options (Lefort 1986; see Gaonkar 2002). In short, Taylor states that the 'social imaginary is not a set of ideas; rather, it is what enables, through making sense of, the practices of society' (MSI, 2).

Although Taylor has never explicitly presented it in this manner, the notion of social imaginaries enables him to address several considerations that were unresolved in his earlier work, and to balance some prior emphases. In most respects, civic republicanism is very much focused on the political domain and an acceptance of the political constitution of society informs its approach to culture. Taylor's indebtedness to this tradition of thought is undisputed, but the notion of social imaginaries allows him, in principle at least, to go beyond some of its limitations. To make this point crudely: the problems of modernity are social and not just political, in the traditional sense of the political sphere. Indeed, Taylor argues that new interrelationships of the social and the political develop in modernity. Likewise, the categories Taylor deploys in the liberalism versus communitarianism debate of 'holism' and 'liberalism', as well as the respective antonyms he presents of 'collectivism' and 'atomism', are primarily typological constructions and distinctions (PA). These categories arguably serve to illuminate political orientations, but the actual combinations of them in practice is far more complex and, in certain respects, more intuitive and habituated than rational. For this reason, Taylor requires a category that can elucidate these practical interconnections and that clarifies the framing interpretation of the connections at the same time. The concept of social imaginary potentially situates the politics of recognition in a wider horizon of meaning and illuminates those moral expectations that underpin the enacting of reciprocal freedom and mutual autonomy in modernity.

Taylor likewise recognised that the context of the discussions of modernity in social and political theory have changed. It was now much more widely acknowledged that it is necessary to account for the diversity of the forms of the institutionalisation of modernity, whilst specifying those shared traits and presuppositions of the forms of modernity. This revised perspective has been reinforced by diverse social developments, from the modernisation during the late twentieth century of East Asian societies, the disintegration of the state socialist variant in Eastern Europe, the challenge that the so-called Iranian Revolution presents to assumptions about historical tendencies, to the debates in the social sciences over a transition to a new phase of modernity, and, more generally still, the way that the ecological crisis opened up the issue of the consequences of an industrial civilisation. Although Taylor does not survey the diversity of the institutionalisations of modernity, the category of social imaginary is clearly meant to constitute a framework for the possible exploration of the varieties of modernity and their historical sources. In this respect, Taylor acknowledges the influence on his thinking of the discussions around the journal *Public Culture*, which published issues on modern social imaginaries and alternative modernities. And this collaborative background is apparent in Taylor's elaborations of modern social imaginaries (Taylor 2001; 2002; MSI; SA).

Taylor's work on modern social imaginaries is conceived as a contribution to the perspective of multiple modernities, with its acceptance of the diversity of forms of establishing modernity (see Eisenstadt 1999b; 2000; 2001; Arnason 2002; Browne 2017b). At the same time, Taylor's adoption of the category of social imaginary draws its initial inspiration from Benedict Anderson's (2006) influential account of the imagined community of the nation. Anderson highlighted how a sense of the 'simultaneity' of experience by a large group or people was significant for the formation of modern nationalism, where such experiences of simultaneity were, for instance, promoted by the creation of newspapers of national scope. Taylor likewise refers to the work of Bronislaw Baczko (1984) on social imaginaries as an important informant of his approach (see Abbey 2006). Baczko's interpretation is congenial to that of Taylor, partly because it highlights the significance of narrative forms. Taylor nevertheless develops the notion of the social imaginary in a unique manner, drawing on elements of his own philosophy and incorporating relevant details from recent social theory. Even so, in his major explications of social imaginaries, Taylor never engages with Cornelius Castoriadis' (1987) and Claude Lefort's (1986; 1988) more distinctive and original conceptions of social imaginaries. Castoriadis is arguably the most important theorist of the social imaginary.

Castoriadis' and Lefort's writings represent an important strand of political thought. For this reason, a direct confrontation with Castoriadis' and Lefort's conceptions of the modern social imaginary and its relation to the political institution of modern society will be used to bring Taylor's key contentions and underlying suppositions into sharper focus. In fact, Taylor's argument that the modern social imaginary generates the 'closed world structure' of the 'immanent frame' through the denial of transcendence is contrary to the secular positions of Castoriadis and Lefort (SA; Castoriadis 1997a; Lefort 1988). Taylor's extended account of a secular age will be examined in the next chapter. This chapter's comparison is principally concerned with Taylor's account and assessment of the institutionalisation of modernity. Similarly, the multiple modernities perspective will be shown to place considerable emphasis on the conflicts and strains of modernity. Further, multiple modernities highlights the salience of the collective subjectivity of groups and movements in their attempts to pursue projects and programmes of modernisation (see Domingues 1995; 1999; 2000). One further feature of Taylor's engagement with modern social imaginaries is worth noting: Taylor's ensuing account of a secular age contests Marcel Gauchet's argument concerning the disenchantment of the world (Gauchet 1997).

A Moral Order of Mutual Benefit

It would be difficult to overestimate the contemporary importance of Taylor's work on modern social imaginaries. It stands at the intersection of the leading debates of the last thirty years in political philosophy and social theory, especially that over the continued commitment to, what Habermas termed, the 'project of modernity' and the alternative perspective of postmodernism, which argued for a rupture with the core modernist notions of the subject, rationality and moral universalism (Habermas 1987b; see Susen 2016; Browne 2008; 2017b). Taylor aims to overcome the antinomies underlying these debates through a renewed appreciation of the social background to modern practices of individual autonomy. His analyses of modern social imaginaries trace the lineages of modernity and how a particular understanding of society took hold (MSI; SA; Taylor 2002). Taylor's earlier account of the development of the formation of modern identity could be criticised for its focus on the history of ideas and theoretical interpretations of the self (SS). It is possible to argue that Taylor did not pay sufficient attention to the actual social contexts and that it is necessary to take into account the extent of the actual diffusion or penetration of notions throughout the entire society, such as those derived from Stoic philosophy or Augustinian ideas about morality. Be that as it may, Taylor's approach to social imaginaries seeks to make a strong connection between the historical forms of theorising, social practices and the social structure.

Taylor's conception of the social imaginary is less stringent and more eclectic than those of Castoriadis and Lefort. For Taylor, a social imaginary is less elaborated than a theory; social imaginaries, instead, bear precisely on how people imagine their society. The moral order crystallises these imaginative projections and the associated understandings are enabling features of practices. Social imaginaries, according to Taylor (MSI, 23), are the 'ways people imagine their social existence, how they fit together with others, how things go on between them and their fellows, the expectations that are normally met, and the deeper normative notions and images that underlie these expectations'. Taylor incorporates into his conception of social imaginaries aspects of such developments in social theory as Bourdieu's idea of *habitus*, the phenomenological concept of the lifeworld, and Habermas' communicative revision of the relationship between action and the interpretative horizon of the lifeworld (Bourdieu 1990; Habermas 1984; 1987a).

The psychoanalytic background to some other usages of the concept of social imaginary is less evident in Taylor's conception. This absence is indicative of Taylor's rather different approach to that of the other major theorists of social imaginaries and the perspective of multiple modernities that is associated with the work of S. N. Eisenstadt (1999a; 2000) and J. P. Arnason (2002). The other major theorists of social imaginaries incorporate into this notion a stronger sense of the conflicts and tensions of institutionalisation, whilst the perspective of multiple modernities considers that the tensions and contestations, associated particularly with the modernising programmes, are a constitutive feature of the multiplication of the forms of modernity. However, as we have seen, Taylor's work does intersect with the perspective of multiple modernities. He considers that modernity has been significantly conditioned by the tension between the dominant tendency of instrumental reason and the expressivist orientation that derives from Romanticism (see Chapter 3; EA).

It may be possible to develop the linkages between Taylor's interpretation of the Romantic Movement's ideal of imaginative creation and the conceptions of social imaginaries in the work of Castoriadis and other figures, like that of Peter Murphy (2012). Castoriadis considers that creation is a defining feature of the social imaginary and that it gives rise to unique and original forms of the institution of society (Castoriadis 1987). In Castoriadis' opinion, there is, however, a permanent tension between that of the instituting social imaginary and the instituted social imaginary, although this tension is generally veiled by the apparent independence of the latter relative to the former. By contrast, Taylor does not define the instituting of the social imaginary as one of radical alterity and historical novelty, rather it is for the most part defined by Taylor as one of enacting established understandings. Although social imaginaries involve utopian projections and representations, Taylor draws attention to historically complicated and long-term processes by which imaginaries are attempted to be instantiated and ultimately achieve a form of practical actuality by being incorporated into widely shared understandings of society (MSI; Baczko 1984). Indeed, according to Taylor, the way that social imaginaries encompass a repertory of practices is crucial to their institution. Taylor claims that the history of social and political movements shows that:

> To transform society according to a new principle of legitimacy, we have to have a repertory that includes ways of meeting this principle. This requirement can be broken down into two facets: (1) the actors have to know what to do, have to have practices in their repertory that put the new order into effect; and (2) the ensemble of actors have to agree on what these practices are. (MSI, 115)

In *Modern Social Imaginaries*, Taylor seeks 'to sketch an account of the forms of social imaginary that have underpinned the rise of Western Modernity' (MSI, 2). He argues that the constitution of a set of uniquely modern ideas about the nature of society started to develop around the seventeenth century and that these ideas partly originated as a response to the effects of the Wars of Religion in Europe. Taylor's major concern is with the emergence and consequences of a new conception of the 'moral order'; its distinguishing feature, he argues, is the idea of society arranged according to the principle of mutual benefit through individual action. Taylor locates the origins of this idea in the natural law tradition, emphasising its descent from Grotius and Locke. Grotius developed a theory of 'political society' that was based on a view of the nature of its members. In this view, according to Taylor, human beings 'are rational, sensible agents who are meant to collaborate in peace to their mutual benefit' (MSI, 3).

Of course, the ensuing implications of a moral order of mutual benefit were far from apparent at the point of its initial positing; they were to be worked out in the processes of its transformation into a social imaginary. In particular, it would lead to a rupturing of the hierarchical schemas of premodern social imaginaries. Premodern imaginaries tended to be organised by notions of 'hierarchical complementarity' (MSI; Taylor 2002). Taylor's illustration of an exemplar of these premodern imaginaries of 'hierarchical complementarity' demonstrates how they justified and gave practical orientations to actions that served the reproductions of a society based on fixed positions and rank:

> Society was seen as made up of different orders. These needed and complemented each other, but this didn't mean that their relations were truly mutual, because they didn't exist on the same level. Rather, they formed a hierarchy in which some had greater dignity and value than others.

> An example is the often repeated medieval idealization of the society of three orders: *oratores*, *bellatores*, *laboratores* – those who pray, those who fight, and those who work. It was clear that each needed the others, but there is no doubt that we have here a descending scale of dignity; some functions were in their essence higher than others. (MSI, 11)

The modern imaginary of the mutually beneficial consequences of individual pursuit of their own interests establishes the centrality of the market economy to the structure of society and of economic behaviour to individuals' ethical conceptions. According to Taylor (MSI, 69), the economy is one of the 'three important forms of social self-understanding which are crucial to modernity' – the other two being the public sphere and 'the practices and outlooks of democratic self-rule' – each representing the 'penetration or transformation of the social imaginary by the Grotian-Lockean theory of moral order'. Social imaginaries consist of previously arcane theories that have become collectively shared projections that intermesh with practices and institutions.

Beside their nucleus in the idea of mutual benefit, civil society appears as the common denominator of these three variants of the modern social imaginary. Taylor's version of modernity is primarily that of liberalism, since the alternatives that he considers appear as tendencies that mobilise dimensions of modern social imaginaries, especially that of popular sovereignty, in seeking to redefine the conditions for realising the principle of the moral order. The connections that Taylor draws between social imaginaries and social practices provide substantial insights into liberalism and reframe its communitarian critique (MSI). Taylor shows why liberalism necessarily involves a form of social self-understanding. In his opinion, moral orders are not limited to norms and normative principles; they contain specifications and representations of the substantive conditions of their practical realisation. At the level of social imaginaries, there can be no deontological morality.

Taylor narrates how a very specific set of notions underwent a process of expansion and adaptation over the course of four centuries. The natural law conception of the priority of the rights and obligations individuals have to one another was initially consolidated in the context of the resolution of the conflicts of the period of the Wars of Religion. At that time, this conception was almost entirely counterfactual, contrasting with the actual order of domination and the legitimating imaginaries of hierarchical complementarity, like the metaphor of a chain of being. Taylor outlines three 'axes' of the new principles of sociality's 'migration': the shift from a relatively elite theory to a broad social imaginary, an extension from one 'niche' of specialised discourse to infiltrating many niche discourses, and the movement towards practical application with the incipient view of a new moral order attaining a more prescriptive rather than hermeneutic status. The last amounts to the exigencies of putting into practice or living according to the new principle of sociality, rather than treating the principle as a theoretical interpretation of how social relations could be organised. In each of the three cases, the changes are cumulative, reinforcing the reconstruction of society around the new social imaginary. During the past four centuries, Taylor claims that

> the idea of moral order implicit in this view of society has undergone a double expansion: in extension (more people live by it; it has become dominant) and in intensity (the demands it makes are heavier and more ramified). The idea has gone, as it were, through a series of 'redactions,' each richer and more demanding than the previous one, up to the present day. (MSI, 5)

Of particular significance, the modern social imaginary becomes independent of its original foundations and points of reference. The religious buttressing of the moral order of mutual benefit became unnecessary, whilst the basis in contract theory of understanding social relations in terms of mutual benefit and mutual service tends to disappear as it is realised and the defending of individuals' rights increases in importance. Grotius had presented an image of society as politically constituted; yet the realisation of the notions incipient in the new moral order would eventuate in a redefinition of society. Society would no longer be equated with the polity, because the social would be considered to contain its own principles of organisation, amongst its first expressions being Adam Smith's idea of the invisible hand of the market. Rather than politically constituted, Taylor argues that what distinguishes modernity is the fact that the 'other dimensions of social existence are seen as having their own forms and integrity' (MSI, 76).

The history of the constitution and evolution of distinctively modern ideas about the basis of social order is related to a number of transformations in the material conditions of social relations. Taylor highlights a long-term process of 'domesticating the nobility', including the subordinating of estates' independent sources of power. He outlines tendencies leading to intensive disciplining and regulating of practices, referring to Foucault's arguments and alluding to those of Elias. Similarly, *Modern Social Imaginaries* largely converges with Max Weber's theses in suggesting that religious groups and Protestant sects carried forward many of the modernising trends deriving from the emergent forms of association.

The familiarity of these arguments with those of classical and post-classical sociological theory extends to the work of Emile Durkheim. Durkheim's account of social solidarity and the division of labour anticipate Taylor's conception of the moral order (Durkheim 1964). Like Durkheim, Taylor relates the rise in individualism to a new conception of society, but he considers that modern individuals are not seeking to realise some higher virtue. Rather, action guided by the modern morality of mutual respect and mutual service is understood to be an end in itself and one could extrapolate from this that Durkheim's conception of society is not entirely secular, despite his insistence that the science of sociology deals with social facts. It could be argued that Durkheim's original conception of the shared beliefs and morality of the *collective conscience* involved a stronger sense of constraint and conditioning power than Taylor's version of the social imaginary, especially in its modern articulation. Even if this is less the case at the level of conceptualisation, it is certainly the case that Taylor tends to attribute a greater sense of constraint and emergent properties to premodern, rather than modern, social imaginaries.

Drawing on an idea present in his earlier writings, Taylor sees modernity as affirming the ordinary. This affirmation undermines hierarchical notions of superior realms of human activity, such as in the withdrawal from the profane, and it is connected to the increasing importance of the economy. In Taylor's view, the economy is the institutionalised realm of modern self-understanding that is most devolved to the level of individual interaction; the public sphere and the idea of popular sovereignty tend to retain a sense of collective action. They are largely constituted by common action and they lead to common action. In addition to the three primary articulations of the modern moral order, Taylor suggests that the increase in bills and charters of rights has been of such consequence that it may be considered a fourth manifestation of its social self-understanding. The growth of rights is closely related to what Taylor considers is the modern imaginaries' empowering of individuals, since the understanding of society they imply accentuates agency and, above all, freedom. Taylor summarises four crucial constant features of the modern moral order in the following terms:

> Summing up, we can say that (1) the order of mutual benefit holds between individuals (or at least moral agents who are independent of larger hierarchical orders); (2) the benefits crucially include life and the means to life, although securing these relates to the practice of virtue; and (3) the order is meant to secure freedom and easily finds expression in terms of rights. To these we can add a fourth point: 4. These rights, this freedom, this mutual benefit is to be secured to all participants equally. Exactly what is meant by equality will vary, but that it must be affirmed in some form follows from the rejection of hierarchical order. (MSI, 21–2)

Modern Social Imaginaries and the Conflicts of Political Formations

Despite Taylor acknowledging the impediments to the historical processes of transformation that resulted in the consolidation of the imaginary of a moral order of mutual benefit and its associated realisation of individual freedoms, he does not explore these impediments in the depth that they warrant. His admission that, in many instances, the effective realisation of the rights and freedoms implied by the modern imaginary is a relatively recent phenomenon, especially as manifested in the restructuring of gender and family relations, could have been recognised to present greater problems for his arguments (MSI). Similarly, Taylor's integration of diverse insights into history veils problems that he has in explaining why a formerly subordinate tendency of the imaginary may subsequently prevail.

Taylor claims that his approach encompasses the questions formerly dealt with under the category of ideology, but this claim does not really appear particularly convincing. The account of ideological consequences of the modern imaginary is limited to some interesting but fairly general theses about contemporary trends. Taylor considers that a 'direct access society' is the correlate of the consolidation of the modern moral order of mutual benefit and that this has come to take on increasing contemporary significance (MSI). That is, individuals increasingly consider that their participation in various dimensions of society as 'direct' and immediately experienced, rather than conditioned by mediations, such as mediated by group belongings. It is not difficult to perceive that the ideal of 'direct access' creates and depends on expectations of equality and openness that capitalist society has difficulty meeting or actually realising. Of course, the idea of a moral order of mutual benefit can be questioned in much the same terms.

This limited consideration of ideology and its legitimation of modern forms of domination and injustice could be explained by Taylor's contention that ideologies are dependent on the understandings constituted by the social imaginary. However, several basic assumptions determine the displacement of the issues of ideology and the oversights indicated. First, the economy is considered by him to be a form of association that partially realises the moral order of mutual benefit and respect. Its centrality is therefore not so much due to the capitalist economy establishing a dynamic of exploitative relations and their consequences. Second, Taylor emphasises the political dimension of the modern imaginary, but he does not conceive the augmentation of power to be an overarching feature of modernity. Indeed, Taylor contrasts the modern imaginary of mutual benefit and equal respect for all not just with premodern imaginaries but also with an alternative subordinate and less realised modern imaginary of command and hierarchy. Third, Taylor argues against visions of modernity as shaped by overarching processes of collapse, crisis and alienation. However, like exploitative economic relations and the augmentation of power, Taylor's analyses of modern imaginaries are too sophisticated to entirely neglect these features of modernity. Similarly, he offers an account of how the 'objectifying' of reality increases; yet the scientific and technological dimensions of modernity are relatively peripheral to its overall position. They are certainly considered far more consequential in the comparable visions of the Frankfurt School theorists and some postmodernist perspectives (Horkheimer and Adorno 1972).

The confrontation with alternative standpoints indicates that Taylor's focus in his reconstructions of the modern social imaginary is primarily upon a couple of exemplary cases and aspects of modernity. Of these, he depicts the public sphere as a particularly significant modern innovation, distinct from premodern conceptions of political assemblage. In Taylor's view, the public sphere is definitely not some deficient version of the classical *agora*, rather its originality consists precisely in its being outside power yet normative for power. He follows Michael Warner in suggesting that the public sphere enables the institution of a space for conflict in the form of debate (Warner 1990). Taylor nicely brings out the importance of imagination to the effective realisation of notions of the public sphere and public opinion. He supplements Habermas' emphasis on the idea of the common agreement of a reasoning public by revealing its extrapolation from the social imaginary. Significantly, the inflection of the modern imaginary in the public sphere contrasts with the immemorial 'time out of mind' of ancient and traditional imaginaries. Modern time is, Taylor argues, secularised; it inhabits the present and radically transforms the character of social practices. Secularity means that there are no transcendental grounds of society, so that it is the common action that is consequential. Irrespective of whether it is in the present, past founding acts or those now 'coming about', society is considered to originate from common action.

For Taylor, secularity constitutes a critical threshold in the formation of modernity and his explication of its connection to the public sphere restates secularisation's original meaning. Secularisation does not amount to the end of religion but the emergence of a context in which the co-existence of belief and non-belief is accepted as legitimate. For some this may appear as a reiteration of the traditional liberal treatment of religion as a matter of private consent. However, as will be explained in detail in the next chapter, Taylor intends to explain the conditions of a secular age in a manner that goes beyond the liberal perspective and its emphasis on the individual. In fact, as we have seen, Taylor always treats the liberal outlook as something to be explained, rather than an explanation in itself. The closest Taylor comes to a systematic conclusion in the book *Modern Social Imaginaries* is acknowledging that the consequences of this transformation to a secular age continue to be negotiated in the present (MSI). In part, modernity is expressed in new public narratives of identity and belonging, especially the nation.

Taylor acknowledges that his endorsement of 'provincializing Europe', in Dipesh Chakrabarty's terminology, is consistent with the general framework of social imaginaries that he sketches but inconsistent with his own work's particular emphasis (MSI; Chakrabarty 2000). Given Taylor seeks to develop a more pluralistic conception of multiple modernities, the discussion of alternative modernities is relatively circumscribed. It largely takes the form of a comparison of 'North Atlantic liberal democracies'. In particular, Taylor contrasts the imaginaries of popular sovereignty that shaped the North American and French Revolutions (MSI; SA). He suggests that the imaginary of the American Revolution was able to find institutional expression in a repertoire of practices and institutions that were already familiar, whereas the French Revolution had far greater difficulty finding the appropriate institutional expression of the new principle of legitimacy that it brought forth. In many respects, Taylor's explications of Hegel's assessment of the perils of Absolute Freedom and the Terror of the French Revolution prefigures this comparison and assessment of the alternative practices that are founded on different interpretations of the democratic form of the modern imaginary (H; HMS).

According to Taylor, the French Revolution's key problem was finding a means to limit itself that was consistent with its understanding of popular sovereignty. It drew specific inspiration from Rousseau's idea of the general will. The consequent scepticism towards political representation produced an extreme emphasis on transparency and Taylor believes that some of the excesses of the French Revolution should be understood in terms of this nexus. Further, the basic dilemma the revolution confronted was sharpened by a tradition of popular insurrection. It was possible to understand popular insurrection as an exemplar of the general will. Taylor describes the French Revolution as failing, in a sense, to resolve its basic problem. Even when popular sovereignty became equated with periodic elections the republican background to the social imaginary persisted and constituted a continuing potential challenge to legitimacy. Many of the tensions intrinsic to the French Revolution are manifest in later historical practices of radical transformation and it instances the possibility social imaginaries contain to overshoot existing conditions.

The French Revolution's descent into the Terror demonstrates the destruction that can result from intending to realise objectives that are radically discontinuous with prior practices and forms of organisation. By contrast, the American Revolution was able to find institutional expression in a repertoire of practices and institutions that were already familiar. Likewise, there was already agreement in America over the democratic meaning of representative assemblies, even though 'the American Revolution started on the basis of one legitimacy idea and finished by engendering another, very different one, while somehow avoiding a radical break' (MSI, 111).

This aspect of Taylor's reflections on the French Revolution can be compared with Castoriadis' and Lefort's specific underlining of social imaginaries' creative and indeterminate character. Lefort appears closer to Taylor in regarding the democratic imaginary as instituting a principle of division and confronting the problem of democratisation being without limits, whereas Castoriadis considers creativity to be an ontological feature of the social imaginary, shaped by the tension of an instituted society to its process of instituting. For Castoriadis (1997a: 78), the chief reason for the supposed 'failure' of the French Revolution and the descent into the Terror was the 'withdrawal of the people'. The 'success' of the revolution, in his opinion, consisted in its break with religion and the instituting of a new horizon of significations. It was, nevertheless, like religion in seeking an overall classification of reality, but differed in its intention of devolving authority onto the people themselves. In a similar vein, Lefort (1988) claims in a discussion of the position of Quinet that the 'revolution failed' not so much because of an inability to find appropriate institutional form but more on account of the continuing hold of past models and images. This was not just a matter of the overhang of the preceding political order of the *Ancien Régime*; it was the work of a theological-political tendency towards repetition that obviated the revolution's creative dimension.

Notwithstanding the substantial theoretical and political differences between Castoriadis and Lefort, their conceptions of social imaginaries emerged from an engagement with several shared considerations. Taylor's account of the long-term elaboration of the imaginary of the moral order of mutual benefit and his analysis of its three-fold articulation would need to be considerably refined in order to come to terms with a phenomenon they considered decisive: the totalitarian potential immanent in modernity and its historically consequential realisation. In Taylor's view (MSI, 181), the twentieth-century totalitarian regimes were largely a product of discontent with liberal democracy; inspired by different critical diagnoses of its debasement of human capacities, they mobilised around 'heroic' visions of different orders. Although the argument is by no means effectively developed, Taylor implies that in the construction of totalitarian regimes the alternative projects of either republican virtue and full equality or the anti-humanist politics of will and force were combined with interpretations of the modern 'modes of narrativity – progress, revolution, nation' (MSI, 177).

This contention undoubtedly opens up an important line of analysis, but the brevity of Taylor's remarks is surprising, given that the overall intention of his adopting the category of social imaginaries is that of the reinforcement of the perspective of multiple modernities. The failure of modernisation theories, particularly those that took liberal democracy as their model, to effectively conceptualise the distinctive patterns of totalitarian formations constitutes a major justification for the introduction of the perspective of multiple modernities. It is likely that a more developed explication of the imaginary of totalitarian formations would focus on a broader set of sources, including the synthesis in the Soviet model, as Arnason's investigations disclose, of imperial background and revolutionary project (Arnason 1993).

Lefort considers that totalitarian regimes enact a kind of reversal of the logic of democracy and for this reason enable a unique insight into the political institution of democracy and the veiling of the political in modernity. He argues that totalitarian projects abolish 'the signs of division between state and society and the signs of internal social division' (Lefort 1986: 286). Like modern democratic regimes, totalitarian regimes take shape in the context of the exclusion of extra-social grounds of legitimation; it is to this idea of social constitution that the concentration of power appeals. According to Lefort, the conjunction in these regimes of power, law and knowledge is the opposite of the division and opening that characterise democracy. Democracy depends on an acceptance of the indeterminacy that is created by the site of power remaining permanently unoccupied (Lefort 1988).

In large part, Taylor endorses this analysis of the 'mutation' that eventuates in the separation of civil society from the state, yet he departs from the full implications of Lefort's contention 'that democracy is instituted and sustained by the *dissolution of the markers of certainty*' (Lefort 1988: 19, emphasis in original). Taylor seems to seek to limit uncertainty by arguing that a shared identity should underpin popular sovereignty in a secular society. In a sense, this republican position is unremarkable. It could, however, obscure what Lefort considers to be the political genesis of the internalisation of division in society and the political framing of a symbolic unity that overarches this division. In fact, this tendency gradually asserts itself in Taylor's conception of political identity, signalling a retreat of sorts from the full weight of the idea of society as founded on itself.

The reasons for Taylor's relative neglect of totalitarian regimes are not difficult to discern. In his opinion, it is 'the victories of liberal democracy in these struggles' with the totalitarian challenges to it 'that seem finally to have entrenched the identity of civilization and the modern order' (MSI, 181). One could wonder whether this position reflects a particular moment in the history of modernity and whether it is compelling from a longer-term and broader historical-sociological perspective. Taylor's statement does not give sufficient weight to the resistance to progressive developments, such as how reactionary movements developed in response to claims for civil rights and the feminist movement (see Eisenstadt 1999a). Similarly, Taylor suggests that the normative horizon of this moral order can be seen in the way that the public sphere and popular sovereignty are simulated in states that resist these spheres' effective institutionalisation. In the first instance, this insight into how the crystallising of the social imaginary transforms the conditions of political legitimacy and their ideological distortion is broadly compatible with the conclusions that Castoriadis and Lefort drew from their analyses of totalitarian formations. At the same time, they believed that it was necessary to develop this insight into the social imaginary in a manner that differs in important respects from the position that Taylor sketches.

Notably, a broadly shared recognition of the closure of meaning that is typical of instituted imaginaries gives rise to divergences in the explications of the origins and character of the veiling. Castoriadis, for instance, believes that the elucidation of the social imaginary and the critique of the priority of theory in relation to instituting practices are one and the same task (Castoriadis 1987). The priority of theory is one of the means by which social imaginary significations deny the processes of their own social instituting and serve to legitimise the hierarchical structure of social orders. Even though certain overlaps can be identified, Taylor's genealogy of modernity highlights precisely the process of translating theoretically elaborated conceptions into collectively held imaginaries. The contrast between these conceptions of instituting is implicit in Taylor's comment that the modern understanding of freedom has led to 'the constant attempt to transform what are at first merely objective sociological categories (e.g., handicapped, welfare recipients) into collective agencies through mobilizing movements' (MSI, 81).

Taylor's account of the interplay of theories and practices in the processes of constituting and institutionalising modern social imaginaries highlights the emergence of a 'bi-focal' vision of the world (MSI). That is, Taylor considers that an objectivist interpretation of reality is the counterpart to the moral order of mutual benefit. It represents a radical departure from the premodern social imaginaries that originated in the classical world; they were organised by the idea that social and natural reality are essentially forms that fulfil teleological patterns of meaning. In Taylor's opinion, the rupturing of this ontological linkage of being and meaning is critical to the modern imaginary since, as has been noted, it makes possible a vision of the social order that is no longer conditioned by notions of hierarchical spheres of activity.

In certain respects, this analysis complements Castoriadis' critique of the veiling of the institution of the social imaginary through its explication of a transformation in understanding and perspective. Indeed, Taylor comments that: 'In one way or the other, the modern order gives no ontological status to hierarchy or any particular structure of differentiation' (MSI, 12). No doubt this statement could be faulted for overestimating certain tendencies; it reflects the extent to which Taylor's conception misses a striking feature of Castoriadis' interrogation of philosophy. Castoriadis' critique extends to the rationality of modern reason, seeking to disclose the occlusion intrinsic to the constitution of the logical order of the world. In other words, Castoriadis intends the 'self-transcendence of reason', something Taylor endorses but pursues differently.

Castoriadis' disclosure of the rational or quasi-rational modes of occlusion identifies salient continuities between objectivist interpretations of the world and the classical vision of forms, evident in a shared commitment to the thesis that being is that which can be determined and their incorporation of dimensions of identity thinking (Castoriadis 1987: 221). Taylor's general description of the disjuncture of modern reason is largely consistent then with its self-interpretation, especially the conception of rationality that underpins liberal-contract theories of society. However, for this very reason, it potentially obscures what Castoriadis regards as the element of truth incipient in the ancient vision of the world and that found expression particularly in the philosophical conception of *form*, which was, for instance, a central consideration of the thought of Plato and Aristotle. That is, Castoriadis argues that the form-giving property of the imaginary is a critical feature of its institution (Castoriadis 1987: 372). The ancient classical interpretations of form cannot be simply allocated to either the modern rationalist or romanticist frames of meaning, but rather serves as a counterpoint that draws attention to their social-historical institution and, indeed, arguably some of the limitations or downscaling that characterises modern thought.

By focusing on the historical constitution of the idea of a moral order of mutual benefit, Taylor is able to reveal the horizon of interpretation in which security and protection became key values of the modern imaginary. These two core values of modern liberalism were already well in place by the time of the institution of the economy as a distinct sphere. On this development, Taylor is insightful without fully justifying the presuppositions of his analysis. He does not specify the degree to which the concept of 'interlocking advantage' actually permeated the subordinate classes of late feudalism and early capitalism. Rather, he introduces with reference to the arguments of classical political economy the unsubstantiated and unconvincing claim that the subordinate classes extend this principle to their economic superiors. Although the idea of an exchange for mutual benefit is presented as facilitating a general interest in prosperity, this is an idea of the social contract that subordinate classes have rarely been in a position to effectively put to the test. It has persisted because it is a kind of functional metaphor, equivalent, Taylor notes, to 'a good engineering design, in which efficient causation plays the crucial role' (MSI, 70). In this way, Taylor reveals how a moral conception is intertwined with the notion of the economy as an ordered system of regularities.

Taylor's depiction of a common source of the market economy and the institution of the liberal polity may appeal to critics of Castoriadis' juxtaposition of two dominant modern imaginaries. In Castoriadis' opinion, the conflation of the project of individual and social autonomy with the alternate capitalist imaginary of unlimited rational, or properly pseudo-rational, domination and control is a mistake, one especially common to contemporary discussions of liberalism (Castoriadis 1997a: 61; 1997b). These two projects, he argues, differ from one another in their genealogies and they conflict in their principles. The 'germ' of the project of autonomy is ancient Greek democracy, itself a creation infused by the secular breakthrough of an appreciation of the indeterminacy of the world. It introduced for the first time the imaginary of the social foundation of the institution of society, and Castoriadis traces this project's modern revival to the emergence in the twelfth century of self-governing city states. Whereas the most significant premodern antecedent of the capitalist imaginary is the Judeo-Christian religious signification of 'infinity', its subsequent change from originally a transcendent reference to a category of this world enabled it to fuse with the understanding of reason as oriented towards the domination of nature (Castoriadis 1991; 1997b).

Castoriadis' contention that the significations of these two dominant imaginaries animate the modern moral order poses the question of whether the social imaginary of the economy should be identified with the self-description of classical economics. The criticisms of classical economics have drawn attention to its disregarding factors inconsistent with its logic and moral indifference to injustices, such as those relating to gender and colonial exploitation. Because Taylor (MSI, 79) has defined the market as 'the negation of collective action', his sketch of the self-understanding of the modern economy has little capacity to throw light on the shift that Peter Wagner (1994) describes from liberal modernity to organised modernity. Similarly, Taylor's description of the emergence of the economy neglects the nascent world market and potential constitutive significance of interchanges. He recognises these interchanges' inconsistency with the moral schema of mutual benefit in delimiting his analysis to the social imaginary of 'Western modernity', implying that global interchanges should not be reduced to the sole dimension of economic exchange.

Even if Taylor's conception of a moral order of mutual benefit could incorporate these complications, Taylor's neglect of the most important other discussants of social imaginaries means that the presupposition of this understanding of the economy remains open to question. Lefort and Castoriadis have been able to place in question the self-consistency of economic significations through their respective elucidations of social imaginaries (see Browne 2016). In their view, the coherence of significations is a result of the constitution of a perspective on reality and at the same time a function of the closure of meaning. This double process is indicative of the tensions that they consider intrinsic to what Lefort describes as 'the political' and Castoriadis the imaginary institution of society (Lefort 1988; Castoriadis 1987; 1997a). Taylor's explication of social imaginaries recognises some manifestations of this constitutive tension, though ultimately its implications are downplayed in favour of a vision of religion's new political relevance in a secular society.

Taylor's justification of the place of religion in secular societies represents a variation of the familiar argument that democratic societies can be undone by the freedom they create. He argues that the legitimacy principle of popular sovereignty demands the foundation of society in collective action, but that such an order requires a political identity that should not be entirely identified with this common will. The exercise of the common will contains a potentially antinomian dimension. Democratic societies precisely require bonds to a political identity that are strong enough for groups and individuals to accept expressions of the common will with which they do not agree and that may be adverse to them (MSI). Taylor believes that these demands of republican freedom can be buttressed by a political identity that takes religion as a point of reference, while sustaining the independence of the public sphere. Whether Taylor appreciates the complete ramifications of this paradox is open to question; however, he draws support for it from his analysis of the practices that facilitated the passage to modern popular sovereignty and the imaginary communities that developed in response to its formal instantiation.

Taylor claims that popular sovereignty originally had another point of reference beside collective action itself: the myth of an ancient constitution, in which parliament had its 'rightful place alongside' the king, and individuals possessed time-immemorial rights. In fact, the sense of justice incipient in this myth worked its way into the new understanding of society. It justified the popular struggle of the English civil war and in mobilising the colonists it did much of the 'heavy lifting' in the revolutionary American War of Independence. This traditional, or 'backward looking', dimension of the change to popular sovereignty in the form of representative assemblies would be obscured by 'the reinterpretation of past actions as the fruit of the new principle' (MSI, 112). Similarly, Taylor suggests that the risk of popular sovereignty destabilising identity, as in fact the spreading of this notion was experienced in parts of Europe after the French Revolution, led to many accepting the view that the 'unity needed for collective agency' presupposed an 'antecedent unity of culture, history' or language. 'And so behind the political nation, there had to stand a preexisting cultural (sometimes ethnic) nation' (MSI, 191).

Conclusion

Taylor's work on modern social imaginaries simultaneously amounts to searching critique and profound justification of liberalism. The modern moral order enables the social enactment of the liberal ideal of individual freedom, on the basis that such freedom and agency are mutually beneficial. Of course, if Taylor is correct then this social imaginary is now so ingrained in modern individuals' background understanding of the world and social relations that it is largely perpetuated independently of the demands of explicit political legitimation.

Taylor's tracing of the long-term processes of the evolution and social extension of the modern imaginary reveals how 'the different ways the original path breaking forms of the modern imaginary – economy, public sphere, and self-governing polity – ended up transforming the understanding of other levels and niches of social life' (MSI, 152). Taylor shows that the attributes of the modern moral order constitute a horizon of understanding that modern individuals are virtually incapable of thinking beyond, yet are simultaneously dependent on for their freedom and autonomy. In fact, Taylor believes that the secularisation corresponding to the modern social imaginary means that it has the potential to become a 'closed world' structure owing to the loss of a sense of transcendence (SA).

In certain respects, this contention amounts to an inversion of the theses of Castoriadis and Lefort, which emphasise how the modern social imaginary of the project of autonomy and the democratic political form derive from the exclusion of extra-social explanations of the world and depend on the secular notion of society as entirely founded upon itself. It has been suggested that Taylor's synthetic approach downplays some of the specificity that the notion of social imaginary has in the work of these theorists. Taylor highlights the enabling character of social imaginaries, but this generative perspective is not the same as Castoriadis' elucidation of the social imaginary as the ontological creation of the institution of society. In a similar vein, Taylor's treatment of the Western model of liberal democracy as paradigmatic may be justified, but it is hard to perceive how his formulation of the imaginary of a moral order of mutual benefit can fully comprehend the multiple forms of modernity. For instance, Castoriadis' claim that modernity contains not only the imaginary of the project of autonomy but also that of the unlimited (pseudo-) rational domination and control of nature and society appears relevant to grasping the totalitarian mobilisation of the modern imaginary (Castoriadis 1991).

Given that the previous chapter noted some parallel conceptions in Taylor's view of the preponderance of instrumental rationality and the influence on his thinking of Tocqueville's analysis of the undermining of democracy, the interesting question is why Taylor did not develop these conceptions in his works on the modern social imaginaries into a more complete account of modern political forms. The comparisons that have been drawn in this chapter demonstrate that Taylor's approach to social imaginaries is framed by a different set of concerns. He has sought to set out the underpinnings of his account of a secular age in his explication of the modern social imaginary. The notion of social imaginaries in the work of Castoriadis and Lefort was equally connected to a reconsideration of the potentials for radical democracy, despite the considerable differences between them concerning whether this should be regarded as antithetical to liberal democracy or a possibility sustained by it. Taylor acknowledges the potential for radical democracy that derives from the modern imaginary and its basic principles, but one can perceive that he accepts many liberal arguments on the need for restraints and regulations of political mobilisation and popular sovereignty. In some respects, he regards the social extension of the democratising tendencies of the imaginary to be more important than the higher intensity of democratic participation in the ancient Greek *polis*. The polis was not just restricted in its membership, in Taylor's opinion, but limited by following 'much more closely traditional laws and mores than the Republics of the modern world' (Taylor 2009: 97).

6

Living in a Secular Age

Introduction

In this chapter we examine Charles Taylor's book *A Secular Age* (2007). The book created a stir upon its release because it challenged many long-held assumptions about both religion and secularism. Taylor argues in this work that religion continues to have much to teach us about how to negotiate social life in the twenty-first century. *A Secular Age* is a long, ambitious and detailed book which would take up a book length analysis in its own right to cover in depth. All we can hope to achieve in this chapter is an overview of its main ideas while focusing on some of its important themes. Before beginning, some caveats about the book should be mentioned. The book focuses on religion and secularism largely from the Western perspective, and the religion that is principally addressed in the book is Christianity. The shift towards secularism that Taylor assesses is the secularism to be found in Western, often democratic and capitalist, states. For some authors the concept of secularism, and post-secularism which follows on from it, are ethnocentric terms with origins in Western social science that leave many cultural assumptions unexamined (Leezenberg 2010: 111). However, with this criticism foremost in mind, we will endeavour to unpack Taylor's theory of a secular age and consider its consequences for contemporary times.

In *A Secular Age* Taylor employs a number of innovative concepts, such as 'the buffered self', the 'immanent frame', 'secularity 3' and 'exclusive humanism'. The 'buffered self' stands in contrast to the porous self of antiquity and the Middle Ages, where people had a close relationship to the natural and supernatural worlds. The buffered self, as we shall see in more detail below, is closed off by boundaries between the self and the spiritual. The 'immanent frame' is that aspect of society where social agents conduct their daily affairs without much concern for the spiritual dimension. 'Secularity 3' is understood as a novel way of interpreting secularisation, and involves an increase in spiritual options that modern social agents may choose from, and which can include membership in established churches or personalised spiritual outlets. For Taylor, those who worship in churches can be described as 'dwellers', while those who pursue other options in spirituality he terms 'seekers' (see CP). 'Exclusive humanism' is a form of humanism that stresses that people possess all of the necessary resources for human fulfilment, and that there is no need to look beyond this world or individual human endeavour to live a full and meaningful life. Here reason and individual action is elevated to the highest level, and God or any other form of supernatural help is rendered redundant. We will return to these and other concepts examined by Taylor later in this chapter. Before doing so, however, it is necessary to explore some of the foundational ideas that are integral to *A Secular Age*, and for understanding where the book sits in debates about religion and modernity. These include secularism and the secularisation thesis, Deism and the Enlightenment, and the Axial Age and multiple modernities.

The Religious and the Secular

In *A Secular Age*, Taylor considers the separation of church and state that is sometimes taken for granted in Western capitalist democracies. This is understood by many to be what is meant by the word 'secularism', and it is an idea that Taylor sets out to challenge. Secularism did not come on the scene suddenly, but rather took some time to develop, and was the outcome of social unrest and armed conflict over religious doctrines over many years. Taylor is critical of this understanding of secularism, but for now it is important to outline its development. Émile Durkheim notes that many cultures and societies draw a distinction between what is sacred and what is profane (Durkheim 1995: 34). Durkheim claims that sacred things include not only gods or spirits, but also material objects that are imbued with a sacred identity because they are used in rituals, or have a spiritual significance. A chalice used in a Mass or Communion Service, or a pilgrimage site, are modern day Christian examples. Overall, for Durkheim, sacred things are 'regarded as superior in dignity and power to profane things' (Durkheim 1995: 35). Although this distinction between the sacred and the profane may seem simplistic, Taylor suggests that it is the basis for our understanding of the political dimension of religion and the boundaries of the secular (SA, 454–5). This is because Durkheim's sacred/profane binary creates the conditions by which communities are able to distinguish between 'religion and the state' (SA, 455). Furthermore, it underpins a sense of religious membership, which is in some countries closely linked to political identity (SA, 455). Thus, Durkheim's sacred/profane distinction is a significant development in the understanding of secularism, but religious reform also played an integral role.

As Taylor points out in *Sources of the Self*, the Reformation, and especially Puritanism, was a major element in the establishment of what he calls 'the affirmation of ordinary life' (SS, 227). By this Taylor means that while pre-Reformation Christianity championed the life of monks and the priestly class over the everyday lives of ordinary people, the Reformation overturned this and put common people's lives and concerns at centre stage. Previously, members of religious orders were seen as superior and more holy because of their celibacy and lives of prayer and mortification, and because they were educated in the study of Latin and theology and could read and interpret the Bible, whereas the Reformation celebrated the life of ordinary people and encouraged them to live a holy life in the midst of their daily work. The scriptures were translated into vernacular languages, ministers were allowed to marry, and churches were stripped of their ornate decorations and statues, so that the focus was on God rather than on the saints. The sermon, in which the minister explains the Gospels and teaches the congregation, became of central importance to the liturgy in Reformation lands, and the importance of a direct relationship between God and the individual was preached.

The French and Industrial Revolutions also had a marked impact on the development of secularism. As we will see in more detail below, the Enlightenment and the Romantic period that followed played a significant role in embedding secularism in Europe. The Enlightenment's call to examine the world through the lens of reason rather than religion was a major factor in promoting the idea that religion should be relegated to the private sphere rather than the public sphere, another key element of secularism which Taylor takes issue with. This aspect of the Enlightenment was symbolised by the publication of the *Encyclopédie* by Denis Diderot and Jean le Rond d'Alembert in 1751, with later editions following, which claimed to contain a collection of human knowledge gathered through rational methods. Furthermore, Owen Chadwick (1975) analyses how the European mind became steadily secularised over the course of the nineteenth century, the result of greater levels of urbanisation, a free press, scientific discoveries, and criticisms of religion from intellectuals such as John Stuart Mill and Karl Marx.

Today, secularism is an assumed aspect of modern life in Western nations. Churches do not concern themselves with the political process, unless it is to raise awareness about a social issue, and governments for the most part do not promote or suppress any religion or denomination. This is not the case everywhere, and religions such as Islam see no distinction between faith and the social order, the idea of a secular realm being a foreign one. In Islam, religion is a complete way of life and it sees little distinction between the sacred and the profane (Nasr 2003: 26). The world Islamic community, the *ummah*, is a united whole in Islamic teaching and is guided by the Quran and the *Sharīah* law, and religion and the state are combined in this system. Secularism is an important aspect of contemporary discussions about religion, and we will return to it below and analyse what Taylor has to say about it. Before doing so, however, it is important to discuss a related set of ideas in religious studies which have also been of great significance to Taylor's book. This is the social process known as secularisation.

The Secularisation Thesis

Steve Bruce argues that secularisation is manifested in three overall social changes, which include a decline in people's church involvement and attendance, the lessening of influence that churches and other religious institutions have in society, and a decline in religious faith, so that more and more people make the claim that they do not believe in the existence of God (Bruce 1996: 26). The idea that as modernity increases, religion decreases, is called the secularisation thesis, and although it has undergone several revisions and much criticism, it is a thesis that retains a number of supporters (Bruce 2011). In *A Secular Age*, Taylor calls analyses of secularisation that focus on the loss of religion 'subtraction stories', and he points out that they see in it only a negative development leading to the decline of religion, while not allowing that the secularisation process, and the idea of a secular order in society, may have something to offer by generating creative ways of organising society and politics.

Taylor writes that the word 'secularization'

> describes a process which is undeniable: the regression of belief in God, and even more, the decline in the practice of religion, to the point where from being central to the whole life of Western societies, public and

> private, this has become sub-cultural, one of many private forms of involvement which some people indulge in. (SS, 309)

Taylor suggests that the second part of his definition of secularisation, the decline of the practice of religion, is more widespread today than is the first, a lack of belief. In other words, many people go on believing in God, but stop attending church. Taylor asks why people from earlier epochs found it difficult *not* to believe in God, while today non-belief is much less challenging. Taylor briefly considers the usual causal explanations for secularisation, including industrialisation, technological change, science, education and urbanisation, but discounts each of these as being able to radically change the nature of belief so that faith in God becomes problematic. Taylor questions the idea that what encourages secularisation is the removal of obstacles to unbelief, as if science, or education, are able to demystify the world and open the way for attitudes that question the necessity of God. Although science and education, as well as industrialisation, might broaden a person's outlook, this alone is not enough to be a cause for greater levels of agnosticism, or a widespread turning away from religion. In *Sources of the Self* Taylor says that what makes atheism and the decline of religious practice possible is located in what he calls 'moral sources'.

Taylor describes how in earlier periods, such as in the Christian West in the Middle Ages, the source of all morality and moral decision making was found in God and the law recorded in the Ten Commandments, and through the teachings of Jesus Christ. God was the only source of morals for people living in these times, and any other source of morality was considered heretical and erroneous (SS, 310–11). However, beginning in the Renaissance, and continuing into the Enlightenment period, other sources of moral decision making begin to gain credibility, including reason, and the idea that our human nature can teach us what is the best thing to do in any given situation. Both of these are the origins of our modern day conception of individualism and the self. Apropos to the use of reason and the notion of individual decision making, and crucial for them to be put into practice, is the drive towards greater human liberty integral to the French Revolution. Reason and freedom, Taylor writes, are prominent in the Enlightenment and the Romantic period. The Enlightenment, which Taylor calls the 'Radical' Enlightenment (SS, 321), introduces the importance of using our reason, evident in Immanuel Kant's essay 'What is

Enlightenment?' Kant emphasised the central place that reason and rational thought should hold. Romanticism, on the other hand, emphasises the importance of nature, both in the world around us and our own human nature, and how our feelings are the measure for our moral decision making, because if we feel that something is right or wrong, then this will direct our decisions when faced with moral choices (Lundin 1993). In other words, the sources of morality 'now lie within us' (SS, 315).

This Romanticist turn inwards in moral decision making has been identified by Taylor and other authors (Wagner 1994) as an important element in appraisals of moral decision making in recent times, such as the shift towards greater sexual liberation in the West since the 1960s. The turn inwards has also been viewed as a key element in discussions about postmodernism, which encourages individualism, where people are seen as creators of their own sense of self, and maintain and promote an image of themselves that they hope others will react to in a positive manner (Harvey 1990: 288). As we shall see below, the Enlightenment, based as it is on ideas of reason and a rational social order, and Romanticism, which champions emotion and the wildness of nature, contain much that sets them at odds with each other. Nevertheless, for Taylor, they are critical historical epochs, marking out the modern world, and he calls these massive changes in moral sources which opened up an alternative to theism a 'cultural mutation' (SS, 316). For Taylor:

> Our sense of the certainty or problematicity of God is relative to our sense of moral sources. Our forebears were generally unruffled in their belief, because the sources they could envisage made unbelief incredible. The big thing that has happened since is the opening of other possible sources. (SS, 312–13)

These new sources of morality compete with religion as the only source of morals, and in doing so dislodge God as the sole source of moral law. This in turn leads to the possibility that if there are other sources of morality, then the existence of God is no longer certain. For Taylor, therefore, secularisation is not so much about *loss*, the *loss* in belief of God, or the *loss* of religious practice, as it is about a significant gain, the gain of new ways of understanding the moral and ethical decisions that concern us. Taylor calls this addition of new moral outlooks an 'epistemic gain' because they broaden human potential, although how exactly they do so Taylor is not so clear about

(SS, 313). We will return to these issues later. As we have suggested, the Enlightenment and the intellectual movements which it inspired are of key importance to Taylor's overall argument in *A Secular Age*. We will explore them in more depth in the next section.

Deism, the Enlightenment and Romanticism

Deism is for Taylor an important precursor to the Enlightenment, and he treats it in detail in *A Secular Age*, as well as in his earlier book *Sources of the Self*. Taylor sees Deism as a crucial stepping stone in the historical development from an age of belief to a secular age. The philosophy of Descartes, in Taylor's opinion, leads to a mechanistic view of the universe, which underpins Deism (O'Shea 2012: 146). Deism holds that there is a God who created the universe, but that after this act of creation God steps back and lets the world and human affairs take their own course. This view of God is akin to being a watchmaker, where God creates the watch, winds it up and then lets it run without further interference. For Deists, worship and prayer are of no use because God does not involve himself in human activity. Deism serves as a midway point between theism and atheism, because although belief in God is maintained, apart from creating the universe he serves no real purpose in everyday life or in society at large. One of the problems with Deism, according to Taylor, is that it provides no moral guidance. Because God has created the universe and then stepped back from it, and is no longer involved in it or in people's lives, it is pointless to call on God as the judge about morals, because whatever we do during our time on earth falls on deaf ears, and has no impact on what might happen to us after death. The idea that God is not involved in the world after its creation allows for the view that we live in an impersonal order (SA, 221), an order in which the laws of the universe are provided for us to follow and we do so, or decline to do so, as we see fit and at our own peril.

Furthermore, Deism encourages the notion that there is a natural religion that has been buried over the centuries under ritualistic and theological baggage. These accretions constitute a corruption of religion, and the Deists believed that by casting these aside we could reconnect with the true nature of faith. Overall, the Deists wanted a rational faith for a rational age, one that did away with the authority of churches and which allowed people to understand God's moral order without recourse to rites or abstruse theological discussion.

Taylor believes that the popularity of this faith among European élites in the seventeenth and eighteenth centuries paved the way for 'exclusive humanism' to take root, because Deism demolished the monopoly that the Christian churches had on how God and human faith were to be understood.

The Enlightenment highlighted the promotion of reason in the study of the natural world and the social order (Edelstein 2010). As well as Kant, mentioned above, another important Enlightenment thinker was Rousseau (1968: 49), who wrote that 'Man was born free, and he is everywhere in chains.' Rousseau was commenting on an unjust society where people had few rights, where poverty was commonplace, and where the wealthy, who were from the aristocracy of the *Ancien Régime*, and the upper echelons of the clergy, enjoyed a life of wealth and ease on the backs of a poor and hardworking populace. Freedom was an important element of the Enlightenment project, and the thinkers of this generation sought a social world where each citizen possessed basic human rights. *The Declaration of the Rights of Man and the Citizen* became a central text of the movement, and the ideals of liberty, equality and fraternity sums up its principle aims. The idea of progress was another essential ingredient, and Enlightenment thinkers believed that by applying rational thought to human problems social progress could be made. Religion, especially Christianity, was identified as a source of the backwardness of Europe by Enlightenment thinkers. Voltaire made the claim that 'it is infinitely more useful in a civilized city to have even a bad religion than none at all' (Voltaire 2005: 23). For Voltaire, religion maintained a stable, but unjust, social order. It is no surprise then that this thinking was typical among Enlightenment *philosophés*.

Although writers of the Romantic era praised the power of nature and drew attention to the affinities between the natural world and our inner, or human, nature, they were also aware that this reliance on nature needed to take into account the impassive destructive capacities of nature, and the tendencies towards evil in the recesses of human nature (Blanning 2011: 60ff). In the novel *Frankenstein*, Mary Shelley combines the confidence of the Scientific Revolution with the hubris of human pride in her portrayal of Dr Victor Frankenstein, who breaks the natural order by creating a new being out of dead body parts and sparking it into life with electricity. This new creation, whom Shelley calls only 'the Creature', turns on its creator and hunts Frankenstein down and kills him in an act of vengeance for breaking the natural order and bringing something into being without thought for how it would fit into a world that was not ready to accept it. The warning in Shelley's story is that manipulating nature through science might be possible, but such power has the potential to upset the natural order with dire consequences, and may very well reflect back to us the ugly side of our own human nature. Now that we have examined the importance of Deism, the Enlightenment and Romanticism for the rise of secularism and the process of secularisation, it is also important to briefly analyse other significant concepts that Taylor utilises in his examination of a secular age. These include the Axial Age civilisations, and the idea of multiple modernities.

The Axial Age and Multiple Modernities

The idea of multiple modernities has its provenance in debates about the Axial Age, particularly through the work of S. N. Eisenstadt (1986). The idea of the 'Axial Age' was prominent in the work of the Swiss-German philosopher Karl Jaspers (1953). Jaspers argued that during the period around 800–200 BCE, fundamental changes took place in religion, changes that would have a marked impact on subsequent history (Bellah and Joas 2012). These changes involved a transformation in how humans conceptualised the spiritual world. Prior to these changes, pagan religions emphasised a non-material world that was in many respects coextensive with ordinary life. The gods of the pagan pantheons were little more than super men and women, who had little interest in human affairs beyond serving their own interests. Upon death, people entered an afterlife in which they became shadowy versions of themselves, with few memories about their life on earth, and the afterlife, called Hades or the underworld, was not a pleasant place. Furthermore, early religions among tribal peoples did not see a split between the spiritual world and the everyday world. Animals and places could be imbued with sacred power, and spirits and gods could be found in earthly events and places.

But during the Axial Age this model of the spiritual world was radically transformed. In ancient Greece, China and India, and in ancient Israel, a new group of spiritual leaders argued that there was a transcendent world beyond what we could see, and which had an impact on the fate of human beings (Bellah 2005). After death, people go to an afterlife that is a place where they will live in eternal bliss or punishment, or be returned in a cycle of reincarnation. The Axial Age revolution created a belief in transcendence, and religion was about getting 'beyond the world' (Browne 2009: 39). In other words, God is no longer a part of nature or of the world, as immanence taught, nor is he remote from the world as the Deists believed. Rather, a transcendent God is separate from nature yet concerned with the affairs of his creation (Lilla 2007: 28). Salvation and how one will spend eternity becomes of greater importance in consequence of the Axial Age revolution. Once this notion of a transcendental spiritual order is established, the mundane world is understood as being insufficient, and in need of reconstruction, and social reformers elevate the everyday world so that it aligns with the idealism of the transcendent. The political order, therefore, has to be realigned so that it conforms to the need for salvation that a transcendental order demands (Eisenstadt 1996: 13–14). What the teachers of these new views about religion agreed on was that a person needs to act with virtue in this life to attain the benefits of eternal life; if not, a place of punishment awaits them, or they will be returned to this life in a lowered form with a chance to make amends.

For Eisenstadt, if there is indeed several disparate areas of the globe where the Axial Age could simultaneously occur, then the same was true of modernity and its massive impact on history and society. The concept of multiple modernities follows a similar pattern of social change across diverse cultural centres (Eisenstadt 1999; 2000). Although modernity began in Western Europe, Eisenstadt points out that modernisation and Westernisation are not the same thing. He argues that after originating in Europe, modernity spread to European colonies, such as America and Canada, Australia and New Zealand, before spreading to other parts of the world. Nations such as China, India, Japan and many others then formed their own versions of modernity, as Eisenstadt showed in his study of Japanese modernity (Eisenstadt 1996). Eisenstadt argues that Japan shares many of the cultural and structural denominators that constitute modernisation in the West, but reached this modernisation through very a different historical trajectory. The key idea behind the theory of multiple modernities is that specific cultures and social and political contexts shape how modernity develops in distinct locations (Eisenstadt et al. 2002). However, it should also be pointed out that modernisation can form in different ways in the very European nations in which it originated. Fascist, communist as well as capitalistic variants of modernity can be identified throughout history.

Furthermore, the institutions, practices and ideas of modernity also found their way into various countries through Western colonisation.

This was partly due to the way in which Western colonisation disrupted the traditional cultures and social structures of these nations. Once the traditions of people in these nations had been displaced, they searched for new ways to organise and structure their societies, and so Western and modern ways of doing things became attractive, mainly because of their efficiency and ability to deliver a high quality of life to the majority of citizens. The importation of these Western ideas was not done without a critical view of their limitations, however, and nor was it forgotten how modernity in the guise of Westernisation had disrupted social life in these nations to begin with. What emerged, therefore, was a hybrid form of modernity, a new interpretation of modernity that adopted its more helpful innovations, while at the same time encouraged political and cultural forms of resistance to the intrusion of Western markets into these nations.

Towards a Secular Age

Having analysed some of the foundational theories that are essential to Taylor's *A Secular Age*, we are now ready to examine the book in more detail. In the book, Taylor wants to outline how we have moved from a situation where most people believed in God, to one where faith is a struggle for many. One of the key aspects of this change is the shift from a hierarchical social order to one which is much more level (Browne 2009: 37). Taylor argues that democracy plays a role in this process, and the French Revolution was a momentous turning point towards greater social and political participation by a larger number of citizens. Prior to the modern age, in the time of monarchies, citizens had much less input into decision making at the social level. It was only with the birth of parliamentary democracy, which evolved gradually in countries such as England, or was established after revolutions in France and the United States, that the common person was able to have a say in the course of the direction of their country. Furthermore, in the early years of modern democracy, it was only men who could vote, women not being able to vote until the late nineteenth/early twentieth century.

As well as democracy, what is also crucial for the development of a secular age is what German sociologist Max Weber calls the 'disenchantment of the world'. This disenchantment arises whenever science and intellectual thought, based on rational methods of inquiry, demystifies the world and provides rational explanations for phenomena that might have previously been left unexplained, or believed to be caused by the supernatural (Weber 2009b: 350–1). Taylor sees much in Weber's ideas for explaining how secularism was able to take root and become a powerful way of ordering the world. Another aspect of this is the way in which rationality is used to order the social world through greater efficiencies that are encased in bureaucracy. The application of rational systems to create social order and produce goods and services much more efficiently leads, Weber argued, to a sense that we are caught up in an inevitable drive towards order, and as this takes place the spiritual elements of life are pushed further and further to the sidelines. The ultimate outcome of such a state of affairs, Weber warned, would result in an iron cage of rationality that would trap us all (Weber 1995: 181). Weber referred to this as 'a polar night of icy darkness' (Weber 2009a: 128). Weber has at times been criticised for being a pessimist, but there is a great deal in what he had to say that Taylor finds relevant to social life today.

Taylor's main concern in *A Secular Age* is to examine the process whereby faith was transformed from being the only option in a society that put God at the centre of people's lives, to one where faith became one option among many other ways of understanding the world. In Taylor's own words,

> the change I want to define and trace is one which takes us from a society in which it was virtually impossible not to believe in God, to one in which faith, even for the staunchest believer, is one human possibility among others. (SA, 3)

What is key about a secular age for Taylor is the fact that people today have alternatives when it comes to how they understand the world. Whereas in past societies such as medieval Europe, people could only understand the world and their place in it through the Christian interpretation of reality (Duffy 2005), now science, atheism, new religious movements and agnosticism are all available for people to draw on in defining their place in the cosmos, particularly those living in the West. From the mid-nineteenth century onwards, therefore, faith becomes much harder to sustain in the face of these alternatives, which are presented as being plausible explanations of human existence. The consequence of these alternatives means that some people will struggle with their faith, while others will give it up altogether (SA, 3). How did Taylor come to this understanding of secularism?

At the very outset of his study into the secular, Taylor is careful to demarcate three distinct understandings of what is meant by the word 'secularism'. The first, as we saw above, is concerned with secularism at the state or public level (see SFC). This is the separation of church and state, in which the state is concerned with maintaining institutions for the efficient running and maintenance of the social order, such as schools, hospitals, the military and the political process. Here, according to the advocates of the separation of church and state, religion and churches should have no place in public policy, and decisions about the administration of social institutions should be left to state officials who are not influenced by religion. These officials work for the common good of society, and although they may belong to a church in their private life, their public life should be dedicated to the state and they should act objectively, not from religious motives. This form of secularisation can be called 'the functional differentiation of religion' (Gräb 2010: 116–17). In this understanding of secularism, religion is forced out of the public sphere and is a private matter for individuals (SA, 1).[1] Taylor sums up this form of secularism by pointing out that it has to do with public spaces that have now been 'emptied of God', and that we now go about our daily life without seeing any reference to God when making political, economic, educational, professional or even recreational decisions (SA, 2). Taylor calls this view of secularism 'secularity 1' (SA, 2).

Taylor's second way of understanding secularism focuses on people's turning away from God, and losing their faith. Whereas his first definition of secularism is concerned with how the state organises the separation of church and state, this understanding of secularism is more akin to the understanding of the secularisation thesis outlined above. One of the indicators of a lack of faith, Taylor suggests, is the drop in church attendance that has been a defining aspect of religious life, especially during the twentieth century (SA, 2; see Brown 2001). This view of secularism Taylor calls 'secularity 2' (SA, 2). Of course, it should be noted that although people may stop attending church, it is difficult to assess whether or not this reflects a loss of faith in God or a loss of faith in churches. The British sociologist of religion Grace Davie (2000) has argued that what has taken place in England, and much of Europe, is what she calls 'believing without belonging', whereby people continue to hold their belief in God, but no longer identify with the established churches. We will return to this debate in the following chapter.

The third way of understanding secularism, which Taylor calls 'secularity 3' (SA, 3), is the way belief in God has become optional – social agents no longer have to believe in God to live successfully, although they may choose to do so. Other ways of understanding the world are on offer, and these include science and ideas from modern philosophy. In this view, secularity is not defined as people believing less in God, but rather as a change in belief itself, as belief is shifted onto a range of possibilities that people can believe in (Warner et al. 2010: 9). This view of secularism draws on elements of the previous two ways of defining it, because faith becomes private rather than public, and many people struggle to retain their faith and some will cast it away. It is this understanding of secularism which is Taylor's unique contribution to thinking about the concept, and much of what follows in *A Secular Age* is Taylor's attempt to explain and analyse how this situation came to be.

In the first chapter of *A Secular Age* Taylor wants to address the way in which belief today is contrasted with belief 500 years ago. Specifically, he asks 'why was it virtually impossible not to believe in God in, say, 1500 in our Western society, while in 2000 many of us find this not only easy, but inescapable?' (SA, 25). A part of the reason Taylor gives to answer this question is a profound shift in subjectivity. Taylor argues that pre-modern people had a sense of the self which he describes as 'porous'. The porous self is one that is open to the spiritual world. Taylor gives the example of demonic possession (SA, 35). Pre-modern people feared being possessed by unclean spirits or demons, because they understood their relationship with the spiritual world as a close one. They lived in an enchanted world populated by angels and demons, and illnesses were often understood as having supernatural origins. For believers, prayer is an efficacious way of warding off evil and calling on God's grace for protection, and for success with anything from crop fertility through to curing illnesses or melancholy. But Taylor suggests that this porous self, with its close connection to the supernatural world, has given way to what he terms the 'buffered self' of modern times (SA, 37). In contrast to the pre-modern porous self, the buffered self is bounded, and this boundary exists between the human subject and the supernatural world. Illness or depression no longer have supernatural causes, but are now understood as medical problems which can be corrected through medicines developed from scientific research (Smith 2014: 107).

Taylor describes the buffered self as being a 'very different existential condition' (SA, 38). To drive home the fact that this shift has taken place, and to highlight the contrast between the two states, Taylor mentions the nostalgia that people today often feel for a time when the porous self was common, and when people seemed to have a closer and more active relationship to the transcendent (SA, 38). An example is the research undertaken by Paul Heelas and his fellow researchers into what is often called 'New Age' faiths (see Heelas and Woodhead 2005). Heelas found that they were a popular form of spiritual practice for those who did not belong to a church, but who wanted to explore spiritual outlets for health reasons, or because they 'felt' that the spiritual dimension of their lives was undernourished. Heelas' study reveals that some people living in secular times may give up their belief in God, but seek other ways to achieve 'fullness'. It also shows that a need to connect with the transcendent continues to exist in a social world that appears for all intents and purposes to be secularised.

The development of the buffered self is for Taylor a clear indication that there has been a significant shift in peoples' understanding of the supernatural world, and is a key stepping stone on the path to secularism. Although Taylor is critical of seeing the idea of disenchantment as the main story for how secularism has come to flourish in the West, he nevertheless concedes that the disenchantment of the world through science and rationality has contributed to a buffered self. As he states, 'disbelief is hard in an enchanted world' (SA, 41), for the very fact that supernatural events are understood in light of God's actions in the world. Once disenchantment has set in, however, the likelihood of finding other explanations for why things happen becomes possible. The shift from a porous to a buffered self is crucial to what Taylor calls 'exclusive humanism', which is also a significant aspect of a secular age.

In Taylor's view, exclusive humanism is the way social agents are able to realise a full life not through a relationship with God, but through relying on their own resources, their own reason and their own actions. In other words, social life becomes much less reliant on the transcendent, and people are forced to find their own way without guidance from the supernatural. In Taylor's words:

> I would like to claim that the coming of modern secularity in my sense has been coterminous with the rise of a society in which for the first time in history a purely self-sufficient humanism came to be a widely

> available option. I mean by this a humanism accepting no final goals beyond human flourishing, nor any allegiance to anything else beyond this flourishing. Of no previous society was this true. (SA, 18)

Such a situation may give rise to some anxieties when people realise that they face the world alone, but it also produces the exciting prospect that social agents have the autonomy to live their life, and make decisions based on their own inclinations, rather than relying on external authorities. The impact of the Enlightenment and the Romantic period can be clearly identified in this description of humanism, as well as the attraction that many élites had in the eighteenth century to Deism and its teaching of a God that created the universe and then left men and women alone to live their own lives. Another important element of exclusive humanism, however, is that it became accessible to greater numbers of people, rather than being the privilege of élites (SA, 19). What is also discernible in this view of a self-sufficient humanism is the individualism that is dominant in our own era, and which was highlighted during the 1960s decade when young people called for greater social freedoms, and made personal decisions based on their own views about the world and what they wanted to do with their lives. A number of scholars, including Taylor himself, have underscored the importance of this kind of individualism to society since the 1960s decade (SA, 473; also Brown 2001; Wagner 1994; Isserman and Kazin 2000). Taylor dedicates a sustained discussion in *A Secular Age* to how exclusive humanism came about (see SA, 221ff).

The importance of exclusive humanism to Taylor's argument in *A Secular Age* cannot be overstated, as it is the linchpin that holds his thesis together. Taylor is critical of theories about secularism that see it simply as the decline of religion and the beginning of a new era where people no longer believe in God. For Taylor, this is a gross simplification of the state of affairs in our own day, and as mentioned earlier, he calls such narratives 'subtraction stories'. By subtraction he means that religion is removed from the equation and what we are left with is a modern world that is largely agnostic. Rather, Taylor argues that what has occurred is that religion and belief have been *replaced* by something new, and he is at pains to point out that his discussion will show not only how belief has receded, but 'how something other than God could become the necessary objective pole of moral or spiritual aspiration, of "fullness"' (SA, 26). Fullness is the capacity to experience more in life than the day to day, mundane activities that take up much of our time and attention. Fullness is the experience of the transcendent. This 'something other than God' is exclusive humanism, and it has taken over the space once filled by God as the compass point people refer to when acting as social agents.

To sum up so far, Taylor argues that what makes a secular age unique and undeniable is a form of secularism, which he calls secularity 3, whereby faith becomes one option among others that social agents may choose from to understand the world, and when making moral choices. What helped to make this possible was the disenchantment of the world that was brought on by a number of massive social changes since the Reformation, which include the Enlightenment and Romanticism, and the French and Industrial Revolutions. These encouraged a shift from a porous self, which had a close relationship with the supernatural world, to a buffered self, where the connection between the self and the spiritual is not so obvious, and other explanations beyond the supernatural can be found to explain social and natural phenomena. Deism arose in the eighteenth century and created a mindset which challenged the idea that humans needed God to assist with every element of their lives, and a new form of humanism arose, called exclusive humanism, whereby people could rely solely on their own resources in working out their life course. This view challenges the commonly held ideas about secularism and the secularisation thesis, which argues, on the one hand, that religion has declined because it has been pushed out of the public sphere by the separation of church and state, and on the other hand, because science, technology, urbanisation and greater levels of education have made it difficult for people in the modern West to maintain a belief in God in the face of these developments.

What arises from these changes Taylor calls the 'immanent frame'. The immanent frame describes a space distinct from the transcendent, in which individuals can go about living their lives without supernatural explanations for everything that happens to them. The immanent frame becomes possible because a buffered self creates the conditions for large-scale changes in how we interact with others, and with the world around us. Taylor writes that the buffered self makes possible the idea that we have an inner self, and thoughts and feelings come to be identified with our minds, this being an outcome of the philosophical revolution precipitated by Descartes and his formula *cogito, ergo sum* (SA, 539). With inwardness firmly established, people develop a greater sense of individualism, and this leads to social changes, such as the need for greater privacy, so that individuals can be alone to probe their inner lives. Privacy, Taylor suggests, changes how we understand intimacy. Acts of love and intimacy are no longer undertaken in crowded conditions, where extended households spent large amounts of time together (SS, 290–1). Rather, intimacy moves into private spaces, and a strict demarcation arises between adults and children, between men and women, and between masters and servants. Manners and refinement are given greater prominence, and the 'civilizing process' outlined by Norbert Elias (1994) establishes a code of conduct for people, especially for the upper classes (SA, 540).

As well as these changes, time is increasingly measured, so that it must be used productively and with discipline. This discipline, encouraged by the ideas of the Reformation, which emphasises a personal relationship with God in which people must take responsibility for the state of their own soul, rather than relying on the mediation of a church, means that in Protestant countries in particular, discipline is highly prized, and is understood as a key ingredient in work, which is in turn, if carried out with success, a sign of God's favour. All of these things enforce individualism to a much greater degree, even leading to what Taylor calls instrumental individualism, the notion that 'society is there for the good of individuals' (SA, 541), rather than as a reflection of God's kingdom on earth as it was understood in the Middle Ages. In this conception of society, individualism is key, and human flourishing is a major preoccupation for citizens, so much so that it gives rise to what Taylor calls the 'ethic of authenticity'. The immanent frame is a new understanding of the self in relation to the social order, a social space that is understood as the natural order of things, and which stands apart from the supernatural or transcendent order, where God and spirits dwell (SA, 542). It is, therefore, the development of the immanent frame that is in Taylor's opinion a major reason for the possibility of secularism.

The 1960s and Beyond

Taylor's argument in *A Secular Age* leads him to a consideration of the impact of the social changes that took place in the 1960s. In

Taylor's opinion, the 1960s decade (and much of the 1970s which followed) constitutes the hinge moment in an ongoing cultural revolution that has been underway since the end of the Second World War (SA, 473). For Taylor, what has been emerging since the end of the war is an Age of Authenticity, which is characterised by the greater freedoms that people in Western nations have in order to create their own lives, and give them a sense of meaning and purpose. The events of the 1960s mark the high point of this push towards greater personal freedom. As noted above, Taylor states that individualism has been a part of modern society since it became identifiable in the eighteenth century, spurred on by Romanticism. The ideals of Romanticism, Taylor suggests, have by no means petered out, but are still with us today, and received a boost during the 1960s (SS, 373). Values such as the importance of personal freedom, self-expression and having a unique sense of self have all been carried through from the Romantic era, and have been given added weight through the work of intellectuals and artists, from the writings of Rousseau to those of Freud on the subconscious. Individual freedoms were at the centre of the upheavals of the 1960s youth protests, Taylor argues, and are a manifestation and a harbinger of what he calls 'expressive individualism' (SA, 473).

What is unique about expressive individualism is the way in which social agents are seen as more than individuals living in a complex social order, but are rather agents that are capable of expressing and displaying their own individual and personal characteristics, and in doing so present a self that they have crafted and which fits with the cultural identity shared by their peers. This can be done through fashion choices, lifestyle options, music and artistic consumption, sexual identity, education and political affiliation. The post-war consumer revolution makes this construction of individual identity possible, as well as the rise of suburbanisation. The stifling culture of the conformist 1950s provides the benchmark which the youth of the 1960s reacted to (SA, 473–4). This is reflected in the Beat writers of the 1950s. Poets including Allen Ginsberg and the novelist Jack Kerouac are the most well known of this movement. They called for a rejection of the post-war consensus between capitalism and political conservatism, and they championed creativity and individualism, as the Romantics had done before them (Campbell 1999; see SA, 475). Furthermore, social theorists, such as Herbert Marcuse, in his widely read book *One-Dimensional Man* (1964), provided analytical insight into the conformity of the era and its negative impact. Marcuse argued that consumerism and alienating, predictable jobs, whether on the assembly line or at the office, were repressing people's desire for spontaneity and self-identity. A rational society was, in short, suffocating individuality. Taylor sums up how the rise of expressive individualism as a countermovement to this conformity constitutes what he calls the 'age of authenticity', and he argues that it explains many of the social attitudes and behaviours that crowd our media headlines and celebrity gossip columns today. The Age of Authenticity is, in short:

> the understanding of life which emerges with the Romantic expressivism of the late-eighteenth century, that each one of us has his/her own way of realizing our humanity, and that it is important to find and live out one's own, as against surrendering to conformity with a model imposed on us from outside, by society, or the previous generation, or religious or political authority. (SA, 475)

Beginning with Romanticism and the Enlightenment, therefore, there has been a steady movement towards greater and greater personal freedoms and individual self-management, which reaches its apex in the student revolts and youth counter-culture that found expression in the college campus rallies in the USA in the 1960s, and in May 1968 in Paris, as well as in many other protest movements across the world.

The freedoms that were won during the 1960s have had an ongoing legacy. Greater rights were won for racial minorities and women, and the peace and environmental movements can trace much of their current visibility to the decade as well. For Taylor, what is interesting about the events of this decade is their impact on Western religion, and he argues that the liberties achieved during that time have had an adverse effect on the major religious denominations (SA, 492; McLeod 2007). The sexual revolution that took place in the 1960s goes a long way towards explaining why this is so. Taylor goes as far as to suggest that the sexual revolution of the 1960s is at the heart of the rise of the Age of Authenticity (SA, 485). This is so, Taylor suggests, because churches preached that sexual freedom was antithetical to the teachings of the Bible, and that sexual restraint was integral to social cohesion. But during the 1960s, sex and sexual identity became linked to expressive individualism and the Age of Authenticity. People now understood sex as self-fulfilment, and choices about sex became a way of making a statement about a person's identity, and the values that he or she stood for. Sex became a symbol of freedom and self-awareness, and once these connections were made, it was difficult for the churches to connect with young people who saw their message of sexual restraint as typical of a 1950s conservative discourse. Pre-marital sex, the use of contraceptives that had become widely available since the early 1960s (Kaplan 2009: 229), and the call for greater recognition and rights for homosexual people, all became part of 1960s personalism, which is undergirded by the idea that 'the personal is political' (Farrell 1997).

Conclusion

In *A Secular Age*, Charles Taylor contests the validity of theories of secularity that see it as the necessary decline of religion in the face of modern progress, or as the privatisation of religion. He calls these ideas subtraction stories. Instead, Taylor suggests that what is unique about modern society is that religion has become an option among a number of ways of understanding the world and our place in it. The creation of these options is the result of a buffered self, a self which is not so closely connected to a world of spirits and demons. The buffered self turns inwards and over time is disciplined and individualised, and hence gives rise to a social order that is an immanent frame, a taken for granted world that is distinct from the transcendent and the supernatural. Within this immanent frame an exclusive humanism reigns supreme, whereby people rely on their own resources to achieve the good that they desire, and which is seen as the highest good in society, the freedom to pursue individual authenticity.

In the next chapter we will analyse the debates that Taylor's thesis in *A Secular Age* have generated. This will include an assessment of the work of critics, and their concerns that Taylor has overlooked issues such as the rise of religious fundamentalism. Of particular interest will be how his work has contributed to thinking about post-secularism, the idea that we live in times when religion has returned to prominence, which has received much attention from major thinkers such as Jürgen Habermas (2006; also Butler et al. 2011).

Note

1. In Gräb's view, however, post-secularism constitutes a situation where religion has become personalised rather than privatised, and therefore retains social significance outside official religious contexts (see Gräb 2010: 114). How the public role of religion can be accounted for in this understanding of post-secularism, which is an important element of post-secularism, remains to be seen.

7

A Secular Age: Controversies and Critiques

Introduction: Debating A Secular Age

The publication of Charles Taylor's *A Secular Age* prompted a range of critical responses. In this chapter we will examine some of the debates the book has prompted. Although there is now a sizable literature in response to Taylor's book, we will only have space to discuss a selection. In what follows we will focus on essays collected in the book *Varieties of Secularism in a Secular Age* (Warner et al. 2010), where scholars debate the ideas set out in *A Secular Age*. Taylor responds to the criticisms raised, in a rejoinder to his critics, which allows for a balanced evaluation of the positions in contention. Following this we will look at other critical responses to *A Secular Age* by José Casanova, Richard Madsen and Ruth Abbey.

Critics of Taylor's book have addressed a range of themes including modernity, historiography, (dis)enchantment, Romanticism, secularism and the sacred/profane divide. We will touch on each of these issues below, but three themes in particular will be our focus. These are, first, questions about modernity and its place in Taylor's analysis; second, Taylor's use of history; and third, the concept of secularism. We will begin with what critics in *Varieties* have to say about the central position of modernity in Taylor's writings, which is evident not only in *A Secular Age*, but throughout his *oeuvre*. This will be followed by an analysis of criticisms by a number of Taylor's respondents about his use of history and historical methods, a key theme raised in the *Varieties* book. Finally, moving on from the debates set out in *Varieties*, we will examine what Taylor's critics have said about his concept of secularism.

Modernity and Secularisation

Taylor has been described as a thinker concerned about the crisis of modernity (O'Shea 2012). Modernity is a key element in his work, and the crisis in question concerns its impact on human subjectivity

(EA; SS, 498–9). In *Hegel and Modern Society* he writes about the impact that modernity has on the self, particularly the problem of alienation that was discussed by Marx in his early work. At the heart of modernity is the problem of exploitation, of both people and the natural world. Modernity has a two-fold relationship with the natural world, and with human nature. On the one hand industrialisation seeks to utilise them as resources, while on the other hand they are venerated by Romanticism, which appreciates the majesty of the natural world and its influence on our human nature (HMS, 69). Modernity is also an important component in the rise of a secular age because it underpins theories of modern social change, modernisation and secularisation. Since the Reformation and the Renaissance, developments in science have altered how people understand the world. As O'Shea describes it, 'We shift from an experience of a cosmos of fixed variety to a vast alienating, immeasurable universe of infinite variety' (O'Shea 2010: 171; see SA, 367). Taylor suggests that this situation generates greater levels of unbelief, and he argues that 'In the nineteenth century, one might say, unbelief comes of age' (SA, 374).

By the nineteenth century, many of the components that make up secular modernity are in place, and the world is looking very different from the way it did in 1500 CE (SA, 375). For Taylor, modernity is responsible for a great many social innovations and improvements, but it is also the cause of disenchantment, which, as Max Weber wrote, undermines belief in the supernatural, and focuses human attention on progress, pragmatism and rationality. Indeed, for Weber, modernity and rationality go hand in hand, and although rationality provides for greater efficiency through social mechanisms such as bureaucracy, it also removes any sense of wonder that people once had about the world, and gives way to what Weber described as the iron cage of rationality (Weber 1995: 181; Weber 2009a: 128; SS, 500; SA, 59). Like Weber, Taylor concedes that modernity has made social life much more comfortable in many respects, but it has had profound implications for religion. These include disenchantment, 'fragilization' as multiple religious options potentially undermine traditional faith positions, the atomism of individuals which challenges religious communities, a scientific worldview that seeks to explain the universe without the necessity of God, and a number of others. We now turn to what Taylor's critics have to say about his analysis of these issues.

Robert Bellah affirms that for Taylor, modernity is an important historical development that has ushered in many positives, especially an independent economy for the efficient production of goods and services, a public sphere which enhances freedom of expression and opinion, and the idea of the sovereign people, the bedrock of democracy (Bellah 2010: 36–7). But although modernity introduces these social benefits, it also generates a tendency towards 'cultural fragmentation' and a loss of meaning for individuals and for society as a whole (Bellah 2010: 43). Modernity induces amnesia about the past while pushing us to embrace the present, and it holds out the promise of future progress. Bellah interprets Taylor's work as distinct from theorists such as Maruyama Masao and Jürgen Habermas, who see in modernity an unproblematic break with the past. Maruyama sees this break as inconsequential because he feels that the pre-modern period can provide little guidance for how we are to live in the modern world, while Habermas sees the break with the past as regretful, but ultimately without consequence. Taylor, on the other hand, 'clearly feels that abandoning the premodern, letting modernity obliterate our spiritual past, would be an irreparable disaster' (Bellah 2010: 51). This is a point of interest for Bellah, because he too has sought to trace religious change over the historical long term in his own ambitious research projects (Bellah 2011). The reason for Taylor's passion for the past, Bellah asserts, is because of Taylor's Catholicism. We will encounter the issue of Taylor's Catholicism again in discussions about Taylor's historiography below, but here Bellah believes that Taylor is interested in how people of faith can simultaneously live in both the modern world of rationality, and in the world of religious belief. Furthermore, Bellah suggests, one of Taylor's motivations in *A Secular Age* is to help believers develop an understanding of the modern world as a place that is at once familiar and increasingly foreign, one which maintains vestiges of a Christian past alongside the novel intrusion of secular institutions. The reason for doing so is to achieve an ethical modernity (Bellah 2010: 53).

Bellah's critique of Taylor remains open to some criticisms of its own, however. For one, it is wrong to suggest that Habermas sees little of import in the break between modern times and the past. His work is concerned with the 'project of modernity', and the centrality of reason in understanding contemporary society (Habermas 1983: 9; see Browne 2017b). Although he sees a rupture between modern and premodern societies, he remains acutely aware of the importance of this break. Habermas (2006) has also given much thought to how religion, rather than being privatised, is essential to an open and democratic public sphere. Taylor would see Habermas' views as dovetailing to some extent with his own. Furthermore, the charge that it is Taylor's Catholicism which leads him to harbour an interest in maintaining links with the traditions of pre-modernity misses the key concept of reform that Taylor has written about (SA, 61ff). Taylor argues that reform, such as that which took place after the Reformation, is essential to how religious organisations are able to maintain their relevance in changing social conditions. Bellah assumes to some degree in his critique that religions are largely static, but for Taylor belief is malleable and able to conform to new conditions. If this was not the case, many contemporary religions would undergo the crisis experienced by the polytheistic faiths of the Greek and Roman worlds.

Also focusing on the consequences of modernity, John Milbank raises a series of critical points about Taylor's use of enchantment and disenchantment. As we discussed in the previous chapter, disenchantment underpins secularisation, a point made by Weber. For Taylor, disenchantment creates high levels of secularisation, but it is not necessarily an inevitable outcome of the scientific and political revolutions that ushered in the modern age. Milbank (2010: 60–1) argues that Taylor is correct to question the connection between religious change and disenchantment, but he suggests that there are a number of inconsistencies in how Taylor argues for such a conclusion, which have their source, perhaps, in Taylor's views about modernity. The first of these, Milbank writes, is the way in which the fear of death became central in the Late Middle Ages, a fact attested to by historians such as Eamon Duffy (2005), because death was understood as the final chance to make amends in this world before facing God's judgement. Over time, however, civil authorities felt that the fear of death had encouraged social perversities, like leaving sums of money for clergy to remember a person after they had died by maintaining demanding prayer vigils, and attempted to reign in these popular sentiments. They encouraged a more rational view of death as a natural part of life, with church leaders emphasising God's mercy for the deceased, so that the elaborate demands left in wills and last testaments could be dispensed with. For Milbank, this is not a form of disenchantment, but a rationalisation of religion. The fear of death in the Late Middle Ages was mitigated not by increased levels of disbelief, but by religious intercession and greater theological insight (Milbank 2010: 60–1).

Second, Milbank interrogates Taylor's notion of the 'affirmation of ordinary life' to unpack the way in which Taylor assumes that the 'ordinary' is waiting there to fill the gap once the divide that existed between the everyday life of the majority of people, and the clergy, is narrowed (Milbank 2010: 61). Milbank suggests that this 'affirmation of ordinary life' might actually be produced by a focus on the secular rather than disenchantment per se, aligning secularism more closely with the religious sphere, as Calvin tried to do with his idea that work was a divine calling and a vocation that identified the elect (Milbank 2010: 61). In other words, the key issue is not that society became disenchanted, but that rational ways of doing things developed, regardless of whether people thought that the cosmos was enchanted or not. The conclusion here is that Taylor argues that disenchantment and secularism are linked (to a large extent although not inevitably), but Milbank suggests that secularism can take place without the need for any disenchantment at all.

Milbank raises some important points, but underplays to some extent the impact of the Scientific Revolution and the social changes taking place during the Renaissance, all of which are important to Taylor's analysis (SA, 90). Scientific discovery, including Newton, and Copernicus and Galileo's view of the universe, challenged the conceptual norms of the élite classes in Europe and, along with the Reformation and its focus on the individual, challenged the authority of churches and their teachings about things such as death. The age of exploration opened new horizons, and led to a rethinking about Western civilisation and culture. The turn to science was couched in an interest in nature. But as Taylor explains, this focus on the natural world was not opposed to religion, but carried out alongside it: 'Nature offers another way of encountering God' (SA, 91). Taylor suggests that a focus on science led to the need for a greater reliance on instrumental reason. The world is now seen as mechanical, and human beings must act within it in the context of ordinary life. There is disenchantment here, but its source comes from dependence on human reason, which must investigate the world and demythologise it, a definition of disenchantment that is closer to what Weber first intended (see SA, 97–9).

Continuing with the theme of modernity, José Casanova is critical of one of the major premises of Taylor's entire thesis, namely, that the West, and particularly Western states in the Northern hemisphere, are uniformly secular (Casanova 2010: 270–1). Casanova is concerned about what American exceptionalism in debates about secularisation does to Taylor's argument that in the West people are more inclined towards a secular worldview than a religious one, a situation that has overturned the pre-eminence of belief since 1500 CE (Casanova 2010: 271; see SA, 506; 513). Casanova focuses on what he calls the 'radical bifurcation in the religious situation today between the Western societies of the North Atlantic' (Casanova 2010: 270), a secularised Europe which contrasts with the United States, where many citizens identify themselves as 'religious humanists' (Casanova 2010: 271), a persistent problematic in discussions about secularism which Casanova acknowledges that Taylor is aware of and tries to address. For Casanova, another way of looking at the problem is that rather than seeing the American experience of secularisation as exceptional, a focus on Europe shows that perhaps its secularism is the exceptional case. Casanova highlights the work of Peter Berger (1999) and Grace Davie (1994) and the way in which they have theorised that secularisation is not as pervasive as was once imagined, but may instead be a particularly Western and Northern European phenomenon, which has not been repeated in other parts of Europe, in the United States, or in many other parts of the globe. How did this situation occur, where parts of Europe reveal differing patterns of religious observance, and where modernised nations such as the United States are not as heavily secularised?

Casanova's main criticism here is that when Taylor speaks of 'a secular age', whose secular age is being invoked, that of North Western Europe, or of other parts of the world? Casanova points out that modernity, and the secularism that is identified with it, spread across the world through colonial expansion and, in more recent decades, through the processes of globalisation (Casanova 2010: 277). However, in doing so, secularism has encountered cultures and religions that share different pasts from Christianity, and so the question goes begging about whether those religions and cultures are responding to modernity and secularism in the same way as Christianity has done (Veer 2001: 15). Casanova argues that at present, secularism is giving rise to a post-Christian social order in areas where it is prevailing, but in regions where other religions arose after the Axial Age, and where modernity is appropriated along different patterns, as outlined by Eisenstadt in his model of multiple modernities, then secularism may be different from that experienced in parts of Europe that are seen as heavily secularised (see Casanova 2012: 212). Furthermore, immigration into the United States and Europe may transform how secularism is understood in those countries, as non-Christian religions become embedded in those societies (Casanova 2010: 280; see Putnam and Campbell 2010). Another development that could be mentioned here is how Christianity is being received outside European and American environments. Jenkins (2002) assesses the rise of Christianity in Africa and Asia, which underpins his thesis that we may be headed for a global Christianity with its population epicentre in the global South. If anything, Casanova reveals that the notion of one standardised version of 'a secular age', which is largely assumed in Taylor's book, is problematic, and needs to be critically reassessed.

On the other hand, Taylor has written about the importance of freedom of religion for attempting to reconcile the experiences of secularism by believers from diverse religious backgrounds (SFC). In multicultural societies, the promotion of freedom of religion, and the neutrality towards religion shown by the state, helps to create greater levels of social harmony, and promotes a vision of secularism that is distinct from the Western European model, highlighting how multi-faith societies can successfully work against the backdrop of a secular state (see Chapter 8 for a fuller discussion). Furthermore, Taylor agrees that secularism will be experienced differently in countries like India, for example, from the way in which it will in Western Europe (Taylor 2016a). The question here is can secularism, as it is known in the West, travel to other locations, and be experienced in the same way as it is in European countries? The answer to this question is no. As Casanova (2016) acknowledges, and Taylor agrees, different historical circumstances and contemporary conditions will flavour how secularism is received in different countries. This includes how in some nations secularism may be welcomed, or even embraced as a tool of state ideology, while in others it will be challenged and will be interpreted as not only a threat to valued beliefs and traditions, but also as a Trojan Horse that is bringing in 'Western' ideas to undermine the legitimacy of the state.

Modernity and its discontents are central aspects of Taylor's understanding of how a secular age can develop, but as we have seen above, key elements of modernity, such as disenchantment and secularisation, are more complex and have a number of unexpected consequences when applied to different social situations at different times. Debates about modernity will continue for many years, but what Taylor has identified is that its impact on religion is sizable, whether or not we adhere to theories of secularisation. In the following chapter we will discuss theories of multiple modernities and their influence on Taylor's thesis in further detail. For now we turn to what critics have said about Taylor's use of history in *A Secular Age*, and the implications of this for the larger argument that he wants to make.

The Use of History in A Secular Age

Like Taylor's thoughts on modernity, his use of history is employed in a particular way in his book and in much of his previous writings. His critics have had some things to say about this. As Taylor intimates, his use of history is not that of the archaeologist or professional historian, who emphasises the use of primary sources and evidence extracted from texts or artefacts (see APLS, 314). Rather, Taylor's historical methodology uses genealogy in a similar fashion to that employed by Friedrich Nietzsche (2013) and Michel Foucault (1991; Smith 2002: 8). For these authors history is approached as a series of discontinuities, displacements and lost events (Foucault 1991: 81). Foucault, commenting on the uses of history made by Nietzsche and its impact on his own methodology, is interested in how historical discourses can help us to understand the many gaps and contradictions that historical events and sources bring to light. Foucault states that genealogy as a historical method is useful for trying to 'identify the accidents, the minute deviations – or conversely, the complete reversals – the errors, the false appraisals, and the faulty calculations that gave birth to those things that continue to exist and have value for us' (Foucault 1991: 81). Likewise, such a historiography is open to chance and 'a profusion of entangled events' (Foucault 1991: 89). This understanding of history is evident in the way Taylor handles change, progress and historical developments in *A Secular Age*. What is important for Taylor when discussing history are the broad themes and developments in social and cultural change, including advances in social thought and social practices. Taylor's history is therefore a history of ideas, and how ideas are transformed by social change and technological innovations, and how these ideas then impact on society in a reflexive manner. As Talal Asad (2003: 16) puts it, genealogy should not be understood as 'a substitute for social history, but as a way of working back from our present to the contingencies that have come together to give us our certainties'. In employing a genealogical approach, Taylor is more interested in recounting historical developments so as to pursue an argument that has relevance for contemporary times, rather than presenting historical facts to shine a light on the past, as professional historians do.

Another way of looking at Taylor's use of history is its episodic character. In a similar way to the Marxist historian Eric Hobsbawm looked at history as a series of 'ages', including the Age of Revolution, the Age of Capital and the Age of Empire (all of which were the titles of his best known books), Taylor is also interested in ages, including the Age of Mobilisation, the Age of Authenticity and a Secular Age. This episodic quality of Taylor's historical methodology means that he is interested in how ideas and social movements interact with established views, especially in areas such as social reform, belief, and the impact of social change on religion and assumptions about the self. Taylor is well aware that his writings utilise this structure, and the concept of 'stadial consciousness', that we view history as a set of stages impacting on one another, is central to his narrative in *A Secular Age* (see APLS, 314).

One historical development that is important to Taylor is the Romantic Movement. It features prominently in a number of his works, and is essential to his argument in *A Secular Age*. Colin Jager (2010) interrogates the assumptions that Taylor makes about romanticism.[1] One of Jager's main points is that romanticism has revealed what has been lost by the disenchantment of the world that was a corollary of modernity. Romantic poets, such as Wordsworth, remind readers of the importance of our connection with nature, the supernatural and the sublime. Once the world is disenchanted, which is assumed within the master narrative of secular Enlightenment thought, then the human subject is at risk of losing its connection to what Taylor calls fullness, that appreciation of things greater than us. For Jager, this is a crucial point in Taylor's argument, that modernity ushers in many benefits, but the loss of fullness is a casualty of this process. Jager's criticism, therefore, is that Taylor uses romanticism to help fill the void of what has been lost to increasing levels of secularisation, as if Romantic poetry or the philosophy of Herder might be able to lead the modern subject back to transcendence via a subjective expressivism, all of which is too much to ask of it (Jager 2010: 191–2).

Jager, however, may be asking too much of the role that Taylor ascribes to romanticism. Although Taylor believes that romanticism provides the basis for the experience of fullness, is essential to our modern notion of the self and is the basis of feeling as an accompaniment to thinking, he is also aware that by itself romanticism cannot provide all of the hypergoods necessary for navigating modern society. As he explains in his essay 'Legitimation Crisis?' (PHS, 274–5), modern society also relies on a number of other values to maintain civic harmony. These include the striving for equality between citizens; efficacy, or the ability for individuals to contribute to society and have choices in the decisions that they make; the necessity of production, to produce the goods and services needed for modern living; and citizenship itself, based on the knowledge that society is a collective effort. Romanticism is then, according to Taylor, only one of a number of elements essential for successful modern societies. It needs to be understood alongside secularism, rather than in strict opposition to it.

Historian Jon Butler offers a sharp criticism of Taylor's historiography in *A Secular Age*. While acknowledging that the book is more akin in its methodology to intellectual history than an account of events studied through sources, as we outlined above, Butler nevertheless finds elements of Taylor's use of history far from convincing. The first of these problems is Taylor's somewhat arbitrary use of the year 1500 CE as providing a point of contrast in matters of belief between the medieval and modern periods. As Butler points out, much has changed in those 500 years, making it a dubious claim that the widespread changes in religion that Taylor identifies are in fact so significant (Butler 2010: 199). An analysis of religion now and 100 years ago could still reveal large-scale transformations. Butler also takes aim at Taylor's lack of historical source material to back up a number of claims that he makes about religion in the Middle Ages, and which are important to his overall argument. An example is Taylor's discussion of the porous self that he claims was normative in the Middle Ages, a self that has a closer relationship to the world of nature and spirits than does the modern, buffered self. For Butler, however, these ideas are developed with 'no evidence drawn from the behavior of common people themselves' (Butler 2010: 201). Similarly, in his discussion of Carnival and medieval revelries designed to allow people to let off steam and playfully mock the aristocracy, Butler points out that there is 'no evidence from revelers themselves' in Taylor's account (Butler 2010: 201).

This is not the first time that Taylor has been challenged over his lack of historical specificity. Clifford Geertz questioned Taylor's ahistorical interpretation of science in his book *The Explanation of Behaviour* (Smith 2002: 39). Butler's conclusion is that Taylor's discussion of 'secularity 3', which is about the shift in how belief is taken for granted, to a situation where it is one option among many (SA, 3), is undermined by these historiographical deficiencies. Butler outlines a number of studies that show that belief in 1500 CE was not as normative or axiomatic as Taylor assumes, evidenced by religious controversies, changeable patterns of observance, and tension between church élites and the mass of ordinary people over issues of faith (Butler 2010: 204–7). Butler's points acknowledged, however, Taylor's discussion does need to start from somewhere to reveal the changes that have taken place in society's commitment to religious belief. In his study, Owen Chadwick (1975) examines secularisation and its impact on social life and intellectual thought in the nineteenth century. Brown (2001) looks at the secularisation of Britain from 1800 CE through to the year 2000. McLeod's (2007) argument about religious change is focused on the 1960s. Taylor has decided on 1500 CE because he sees the Reformation and the Renaissance as integral to his discussion. The point is, whichever dates scholars decide to start or end their analyses of secularism, Butler's criticisms do not really detract from Taylor's overall project, which is to show that society is undergoing significant change in regards to religious belief, and his attempt to trace the impact of this change on political and social discourses in the contemporary era. For Taylor, history serves as a backdrop to set out the issues that he wants to examine in the context of society today, which is why it may appear at times that his historiography is not always as thorough as some professional historians might like.

Continuing with criticisms of *A Secular Age* from a historiographical perspective, Jonathan Sheehan interrogates the assumption Taylor holds of a 'before and after' historical break that demarcates present secular times from an enchanted, religious past (Sheehan 2010: 219). If such a break can be said to have occurred, Sheehan argues (agreeing with Taylor on this point), it is to be found in early modernity, which encompasses the Renaissance, the Reformation and the Enlightenment. It is these three epochal moments of change in Western society which Sheehan, again thinking alongside Taylor, considers the linchpins of the shift towards secularism (Sheehan 2010: 220). Or are they, Sheehan asks? Sheehan examines Taylor's idea of reform, and suggests that it is very difficult to come to any accurate historical conclusions about the intentions of Luther or Calvin, or the causes of events stretching from the eleventh to the eighteenth century (Sheehan 2010: 226). However, Sheehan concedes that for Taylor the idea of reform is much older, and enters the picture at the time of the Axial revolutions outlined by Karl Jaspers (1953). Taylor argues that the logic of the Axial Age reforms created a sense of disconnection between society and religious rituals (SA, 151; see O'Shea 2010: 166). Moreover, the Axial revolution set in motion a greater separation between individuals and their communities, and the relationship between the individual and the spiritual world that was essential to early religions, which in turn makes possible the modern idea of individualism. Taylor calls this process the Great Disembedding (SA, 146ff). In other words, reform is something that is always present and continuous, it is 'the unfolding of the logic of axial religion' (Sheehan 2010: 227).

Sheehan is not completely convinced by this narrative. He criticises the way religious history is used to make these arguments. For Sheehan, Taylor is telling a story about the loss of enchantment, and this means that facts from history are hard to verify as evidence for such loss; as he puts it 'the historicity of religion . . . is hard to pin down' (Sheehan 2010: 229). For example, Sheehan examines Taylor's idea of fullness. If fullness is important to religious belief, why does it also have to be important to unbelief? 'One could argue that the unbeliever makes very little use of the idea of fullness at all' (Sheehan 2010: 230). For Taylor, fullness involves some form of transcendence, which might not be obvious to unbelievers. Fullness, as used by Taylor, is a religious feeling, Sheehan argues, and does not necessarily flow into the realm of the secular, a claim which in itself cannot be verified by the 'history of ideas' method that Taylor relies on. The reason for this is because Taylor is not making a historical argument, but a theological one (Sheehan 2010: 231). Moreover, Sheehan finds Taylor's use of history and philosophy – to outline how we have moved from an enchanted, religious worldview to a secular and disenchanted one – as engaging in apologetics (Sheehan 2010: 237). He suggests that Taylor is writing in such a way so that 'a secular age' does not spell the end of religion, but rather religion is the context in which secularism can be understood, a strategy which retains belief at the centre of the argument: 'The past stipulated as religious, as enchanted, thus can assert its power over the present and determine its various forms' (Sheehan 2010: 238).

Fullness, therefore, can now be understood as something that modern subjects who are non-believing lack, a lack which results in anxiety. Taylor makes fullness essential to authentic living, and if it is lacking, as it is in a disenchanted, secular age, then problems follow. What this means is that belief also becomes essential, and its absence results in an age of inauthenticity. A similar game is being played in Taylor's idea of the immanent frame, Sheehan suggests, where the 'closed' secular frame gives rise to the evils of capitalism, greed and totalitarian forms of nationalism, while the 'open' religious frame harbours transcendence and faith (Sheehan 2010: 239). Furthermore,

Sheehan highlights how Taylor's narrative explains how religion, and Christianity in particular, will triumph in the future by reforming and evangelising the very secularism that it gave birth to after secular and religious social spaces were first established (Sheehan 2010: 240).

To claim that Taylor's work is apologetics is a heady charge, and one which Taylor is keen to counter. In his reply to Sheehan, Taylor readily admits that his historiography is one of ideas and stadial thinking, but he warns against dismissing the relevance and potential fruitfulness of such writing. Although Taylor agrees with Sheehan that exact statistics would be preferable when presenting evidence for historical episodes of social change, the fact of the matter is that this is not always possible, especially when trying to chart changes in social imaginaries, which requires trying to understand how people's ways of thinking and acting has changed, rather than attempting to describe a specific historical event, or series of events, to determine their repercussions (APLS, 315). Defending his idea of fullness, Taylor counters Sheehan's criticism, saying that fullness is a category that humans really do think about in relation to their lives, and that to suggest otherwise is really to muddle the issue (APLS, 317). For Taylor, non-religious people can still see meaning in the world and in their lives; otherwise life for them would be flat and banal. Taylor wants his readers to understand that fullness really does exist, but that it can mean different things to different people, and misunderstanding what is fullness for others can lead to a great deal of miscommunication in society.

Finally, in reply to his critics, including Sheehan, Taylor provides a rationale for his writing of the book, which includes his own faith position as a starting point: 'My Catholic faith enters into the equation, but not in the way many people think it must' (APLS, 319). For Taylor, *A Secular Age* is an effort in building bridges and promoting greater reconciliation between people of different beliefs, whether they be religious or not, and as a love of neighbour is essential to Christianity, then if there is an element of apology for the Christian perspective in the book, then this is the reason for it. For Taylor, his reliance on the Christian perspective emphasises enhancing connections with others, as opposed to what he calls Catholicism 'from relatively high places', which puts Christianity before other faith (or lack of faith) positions (APLS, 320). In other words, Taylor is setting out in the latter parts of his book ways in which advocates of the religious and the secular can reach greater understanding, in the hope of improved harmony in the future, rather than an either–or narrative which sets the religious and secular worldviews at odds with each other. These points connect Taylor's work in *A Secular Age* to his larger project of restoring to individuals a sense of meaning that can then be a driver for a more harmonious social and political landscape (Smith 2002: 9).

Revisiting Secularism

As well as the points of criticism discussed above, scholars have also engaged with Taylor's conceptualisation of secularism. José Casanova interrogates the intellectual categories of the secular, secularisation and secularism, showing that each of these categories are much more complex than they first appear, and this has implications for Taylor's argument because he makes a number of assumptions about them. For Casanova, the 'secular' is often uncritically assumed to be what is left once religion is lifted away from the social fabric (Casanova 2011: 56). But Casanova writes that countries such as the United States and South Korea, which have secular political systems while maintaining high levels of religiosity, raise questions about this assumption. Furthermore, the idea that to be secular is identified with what it means to be modern is also problematic. However, this is more evident in those parts of the world, such as Europe, where people understand the world through Taylor's 'stadial consciousness', that is, seeing historical change and social developments in stages. Where a stadial consciousness is less evident, a direct link between modernisation and religious decline is not as readily accepted (Casanova 2011: 60).

Casanova points out that both secularisation and secularism are complex categories of which little should be assumed. Secularisation is made up of a number of subtheses, such as the separation of secular social institutions, including the state, the economy and science; the theory that as societies industrialise they become less religious; and that the privatisation of religion is a key component for the decline of religious observance and disenchantment (Casanova 2011: 60). Each of these subtheses, Casanova stresses, can and should be questioned, and further study of each of them reveals that colonialism, globalisation, the rise of fundamentalism, politics and regional differences all create a number of questions about the theory and its applicability (see Casanova 1994). All of these issues mean that 'it is unlikely that what Taylor calls "our" secular age will simply become the common global secular age of all of humanity' (Casanova 2011: 65). The many complicating factors that Casanova highlights will impact on the 'secular' in ways which it is difficult for us to understand.

Similarly, the concept of secularism for Casanova is not a simple one. Secularism may be used as a tool by governments to maintain the distinct spheres of state and religion in their societies through practical measures. Or secularism can be seen as an ideology which upholds the benefits of a secular worldview over a religious one. This second kind of secularism, which Casanova identifies as political secularism, involves theories that reinforce the separation between the state and religion:

> But the fundamental question is how the boundaries are drawn and by whom. Political secularism falls easily into secularist ideology when the political arrogates for itself absolute, sovereign, quasi-sacred, quasi-transcendent character or when the secular arrogates for itself the mantle of rationality and universality, while claiming that 'religion' is essentially nonrational. (Casanova 2011: 69)

What Casanova is highlighting here is that secularism can become a motivating force for policies aimed against religion. However, for all of the talk about secularism, Casanova notes that many European states retain close connections with their religious heritage and with the churches that reside within their borders. As he points out, from England to Greece, establishment churches continue to receive preferential treatment from the state, and in nations such as France the separation between church and state only goes so far, with Catholic schools and other institutions receiving generous government support (Casanova 2011: 71).

In summary, Casanova draws our attention to the way in which the secular is far from a simple category understood through a dyadic contrast with religion. Rather, secularism is an untidy category which involves a number of counter-trends and uncomfortable contradictions, which need to be taken into account if any discussion about a secular age is to be useful. On the other hand, Casanova does not give Taylor a great deal of credit here for his examination of the secular in *A Secular Age*. Taylor's book is largely based on the idea that simple notions of secularism and secularisation will not do in efforts to understand the current condition. For Taylor, early versions of the secularisation thesis have come under intense criticism because they have not provided an adequate account of what secularism is all about. For example, Taylor focuses on the issue of belief (SA, 4–5). Secularisation theory stated that modernisation and science led to an undermining of belief – people no longer believe because there are alternative ways of understanding the cosmos. But, Taylor argues, it is not that simple; rather, people have changed how they believe, but continue to believe.

Sociologist Richard Madsen is interested in the cross-cultural applicability of the model of secularism presented in *A Secular Age*. Madsen revisits Taylor's three notions of secularism, which are, to recap, (1) the political separation of religion and the state, (2) the decline of religious belief and practice among a greater share of the population, and lastly (3) changes in how people believe, with religion now becoming one option among many legitimate others. Using this as his point of departure, Madsen asks 'Can this analytic framework be applied outside of the North Atlantic world, particularly to Asian societies?' (Madsen 2011: 248). In Asia, Madsen argues, some of these forms of secularism are evident while others are not. Like many Western nations, a number of countries in northern and south eastern Asia are politically secular, with a clear demarcation between state institutions and religious organisations. On the other hand, however, Madsen points out that much of Asia is 'religiously dynamic' (Madsen 2011: 251). Although Taylor's secularity 3 (religion as one option among many) may be common in the West, Madsen writes that this is not the case in many parts of Asia. Religious dynamism in Asia is not found, however, in private belief, but in collective faith that is expressed in rituals and through the maintenance of religious temples and shrines. This, Madsen suggests, is similar to what Taylor calls embedded religion, where there is a strong relationship between faith and cultural practices shared by members of a community. Taylor theorises that such forms of religion were dominant in the Middle Ages in Europe, but have steadily been replaced by private faith in societies where belief is considered to be an individual preference, or choice. In Madsen's view this form of embedded religion remains normative in many Asian societies, with ramifications for modernisation and politics. He outlines how during the Cold War a number of Asian nations suppressed religion in an effort to build social consensus so that they could align themselves with the two major rivals, the USA and the USSR.

Madsen examines the case of China, a country where religion was actively suppressed by government authorities after it became communist in 1949. Government officials created a complex bureaucratic structure to control religious groups, and some were outlawed altogether. Ministers of religion were in some instances exiled and others imprisoned and even executed, and a number of holy sites were destroyed (Madsen 2011: 257). During the Cultural Revolution in the 1960s a form of state religion was developed, which centred on the mythical idea of communist success over external enemies, and the elevation of Chairman Mao to cult status. This continued until Mao's death and a drive for reform under China's new leader Deng Xiaoping. Part of these reforms in the 1980s included a renewed recognition of China's polytheistic past, and in light of this a number of new religious movements sprang up in China, some of which were seen as a challenge to state authority (Madsen 2011: 260). Today the Falun Gong movement is targeted by the Chinese government as a group which is a threat to national security, and many practitioners of the movement have been arrested and detained for lengthy periods of time. How do these developments help us to understand Taylor's views about secularism?

Madsen suggests that Taylor's understanding of secularism can be helpful for deepening our understanding of religion in Asia, but emphasises that a neat fit between a model based on the European experience and Asian societies will not be possible (Madsen 2011: 266). Rather, Taylor's model reveals that religion in Asia has not moved from public faith to private belief as has occurred in the West. In Asia, patterns of syncretism are evident whereby people actively pick and choose elements from different religions that apply to their life experiences, and religion remains something that is practiced among communities over many generations, rather than a set of beliefs harboured privately. The collapse of the bipolar world order that was established during the Cold War has meant that governments across Asia have lost the ability to justify the continued repression of religion, and since that time a plethora of new religious movements and imported missionary faiths have swamped the religious marketplace in these countries, leading to a revival of religious expression (Ashiwa and Wank 2009). What Madsen's analysis reveals is that although Taylor's work may not be applicable to all social settings, it is valuable for developing conceptual tools in aiding scholars to understand the religious transformations that are taking place across the globe.

Casanova and Madsen are not the only theorists to take issue with Taylor's theory of secularism. Ruth Abbey, one of the world's foremost Charles Taylor scholars, has published two essays where she takes a second look at what Taylor calls secularity 3 (Abbey 2010; 2014). In her first essay, she highlights how secularity 3 is about *how* people believe in the modern world, rather than what they believe in. Abbey emphasises the phenomenological aspects of belief that underlies secularity 3, and the stress on experience, or 'what it is like to be a religious believer or non-believer in contemporary western societies' (Abbey 2010: 9–10). Abbey suggests that Taylor is overstating just how secular our secular age really is. She argues that Taylor has not analysed recent data sufficiently to support his claim that modern society, including industrialised Western societies, exhibit widespread secularism: 'the secular age is not as secular as Taylor often suggests' (Abbey 2010: 10). In some respects Abbey's criticism is along similar lines to that of Sheehan outlined above. Sheehan questions Taylor's lack of *historical* evidence, while Abbey is critical of his lack of *contemporary* evidence.

Abbey is concerned that when Taylor claims that the majority of Westerners no longer believe in God, this claim is not supported by research into religious belief in modern societies of the North Atlantic world (Abbey 2010: 17). She cites a number of studies that confirm her suspicion that Taylor has overplayed his hand in his claim that we live in an increasingly secular age. These include the Pew Forum on Religion and Public Life, the European Values Survey and census results from across the world. She examines data for the United States, the United Kingdom and Ireland, Europe, Canada, Australia and New Zealand. Looking at this data reveals that in each of these locations non-belief remains in the minority, which undermines what she refers to as Taylor's alarmist notions that the world is becoming more secular, while paradoxically reinforcing his overall argument that religion has not disappeared, but rather there has been a profound change in how people believe today. Abbey also points out that Taylor's arguments would be greatly supported by use of qualitative methodologies, which might take the form of interviewing people about their religious attitudes (Abbey 2010: 18–19; also 20–1).

In her second essay, Abbey continues with the theme of critically evaluating secularity 3. She examines Taylor's notion of an Age of Authenticity and his suggestion that contemporary times show evidence of cross pressures and fragilisation when it comes to religious belief and non-belief. The Age of Authenticity is about the trend towards greater levels of individualism in religious expression, especially among the young in advanced industrial societies. For Taylor, the social events of the 1960s decade are integral to a drive towards greater personal authenticity and autonomy for individuals. As he puts it: 'The 60s provide perhaps the hinge moment, at least symbolically' (SA, 473). During the 1960s expressive individualism becomes more widespread, even democratised, rather than being the privilege of a wealthy few as was the case during the Romantic era (SA, 475). After the Second World War a number of social changes take place to make this possible, including the consumer revolution, increased suburbanisation and the creation of a youth market (SA, 474). Taylor's idea of cross pressures and fragilisation refer to the way in which modern social agents live in a world where there are many more options for how one may believe, and what one may or may not believe in, which is central to his notion of secularity 3. People today can change their religious affiliation, or drop it altogether, which was not so easily done in past societies, and this is made possible by the greater options about belief that they now have: 'the religious life of Western societies is much more fragmented than ever before, and much more unstable, as people change their position during a lifetime, or between generations' (SA, 594).

Abbey sets out some criticisms of these ideas. First, when considering the idea of authenticity, she asks whether or not an Age of Authenticity is really the recent phenomenon that Taylor claims that it is. Weren't the Reformation, and Romanticism, which Taylor traces in some detail, examples of a striving for transcendent authenticity (Abbey 2014: 104)? Furthermore, Abbey asks if exclusive humanism is really so central to individualised authenticity. What about a situation where everyone was religious, yet sought greater authenticity (Abbey 2014: 104)? Similar criticisms can be made for the ideas of cross pressures and fragilisation. Abbey identifies two aspects of cross pressures and fragilisation. One is structural and the other psychological (Abbey 2014: 107). One the one hand, there appear to be a number of social pressures that encourage people to shift their beliefs, and on the other hand there are psychological reasons that people do so without sensing guilt or loss. However, as Taylor points out, and which Abbey acknowledges, people may live in a pluralistic religious landscape with attractive options, but this does not mean that they will necessarily change their beliefs (Abbey 2014: 109). Abbey criticises Taylor for not making clear how, at the societal or individual level, the mechanisms of cross pressures or fragilisation actually work. If these pressures are cultural, then why are they not having a larger social impact? If they are psychological, then how exactly are they manifested in society? For this last point Abbey recommends further empirical evidence, 'information from people who have undergone such transformations' (Abbey 2014: 111).

This, however, would be a major undertaking from a research perspective, with potentially ambiguous results. Rather, Taylor is arguing that what he refers to as cross pressures are symptomatic of the shift towards options: 'We have undergone a change in our condition, involving both an alteration of the structures we live within, and our way of imagining these structures' (SA, 594). Finally, like the Age of Authenticity, Abbey questions whether or not exclusive humanism is essential to cross pressures and fragilisation. Imagine a society where everyone is a believer, but where they are affected by cross pressures and fragilisation from a plurality of belief systems and the option of moving between them (Abbey 2014: 112). In such a scenario exclusive humanism and secularism could be absent, while cross pressures and fragilisation are still evident.

Conclusion

In this chapter we have analysed the work of a number of scholars who have engaged with *A Secular Age*. As the discussion has made evident, Taylor's book is immensely helpful in charting how we have arrived at our current destination with regard to religion and the secular. However, these authors have shown that there remain unanswered questions in Taylor's account of the dawning of a secular age. Taylor's narrative traces the disenchantment of the world and the move from transcendence to an immanent frame of worldly concerns. In doing so his book assists scholars, and the public at large, in their efforts to understand how religion and belief have changed over the long term. Although their insights into Taylor's book are not without their own weaknesses, these critics show that Taylor's book is by no means the end of the debate about these issues.

Robert Bellah agrees with Taylor that modernity has ushered in a number of positives, but sees in Taylor's discussion of modernity a concern to emphasise connections with the past, a concern which manifests itself in the long historical sweep that many of Taylor's writings utilise. As Bellah understands it, it is Taylor's Catholicism which motivates him to reinforce connections between the pre-modern past and the modern condition, largely because Catholicism as a faith position requires one to value the beliefs and achievements that came before modernity. A response to this, however, is that Taylor does argue that modernity's break with the past is decisive, but that the pre-modern past continues to impact on the present in ways that we need to try to understand. John Milbank questions the role that Taylor gives to disenchantment as one of the steps towards secularism. Milbank proposes that rather than the world becoming disenchanted, religion was becoming more rational, so that social issues such as death and dying could be controlled by the state. Taylor, however, emphasises the importance of the Scientific Revolution that studied nature within a framework established by theology, creating a greater reliance on reason. The rationality Milbank relies on is, then, not antithetical to a religious outlook.

José Casanova challenges the assumptions Taylor makes about secularisation, an important influence on religion that began with modernity. Casanova is cautious about seeing the West as uniformly secular, pointing out that secularism and religious belief are unique in different parts of the world. Perhaps, Casanova claims, it is Europe that is the odd one out, with high levels of religiosity evident in many other parts of the world, including the United States. But Taylor agrees with these points, and raises the question of whether or not secularism, as it is experienced in the West, can travel to other locations, and he is sceptical that it can without being altered.

We have also considered Taylor's use of history. Colin Jager interrogates Taylor's emphasis on the importance of romanticism in his historical narrative. This seems to Jager to be linked to his ideas about disenchantment, and romanticism is used to fill the void in meaning, for individuals and for society, when the world has lost its enchantment with the onset of the Enlightenment and the Industrial Revolution. But is this too much to ask of romanticism, which is at its core a literary and philosophical movement promoted by a small number of European élites? Jon Butler then examines some of Taylor's historical claims in an effort to find empirical evidence to support them. But because Taylor is more a historian of ideas, rather than a professional historian relying on sources, such evidence is lacking. Butler prompts readers to think about the implications for such a lack of evidence for Taylor's argument.

Similarly, Sheehan examines a number of concepts that are essential to Taylor's narrative and finds that they lack supporting evidence. These include enchantment, fullness and discussion of the Axial revolution and its impact on religion. Finding these areas lacking in support from historical sources, Sheehan poses the controversial question of whether or not Taylor is engaging in apologetics, an argument for why religion, and the Christian religion in particular, is crucial for civilisation. Taylor challenges this supposition, pointing out that if his faith enters the book then it is manifested in his efforts to present religion as a potential vehicle for overcoming social fractures and promoting social harmony.

Finally, we examined the key concept of secularism in Taylor's work, and how his critics view it. Casanova assesses secularist categories, beginning with the secular as a social fact, secularisation as a process of modernisation and secularism as a political ideology. He concludes that these categories are more complex than they first appear, and that it is perilous to make assumptions about them. For example, although nations such as the United States or South Korea understand themselves as being secular, they are in fact highly religious societies. Richard Madsen addresses the cross-cultural applicability of Taylor's model of secularism. He suggests that although many Asian nations maintain a secular social order with a separation of church (or temple) and state, they reveal, as in the case of China, diverse and complex patterns of religiosity. Lastly, Ruth Abbey critically examines Taylor's theory of secularity 3, which says that although religion has not disappeared from modern society, social agents are now presented with options, to believe or not believe, or to choose from a diverse range of spiritualities. Like some of Taylor's historical critics, Abbey is concerned that Taylor has not included enough evidence from contemporary research that challenges the notion that the world is increasingly secular.

Furthermore, Abbey writes about how Taylor's efforts to show that people today have a number of religious options, summed up in his views on authenticity, cross pressures and fragilisation, could undermine his idea of exclusive humanism, an important part of what makes increased secularism possible. Is it possible that exclusive humanism might not exist, while everyone in a highly religious pluralistic society could still exhibit authenticity, and choose widely between divergent belief systems? A reply to these points is that Taylor is interested in the form, or shape of, contemporary secularism, as opposed to its degree. Taylor is arguing that secularity today is about religious options, rather than how many people are reported to engage in prayer or worship.

Taylor's *A Secular Age* is an ambitious project which will continue to spark debate for many years to come. The issues raised here are only a sample of the many claims and innovative concepts that are found in the book, and which find their place in Taylor's other writings. However, just as the debates about *A Secular Age* do not end here, neither have Taylor's efforts to understand life under modern social conditions. Since the publication of *A Secular Age* Taylor has moved on to other projects, including further writings about secularism, and a lengthy report written for the Quebec Government with the aim of bringing to light issues of diversity and pluralism in Canadian society. In the next chapter we will examine some of Taylor's most recent work, in an effort to assess his ongoing contribution to social analysis and politics. We will also explore how this work fits into debates that are currently occupying scholars, including issues such as multiple modernities, multiple secularities and the rise of post-secularism.

Note

1. Jager uses a capital 'R' to denote the Romantic Movement of writers in the seventeenth century and after, who challenged what they considered the sterility of Enlightenment thought about progress, and a small 'r' to denote romanticism as a broader set of ideas. We will follow this convention in this section.

8
Charles Taylor's Work after *A Secular Age*

Introduction

As we saw in the last chapter, since publishing *A Secular Age* Charles Taylor has been involved in various symposiums where his book has been critically assessed, and has contributed papers to edited collections which examine some of its key themes. However, Taylor has also been working on a number of other projects, some that have engaged his passion for politics, while others remain focused on his interests in debates about religion, secularism and multiculturalism, and other social issues. These include his work for the Quebec Government in producing a major report on multiculturalism called *Building the Future* (2008), and his work on freedom of religion (SFC). Furthermore, in 2015 Taylor published a book with co-author Hubert Dreyfus called *Retrieving Realism*, in which they argue that philosophy should base its conclusions more firmly in empiricism. Finally, Taylor has published a book called *The Language Animal* (2016), which shows the impact that Romanticism has had on our thinking about language. In this chapter we will examine Taylor's contributions to these topics, revealing how he continues to be one of the world's foremost intellectuals who is able to participate in a wide range of political and social debates.

What these projects also reveal is Taylor's continued interest in the breach where individualism and society collide. His focus on Romanticism, along with his work in politics and social philosophy, reveal his understanding about how relationships between the self, other selves and the social body as a whole, is constitutive of a society's ability to create social conditions based on equality, freedom, ethics and other hypergoods. These, he argues, limit the ill effects of atomism, which advocates individual autonomy outside communal contexts. Although the individual has been provided with much greater creative, social and political freedoms since the onset of modernity, there is an ever present tendency for individualism to try to overstep the mark and create conditions where others are seen as a means to an end, rather than as fellow citizens in an open and democratic public sphere. Taylor's aim, in much of his work, is to continue to remind his readers that we must be careful that atomism does not become normative at the expense of a vision of society where collaboration and interdependency are better ways of maintaining a just and fair social order.

Taylor develops these ideas in the work outlined below. We will begin with his work on secularism that takes its point of departure from *A Secular Age* and analyses the importance of freedom of religion in the modern world. This will lead to a discussion of the report that he and Gérard Bouchard produced for the Quebec Government, and which is concerned with the challenges of maintaining social harmony with high levels of multiculturalism and religious diversity in a modern pluralistic society. Finally, we will examine Taylor's views on the centrality of language for self-identity and social communication.

Freedom of Religion in a (Post) Secular Age

After writing *A Secular Age*, Taylor shifted his focus to consider freedom of religion in modern societies. For Taylor, this issue is particularly poignant today due to the high levels of religious diversity that is evident in many societies. But Taylor also suggests that religious freedoms must be worked out in a context which upholds the claims of secularism, for 'there is a broad consensus that "secularism" is an essential component of any liberal democracy' (SFC, 2). But how can this tension between the promotion of religious freedoms, and the maintenance of a secular social order, be worked out? Taylor and co-author Jocelyn Maclure investigate this problem, beginning by subjecting the notion of secularism to critical analysis. They argue that 'secularism' as a concept cannot be reduced only to ideas such as the separation of church and state, or relegating religion to the private sphere. These definitions of secularism are inadequate. Rather, 'secularism must at present be understood within the broader framework of the diversity of beliefs and values that citizens embrace' (SFC, 4). Such a view of secularism echoes theories of post-secularism, which we will discuss below. The authors stress the importance that Taylor made in *A Secular Age* of distinguishing between political secularism, or the separation of church and state, and social secularisation, the process whereby religion becomes less visible due to falling levels of religious adherence, however contested such a theory might be. Taylor and Maclure want to highlight how the separation of church and state, and the state's neutrality in religious questions, is really only possible through the promotion of freedom of conscience, where individuals are free to follow the religion of their choice without coercion or interference from the state or state agencies (SFC, 20). Freedom of conscience is in turn based on a view of the dignity and equality afforded to each citizen, and the protection of their freedoms. Furthermore, the many cultural values held by citizens from diverse backgrounds means that there will be a diversity of religious views and customs that the state must respect. Therefore, a democratic state cannot endorse an official religion, for to do so makes those who do not adhere to that religion 'second-class citizens' (SFC, 20).

However, an overemphasis on advocating secularism can, Taylor and Maclure point out, lead to pathologies, such as what they call 'regimes of secularism' (SFC, 27). This occurs when a secular state restricts religions, seeing them as potentially harmful to secularity, or as competing for the loyalty of citizens. These 'rigid forms of secularism' are found in countries such as China, where religion is restricted because it is seen as a form of social mobilisation which might criticise the state, or question the legitimacy of the Communist Party. Rather, the authors advocate 'open secularism' which protects the right of citizens to follow their religion without hindrance, while the state takes a neutral stance. These points were underscored in the commissioned study that Taylor co-chaired and Maclure worked on for the Quebec Government, which we will discuss further in the next section. But the principal points the authors present here reflect Taylor's faith in 'the people', which became central to democratic countries following the political revolutions of the eighteenth century (Rundell 2014: 203). By granting an open field in the practice of religion, the state takes a step back and lets individuals fill this field of social action. But although this may fit well with modern conceptions of the freedom of the individual, there is a certain degree of idealism at work here. As we stated in Chapter 7, José Casanova points out that most states are not completely dissociated from particular religions, and their support of a religion can take the form of financial assistance via tax concessions, or by granting special status to a religion through legal exemptions. Furthermore, many states are not content to let religion run its own course within their borders, and may subject religious persons to high levels of security surveillance, especially in countries where terrorism inspired by religious ideology is perceived as a threat. Finally, many states are keenly interested in the religious activity of their citizens, be it in regimes of secularism such as China, or in more indirect forms, such as asking people's religion in census data collection. These points challenge the notion that the state is, or will ever be, completely neutral in relation to religion.

A Secular Age was written at a time when theories about secularism and secularisation were being intensely debated. The theory of secularisation has been critically reassessed for a number of years now. Some scholars have questioned its core idea, which suggests that as societies become modernised, they concomitantly become less religious (Asad 2003: 181–2). The United States is held up as an exception to this trend, as a nation at the forefront of technological developments and innovation, but which at the same time has very high levels of church membership (Bruce 1996: 129; Putnam and Campbell 2010). As we saw in our discussion of *A Secular Age*, the secularisation thesis and political secularism are related but distinct terms. Secularism involves the role of religion in politics and public life, and advocates of secularism claim that religious beliefs should be left to the private sphere when it comes to public policy and decision making. This, along with the effects of secularisation, and evidence from statistics that shows lower levels of attendance at religious ceremonies, has meant that for some time now religion has been of minor concern in public life. But as a number of commentators have argued, rather than religion being pushed out of the public sphere, it has in recent decades made its presence felt again more forcefully. Examples include the rise of Islamic fundamentalism which has become more pronounced since the Islamic Revolution in Iran in 1979, and the defeat of Soviet forces in Afghanistan in the 1980s. Another example is the influence of religious groups on politics, such as the Moral Majority in the United States, which was composed of a collection of Christian churches and organisations which supported Ronald Reagan when he won the presidency in the 1980 and 1984 elections. Thus, a number of studies have revealed that religion is making a comeback in modern society, rather than being cast into the waste bin of history as some secularists assumed.

Gilles Kepel (1994) examines the efforts of Islamic groups, the Catholic Church and Jewish organisations in political struggles in diverse settings. His conclusion is that rather than being marginalised in international affairs and public policy, religion has become central to understanding social change and global tensions in numerous countries. Another major study that challenged the idea that religion had lost its relevance in modern times was that put forward by José

Casanova (1994), who also argues that religion continues to play a significant role in regional and global politics. Casanova highlights the deprivatisation of religion, providing examples of how religion has impacted on public life in Spain, Poland, Brazil and the United States since the early 1980s. Examining the role that Catholicism and Protestantism is playing in these places, Casanova argues that secularisation has occurred, but that religions are again

> entering the public sphere and the arena of political contestation not only to defend their traditional turf, as they have done in the past, but also to participate in the very struggles to define and set the modern boundaries between the private and public spheres. (Casanova 1994: 6)

For Casanova, religion is a motivating force for social groups in their efforts to resist secularisation, or to counter the power of authoritarian regimes. It also aids in sustaining social, ethnic and cultural identities, especially when these are under threat from powerful forces, as the case of Poland showed under communism. Casanova highlights, therefore, the political implications of religion as it becomes increasingly deprivatised, and as those of religious faith involve themselves more fully in public debate.

Other criticisms of secularisation focus on 'de-secularization', a term used by Peter Berger (1999). Berger claims that the secularisation thesis has been falsified, and that this has taken place because of the ways that religious institutions have responded to modernity. One response includes religious revolutions, from the revolutionary reforms of Vatican II in the 1960s, through to the Iranian Revolution of 1979, and another is because religious institutions in many countries have stuck to their core teachings rather than adapt to social change, offering a countermovement to secularism (Berger 1999: 3–4). Fundamentalism is an important element, in Berger's opinion, for the religious resurgence since the 1970s. Berger goes so far as to suggest that it is now secularists who comprise a small 'international subculture composed of people with Western-type higher education' (Berger 1999: 10). Rather than an inevitable move towards the creation of a small religious remnant of believers under secularisation, it is secularism that appears to be on the wane.

Overall, these theories are contributions to what has become known as post-secularism, a situation where social life is no longer a space where religious views are silenced, but rather where religion is seen as a prime motivator of social protest, identity and political mobilisation. But in Taylor's opinion, although these points are all valid, he takes issue with the way in which secularism is framed in contemporary analyses such as these. As we pointed out earlier, Taylor is critical of how secularisation has been understood as a subtraction story, where religion is removed from modern society. The reality, Taylor argues, is more complex. The greater preponderance of religious, or spiritual, options for modern individuals means that the kinds of arguments put forward by Kepel, Casanova and Berger, which aim to reintroduce religion after an apparent absence, fail to show that belief has been with us all along in one form or another. New religious movements, shifts away from established churches and towards individualised spirituality, the religions of minority groups in multicultural societies, and the ways in which people seek fullness through both spiritual and secular experiences, all point towards his view that belief, and how it is expressed, has changed, rather than decreased or increased.

Jürgen Habermas' views are closer to Taylor's than other secularisation theorists on these issues. He has argued that in a post-secular social order people's religious views should not only be brought out of the private sphere and into the public arena, but that secular societies need to take into account the religious sentiments that influence citizens' decision making and sense of social inclusion. As he puts it, the 'liberal state must not transform the requisite *institutional* separation of religion and politics into an undue *mental* and *psychological* burden for those of its citizens who follow a faith' (Habermas 2006: 9, emphasis in original). In other words, although a separation of church and state can be maintained, democratic nations cannot compel citizens to disregard their faith in the public sphere or in political debate, for to do so is effectively to silence them. This is a recognition of the varieties of belief found in many pluralistic societies today. Taylor reworks some these principles in his contribution as co-author to the report *Building the Future*, for the Quebec Government, where he advocates that the unique culture and identity of minority groups needs to be sustained as they seek to integrate into Quebec society, rather than expecting them to discard their culture and/or faith. What Habermas is talking about also coincides with Taylor's views on religious diversity, where he and Maclure write that 'the state, to be truly everyone's state, must remain "neutral"' (SFC, 13) when it comes to questions to do with religion. As we mentioned above, although any true state neutrality regarding religion might in practice be difficult to achieve, such a perspective does add credence to the suggestion that we are now living in times when secularism is not as easily definable as it once was, and when belief and the options for expressing it are having a powerful impact on government policy and social cohesion.

Recent sociological research on religion has begun to question the idea of the secular in new and provocative ways. An example is work on multiple secularities. Multiple secularities borrows a key idea from theories of multiple modernities. The concept of multiple modernities suggests that although modernity is evident in many places around the globe, it takes on local manifestations in different regions and countries, depending on the political, cultural and social particularities that are to be found in those regions and countries. For example, the originator of the idea of multiple modernities, S. N. Eisenstadt, studied Japan and its path to modernity, finding that it took on cultural and political manifestations that were different compared to the modernity that originated in Europe and North America. It was the unique social institutions and culture of Japan that led to this distinctive form of modernity developing (Eisenstadt 1996). The key idea underpinning multiple secularities works in a similar way. Although secularism may be understood, in broad terms, as a realm separate from religion, how this works in practice will differ in specific locations. Therefore, just as modernity should not be seen as all-encompassing, which different cultures and traditions should be forced to fit into, neither should the idea of secularity be seen as a one size fits all concept (Burchardt and Wohlrab-Sahr 2013). Although modernity and secularity are well documented social trends, different cultures and societies will influence these trends in different ways when they take root in these cultures. In their paper setting out the research agenda of the multiple secularities concept, Wohlrab-Sahr and Burchardt (2012) outline how secularism has different inflections in the disparate regions where it is found. In the United States, for example, secularism is noted for its emphasis on the rights and freedoms of the individual. Church and state are kept separate to protect individual liberty. In India, secularism is a mechanism for achieving social harmony between different religious groups, in particular Hindus and Muslims. A third form of secularism is evident in France and Turkey, where it serves as a tool for maintaining national and social integration of a number of different religions and ethnic groups, while at the same time enhancing the cohesion of the nation state. Finally, secularism serves in a number of locations as a way of sustaining the independence of state institutions, such as education, science and government bureaucracy, from influence by churches or other religious organisations. Secular schools and a secular political system include social institutions which serve this function.

Taylor's points in *A Secular Age*, and his other works on religion and communitarianism, add to these ideas. Taylor argues that each society has its own social imaginary, a shared conception between citizens about what the state's role is and how the culture that each person is a part of is unique and valuable (see SA, 159ff; MSI; see Chapter 5). In a way similar to Benedict Anderson's (2006) theory of an imagined community, a social imaginary is based on the understanding that citizens share a vision of a common good which binds them together. Taylor expands this notion to argue that what is at stake here is a 'new idea of moral order' (MSI, 5), one which emphasises the rights of individuals alongside the rational organisation of the state. Such rights include freedom of expression in the public sphere, access to social provisions including welfare and freedom of conscience. On the other hand, Taylor's work has been subject to the charge of Eurocentricism (Veer 2001: 160). The stress he places on the impact of Romanticism and the Enlightenment for the development of modern society and the modern self underscore this criticism, as these movements have their origins in the West and reflect Western concerns about society and the individual. On the other hand, Taylor's focus on freedom of religion goes some way at least in developing ideas that are applicable to social contexts where modernity might not be of the same type as that found in Western nations, but where questions about religious diversity are just as urgent. In an essay on secularism in diverse global settings, for instance, Taylor (2016a) has argued that although secularism can be found in many locales beyond the West, he warns that they should not be seen as derivatives of the Western model of secularism, but should be assessed in the context of local conditions.

As well as his work on freedom of religion in the context of post-secularism, Taylor has also continued to contribute to the political situation of his native Canada, especially the question of multiculturalism in Quebec. In 2007 he helped to research and co-author an important report on the issue for the Government of Quebec. It is to a discussion of this report that we now turn.

Building the Future: *A Report on Multiculturalism in Quebec*

In 2007, Taylor and Gérard Bouchard published their report into the accommodation of social diversity in Quebec, with an English language version of the report produced a year later (see BF). This diversity includes multiculturalism, religious diversity, secularism, gender and the status of the French language in a multi-linguistic society. The report was the product of a number of public hearings and research projects that the commission undertook throughout 2007, and the commissioners' mandate, as stipulated by the government, was to look into the success or failure of the accommodation of minorities in Quebec society, and to make recommendations about how these accommodations 'conform to Québec's values as a pluralistic, democratic, egalitarian society' (BF, 17). The authors concluded, after a year of intense research, that 'the foundations of collective life in Québec are not in a critical situation' (BF, 18). In other words, although there have been flashpoints of conflict between native Quebecers and migrants, these have been overblown in the media and are not symptomatic of a crisis in Quebec society. On the other hand, the authors noted that Quebecers remain ill at ease with their status as a majority in Quebec, while at the same time being a minority in Canada. Any long-term solutions to this situation remain to be seen, and the authors note that a similar state of affairs can be found in some European countries (BF, 18).

Building the Future illustrates Taylor's interest in the liberal–communitarian debate on multiculturalism that we outlined in Chapter 4. As we argued, although individual rights are important for the liberal tradition, Taylor stresses that individuals are defined by the cultural and social contexts in which they live; this is particularly so for migrants who experience feelings of vulnerability in their new environment. The communitarian aspect of social life is, therefore, crucial for successful multiculturalism. Recognition also plays a part in this process. Migrant groups derive their sense of identity from how they are treated, or recognised, by the majority. If they are treated as equals and welcomed into society, their ability to become productive members of that society will be enhanced. Misrecognition, on the other hand, leads to feelings of alienation and crisis, with flow-on social problems between migrants and their new society. This occurs when migrants experience high levels of unemployment, are excluded from social services, or when their education and expertise, which they have brought from their home country, are undervalued.

One of the report's major topics is religion in a secular state made up of a large number of different faiths. Quebec was once predominately Catholic, and its Catholicism has been a strong point of identity for French speaking Canadians. However, after increased secularisation in Quebec, and decreasing rates of church attendance and religious identification, Catholicism is now competing with many other religious denominations and faiths, many of which are held by its migrant population. The authors of the report advocate open secularism, which is based on the four principles of moral equality between persons, freedom of conscience and religion, the separation of church and state, and state neutrality towards religion (BF, 20). The separation of church and state, and neutrality, are needed to reinforce the first two aspects of open secularism – moral equality and freedom of religion (BF, 136–7). The authors highlight how Quebec has advocated secularism without enforcing it, and this should continue. Therefore, the banning of religious dress in public, such as the burqa, hijab or the turban, is not recommended. The report takes the stance of state neutrality towards religion as an important ingredient of this process of open secularism. Thus, the state should not support one religion over any others, but rather it should provide the conditions where individuals are able to practice freedom of religion without constraints (Abbey 2009: 82). Because the state should not favour any particular religion they advise, perhaps controversially given Quebec's Catholic history, that the crucifix that hangs in the National Assembly should be removed (BF, 20). Other religious symbolism, they suggest, should on the other hand be left to individuals to decide on, such as the wearing of the headscarf for Muslim women, or any other religious symbols that pertains to individuals. Such symbols are expressions of the right to religious freedom, and contrast with religious symbolism at the state level. In keeping with this approach, the authors point out that educational institutions are not obliged to establish prayer rooms, but that individuals are free to find spaces to pray on campus.

Harmony and friction between different ethnic groups was also investigated at length by the commission. One concern was with investigating to what degree ghettoes and ethnic enclaves, or 'spatial rifts', were forming in Quebec, and the potential here to reinforce geographically the separation of ethnic groups that might be occurring at the cultural level, or what the authors call 'social and cultural divides' (BF, 205–6). During testimony at the commission's hearings, such geographical spaces were highlighted as examples of the failure of multiculturalism in Quebec. However, after analysing data, including census results, the authors conclude that there is little evidence for the existence of ethnic ghettoes or enclaves in Montreal, Quebec's largest city. Although ethnic groups might live in close proximity to one another in specific parts of the city, the report argues that these groups are well integrated into the wider society through employment and education, and through civic involvement.

The status of the French language in Quebec followed on from these considerations, and although the authors admit that addressing this topic was stretching their terms of reference, they offered a number of points for consideration. These included the reflection that any form of 'linguistic tranquillity' will be impossible in a situation where globalisation is subjecting cultures around the world to large-scale structural and cultural changes, and that the decline of the French language in Quebec can be highlighted in a number of statistical reports (BF, 209). On the other hand, the authors point out that French is being learned by many new migrants, and that the government has in place financial resources to support the French language. A sense of crisis over the loss of French is, therefore, overblown.

The major conclusion of the report, then, is that Quebec should continue to strive for a model of diversity that encourages interculturalism. Such a course of action means encouraging migrant groups to adopt the identity and language of what it means to be a Quebecer, without giving up their own unique cultural identity. Such a position protects French as the national language of Quebec and offers a buffer to Quebecers' feelings of insecurity about their position as a minority in Canada and North America, while at the same time providing the social mechanisms for migrant groups and social minorities to participate fully in Quebec society (BF, 265–9; Abbey 2009: 86–7).

The report has not been without its critics. Ruth Abbey takes issue with its conservatism, which for her derives from the theoretical perspective which the authors take. The report in her reading concludes that concerns over accommodation and multiculturalism in Quebec have been overstated, and it emphasises a 'steady as she goes' approach, advocating discussion and monitoring rather than an overhaul of the province's immigration policies. A second reason for the report's 'minimalist response' (Abbey 2009: 75) is the confidence that the authors have that Quebec is already handling accommodation and integration effectively, and so further tampering with the system would be both unhelpful and potentially counterproductive. Because the authors see no crisis of accommodation in Quebec, there is therefore no sense of urgency of action forthcoming from the report. Abbey speculates that Taylor's interest in rights may be a reason why he considers Quebec to be, generally speaking, successful in the accommodation of immigrants. However, we should be careful to attribute all of the report's conclusions to Taylor alone, as he was but one of the two lead authors, and the report is the outcome of a large team of researchers and government administrators who worked on it. Overall, however, the report reveals Taylor's contributions quite strongly in its firm grasp on issues related to secularism, human rights and multiculturalism. Taylor's continued interest in the situation of the French language in a country where English is spoken is also evident in the report. In another major research project, completed since the publication of *A Secular Age*, language takes centre stage, and we shall turn to a consideration of this work in the next section.

Language and the Politics of Human Agency

As we have stated earlier, Taylor has a long-held interest in language (see HAL). He has returned to this topic, subjecting it to sustained analysis. In *The Language Animal* (LA), Taylor outlines over the course of a number of chapters his thoughts on the centrality of language for the human person and as being essential for the formation of human societies and communities. Taylor puts forward two major ways in which language is understood, which are part of a debate about language that has been underway since the Renaissance. The first of these he calls 'designative-instrumental'. In this view of language, words point to, or designate, objects and phenomena, and language assists us in building a picture of the universe, to make sense of the world and to understand our place within it. It is an enframing theory of language (LA, 3). Words help us to grasp universal ideas, and they are used as tools to describe the world, meaning that they have instrumental qualities. But here the limitations of such a theory of language are made evident, because language in this understanding is little more than a collection of signs that have a use-value for human beings.

This view of language is overtly rationalistic and something closer to a code than a shared set of linguistic signs able to produce meaning. This way of understanding language is, according to Taylor, largely post-Cartesian, and is found in the works of philosophers such as Condillac, Hobbes and Locke (Taylor 2016b). As Taylor stresses, 'Condillac belongs to the mode of thought which conceives language as an instrument, a set of connections which we can use to construct or control things' (LA, 12). This view of language is also essential to the scientific method, and underlies the Scientific Revolution and the many advances that science and technology have made since the seventeenth century. The correct use of language, or 'rightness' is important here (LA, 7–8). Furthermore, science relies on a use of language that is objective and value-free, and science uses language instrumentally to designate and describe a wide range of natural phenomena from pulsars to insects. The social, or human, sciences have also been widely influenced by this way of utilising language, in their efforts to study human beings and their social contexts objectively, and free from value judgements and prejudice.

The second way that language has been understood since the Renaissance comes from the Romantic period. This theory of language Taylor calls 'expressive-constitutive'. Language now does more than merely describe the world and the objects to be found within it. Rather, language changes how we live in the world. Language becomes the essential ingredient in how we are socialised and learn moral and ethical rules. It helps us to understand not only what things are, but how we are to act in response to their presence. As Taylor points out, Socrates, Jesus and the Buddha were all reliant on language to convey to others their moral view of the world, and their modern day followers can only access their teachings through language, whether it is through the writings of Plato in the case of Socrates, or through sacred texts in the case of Jesus and the Buddha (Taylor 2016b). A similar case can also be made for the followers of Mohammad. Expressive-constitutive language allows us to express ourselves and our ideas and it also aids us in constituting meaning, to create a meaningful order. Moreover, this view of language reveals how language is a social phenomenon: 'To learn the language of society is to take on some imaginary of how society works and acts, of its history through time; of its relation to what is outside: nature, or the cosmos, or the divine' (LA, 22). Furthermore, according to Taylor, we take on a new vocabulary when we try to work out our life projects and how these projects fit into the morals and ethics we learned as we were growing up. This vocabulary is more nuanced and more abstract than that used under a 'designative-instrumental' theory of language, which we learn first and relies mainly on giving names to things.

With an 'expressive-constitutive' theory of language, words are used to tell ourselves and others what is most important in our lives, and how our life goals fit in with our society's moral expectations. Taylor finds this theory of language evident in the work of Romantic thinkers such as Herder and Humboldt, and he is interested in how such thinkers use language in their construction of a worldview that is based not on description, as it might be in science, but on the idea that we need to make sense of our ethical and moral decisions in the world. An expressive-constitutive theory of language allows for the way in which words and symbols are used to convey artistic expression and emotion, something that was crucial for how the Romantic poets and novelists used language, examples of which includes English Romantic writers such as William Wordsworth, Samuel Taylor Coleridge (Auden and Pearson 1978) and Mary Shelley.[1] It is a way of understanding language which allows for imagery, symbolism and metaphor, and it is integral to what it is to be fully human – it is, in short, 'reflective' (LA, 30). Furthermore, because this way of understanding language goes beyond classification and description, it is a powerful source of new ideas, and it is essential to how we understand new experiences and probe beyond the here and now into the larger questions about life and the meaning of our existence. It is, in other words, essential if we are to *change* our view of the world, and not just exist within the world.

Another important aspect of constitutive language is the way that it forms the basis of ritual, including religious rituals (LA, 343). This form of language also changes how we live in practical terms in human societies. Taylor gives the example of how we address others. In non-egalitarian societies forms of address to superiors are very formal, enhancing the social distance between different classes of people. In egalitarian societies, on the other hand, Taylor stresses that forms of address are much more relaxed (Taylor 2016b). This is an example of language not only describing social relations, but transforming how we act in the world and how human agents interact with one another in real social contexts. Moreover, using language figuratively, imaginatively and creatively forms who we are as human beings, it is embodied, foundational to our own self-understanding, and reveals our place in human communities (LA, 24; 333).

Taylor has pointed out that his interest in language is a product to some extent of his biography growing up in bilingual Quebec (Taylor 2016b). Taylor remembers as a child addressing his parents as '*vous*', which is the respectful form of address in French, but points out that such a form of address is not used by young people today (LA, 271). He also recalls the debate over bilingualism in Quebec. For Canadian English speakers, language was described as a medium for communicating and conducting business. It was all that was needed to run schools and bureaucracies, and maintain a prosperous economy. French speakers, on the other hand, decried this understanding of language, seeing it as impoverished. To them language was much more than only a medium of communication. For French Canadians, language was a repository of their history and culture. It expressed more than linguistic signs, but also conveyed a way of life and a unique understanding of the world (Taylor 2016b). For Taylor, the English speakers in this debate were advocating a designative-instrumentalist view of language, as a tool used by human beings to navigate the natural and social worlds. The French speakers were promoting an expressive-constitutive view of language, as a group of symbols and signs that conveyed ideas such as culture, a shared history and belief. What this example highlights is the ramifications of Taylor's views about language. A designative-instrumentalist understanding of language may well be useful for the scientific method, and for helping humans to solve problems and develop new technologies, but left to itself will in the long term lead to a poorer understanding of the cosmos, and it undervalues human potential. However, by subscribing also to an expressive-constitutive view of language, human agents are able to make sense not only of the objective world, but of their own subjectivities as well, and are able to map out a path in life that allows them to reach their full potential and act as good moral and ethical citizens at the same time. Or at least that is the hope.

Another issue raised by Taylor's ideas on language is how it can be hijacked by those in power for the purpose of manipulating individuals or even whole societies. There are many examples of this in history, including the careful attention given to propaganda by the Nazis in the 1930s and 1940s, and the warnings about the corruption of language for the purposes of holding power that have been astutely set out in literature, including George Orwell's classic novel *1984*. In Orwell's novel an insidious form of double-speak is used, describing social problems such as scarcity and war in positive terms in an effort to mislead people about the reality of the world in which they are living. Similar things could be said vis-à-vis certain political and economic ideologies that are active today. The neo-liberal conception of economics, with a strong emphasis on individualism and its criticism of funding public services, is a focus for a number of intellectuals (Saul 1997; Bourdieu 2010), and its success in many countries is dependent on its ability to use language to justify cuts to social services. For example, publicly owned entities such as postal services and railways have been sold off in some industrialised nations, and this has been done by advocating efficiency, improved customer relations, and austerity now for a more prosperous future. However, a critical analysis of these ideas shows that they are language-forms that mask a drive towards privatisation at a specific time of change in globalised capitalism.

As outlined above, an important consequence of a constitutive theory of language is the way in which it creates meaning (LA, 179). Taylor points out that language is constitutive not only of things and ideas, but also forms the individual, as each social agent uses language in common with others. Language is not, Taylor stresses to point out, simply a code that lies dormant when not used. Rather, language is embodied because we are embodied beings living in complex social relations. This notion of embodiment is an important element for Taylor in his work on language, as well as for his philosophical vision as a whole. It is through our being embodied that we overcome the problem of the mind's ability to know reality (RR, 91). Without bodies, it would be difficult for us to be sure that we know what is really out there in the world. Taylor and Dreyfus (see RR) discuss this point in their thoughts on the mind–body problem, which is neatly illustrated in the film *The Matrix*, where human beings are kept in life support systems and fed images of 'reality' through a computer program. This keeps them docile so that their body's energy can be harvested. This is an example of the 'brains in vats' dilemma outlined by Searle (see RR, 95). Ẑiẑek (2002: 244) defines the Matrix computer program in the film as 'the network that structures reality for us'. Because it is an external force, it is also alienating, a form of symbolic violence that orders our reality without any input from us, and from which we are detached. For Taylor, on the other hand, being embodied helps to overcome this alienation and keeps us from being fooled about the nature of reality.

Taylor and Dreyfus propose a 'contact theory' of knowledge, rather than a mediational one which was promoted by Descartes. A contact theory relies on human agents taking into account their relationship with their world for understanding reality, it 'is a reembedding of thought and knowledge in the bodily and social-cultural contexts in which it takes place' (RR, 18). But returning to the issue of embodied language, Taylor is interested in how language helps to constitute for us a habitus, in the sense of the word used by Bourdieu (LA, 272). A habitus is formed by embodying specific social meanings, and expressing them in a social context where they are recognisable by others. Also, we embody meaning in a habitus which matches 'those of our institutions, hierarchies, understandings of who or what is superior and inferior, and so forth' (LA, 273). In this way our habitus allows us to fit in with what is taken for granted in our community, to understand these taken for granted ideas and express them in our words and actions. It also enables us to challenge them when the need arises. Embodied language, therefore, is constitutive of individuals, social institutions and social relations. Further to this, Taylor argues that it is in more complex forms of language, such as narrative and stories, that meaning is made. Stories help us to make sense of our lives and the world in which we live, and they offer a connection between our embodied self and the social relations that we must navigate on a daily basis: 'This constitutive power is of the greatest importance, because it is through story that we make sense of our lives' (LA, 317).

Just as Mead argued that the self can only be formed within social contexts of mutual communication and interdependence, Taylor suggests that the self requires stories to understand itself, to come to some kind of understanding about who I am and how I fit in with others in the social world in which I live and strive. Moreover, to form a self in the first instance requires not only Mead's 'generalised other', but also narratives through which I can make sense of the world around me: 'It is through the power of making and understanding stories that I have access to myself as a self . . . that I *become* a self' (LA, 318, emphasis in original). Bringing these two ideas together, of language as being embodied and as a creator of meaning, allows us to see, therefore, how language underpins complex social processes such as religion and politics. Through the creation of meaning rituals take shape, be they of a secular or sacred nature, and these rituals provide solidarity and opportunities for restitution when needed (LA, 279). In politics, language provides the means through which communities make sense of their interconnections and the role of power, enabling them to create consensus around the best ways to order society, although this may be initially through conflict. In this case, language comes before the establishment of a political order. Taylor cites the United States Constitution and Greek ideas about politics in ancient Athens as ways in which a political community is formed, or constituted, through language, rather than language expressing a state of affairs which is already in existence (LA, 278; 285).

Conclusion

What we have shown in this chapter is that Taylor's work continues to contribute to debates at the cutting edge of research in the humanities and social sciences. This is testament to both the relevance of his work, and his ability to help set the research agenda across a number of fields. While his work on religion and secularism continue to shape how these issues are understood and analysed, his recent work on realism in philosophy, and on language, will no doubt have a similar impact for a number of years to come. Furthermore, as we have seen above, Taylor has not shied away from pragmatic contributions in politics and public debate, and his work on freedom of religion, and his contribution to the report on multiculturalism in Quebec, have opened up new perspectives on these issues, and will help to keep the discussion of social recognition for minorities, and religion in the public sphere, on the social agenda.

In the Conclusion to this book, which follows, we will bring together and sum up a number of the strands of Taylor's long intellectual career. Reflecting on the issues raised by Taylor's work since *A Secular Age* was published, what is evident is that Taylor remains committed to a vision of the social order that upholds the sovereignty of the individual, which was given impetus during the Enlightenment and the Romantic Movement, with a commitment to a communal conception of society that does not slip into an atomism which pits persons against each other in a struggle for resources. His work on freedom of religion, on diversity in Quebec and on language, highlight his ongoing concern for a vision of society and politics where individuals can strive to build the lives that they find most fulfilling, while at the same time contributing to a social order where equality of opportunity is maintained by being founded on notions of egalitarianism, freedom and conscience. This is, therefore, Taylor's vision of a society that has at its centre a moral order.

Note

1. In his concluding remarks in *The Language Animal* Taylor notes that he aims to investigate the post-Romantic tradition in greater detail in a planned subsequent work.

Conclusion

As we have discussed in the preceding chapters, Charles Taylor has contributed to a diverse range of philosophical, political and sociological issues that are central to unravelling some of the most pressing challenges confronting contemporary societies, in areas such as pluralism, religion and secularism, and national identity. Taylor's wide range of interventions on these issues gives rise, however, to a potentially major problem concerning his work – where is the consistency and coherency in his philosophical and political project? Are Taylor's contributions part of a coherent critique of modern social and political frameworks, or are they rather a collection of penetrating yet isolated writings on a number of haphazard topics which he happens to find interesting? As Nicholas Smith and Ruth Abbey stress, and as we mentioned in the introduction to this book, Taylor is not a systems builder, and his work is not easily summed up or categorised. This may add to its breadth and reach, but does it allow him to offer a consistent analysis of life in modern times from which readers can access comprehensive and sound theories? Although this may seem a difficult charge to exonerate Taylor from, based on the variety of his publications, we would answer the preceding question in the affirmative. This is because examining Taylor's work in its entirety shows that there are indeed a number of consistent themes that run throughout his writings, and which ties the many issues he has commented on together.

These consistent themes include his interest in moral sources, the idea that ethics, values and notions like freedom are based on more than arbitrary categories of thought, but are rather akin to hypergoods, things which we value above others, and which have their basis in something transcendent. Another recurrent and important idea for Taylor is the Romantic Movement and its impact on modern society, our thinking about the self, moral questions and language. The Romantic Movement was more than a reaction to the championing of reason and rationality by Enlightenment *philosophés*, it was also a time when the self and its relationship to nature, other selves and society became central. Third, modernity underpins Taylor's work across his writings. His interest in Hegel as a philosopher of modernity, and the impact that modernity is having on social bonds and pluralism, reveals his attitude towards life in modern times, as providing a number of benefits and efficiencies while at the same time threatening some traditional certainties, and at worst enhancing the social conditions that increase alienation.

Furthermore, each of these reoccurring themes in Taylor's work acts on the others. Moral sources need to be understood within the framework of modernity after the Romantic Movement. Modernity and romanticism provide the conditions whereby moral thinking no longer needs to be based on transcendent authority, such as religious institutions or their leaders. The self now becomes the arbiter of moral decision making, and this became even more pronounced during the 1960s decade. Modernity provided the environment where critical thought, mimicking the scientific method, was able to peel back the layers and see outside moral sources as historically conditioned and, at times, the product of power and inequality. Taylor has some criticisms about this development, as it lacks purpose beyond human whims. Modernity, in its turn, has transformed social life, politics, and how individuals understand each other and their world in profound ways. Central to the modern project is the idea of the freedom of the individual, and that individuals have the required reason to make decisions about how to live their lives. This, however, can lead to crisis when thinking about moral sources, because it becomes apparent that without firm moral guidelines definitions of 'morality' become self-generated – people, in short, decide on their own rules – and the political and legal processes of deciding what is correct conduct in different cases is made ever more complex. The Romantic Movement has in some ways provided fuel to these situations – it has championed the idea of the solitary walker who decides on meaning and the nature of reality outside social contexts, and its reaction to the rationality of modernity can lead to a creativity and expressivism that does not always translate into activating social change.

At another level, these reoccurring themes in Taylor's work reveal challenges for the modern self and for society. For the self, authenticity becomes a key issue, especially in the face of social forces that promote a one size fits all approach to what it means to be human. The numerous debates about difference in many countries attest to the struggle for recognition by individuals of diverse backgrounds to have their identity accepted. This is one reason why Taylor sees the 1960s as such an important decade, because although it may have given rise to a sometimes unrestrained individualism, it was also the time when a number of social movements motivated by questions about difference and identity found their momentum. At the social level, creating greater levels of harmony and inclusion are important as far as Taylor is concerned, to reduce the possibility of alienation and social fragmentation. An atomistic view of society should always be held in suspicion, because an overemphasis on individualism presents grave problems for a society striving for collective goodwill and interdependence. Unconnected individuals, and those left behind in the race for consumer goods, are easy prey to alienation and social isolation, which in turn fractures societies.

Taylor makes this point in his speech on winning the Kluge Prize in 2015: modern democracy requires a very strong sense of bonding between citizens who cannot be forced to pay their taxes or fight in wars (as they might be under other social systems), and this close bonding between citizens means that individuals must trust one another in an ongoing dialogue about what is the best way to organise social relations (KP). However, when segments of a society feel excluded from this conversation, and feel that their interests are not being met, or that they are being discriminated against, then not only does disorder follow, but the core values of the democratic ethos are undermined, or as Taylor puts it, 'it's that distrust which can tear a democratic society apart' (KP). Taylor goes on to point out that democracy today is in danger of contradicting its own principles, and it does this when immigrants are accused of not adopting the values that the rest of the population subscribes to. To overcome this problem, Taylor calls for the recognition of a state of permanent diversity in democracies, that is, a situation where citizens are constantly open to new migrants. Secularism plays a part in this process, by confirming the neutrality of the state over matters of religion and religious symbolism, so that migrants and others who continue to uphold their faith publicly have the opportunity to become a part of the nation without facing religious discrimination, which in turn breeds alienation and resentment (KP). This state of permanent diversity not only includes, Taylor argues, the welcoming of migrants, but also a redefinition of the relationship between the state and indigenous populations. Language is another key component, because the language we use to define what it is to be 'we the people' is crucial to a nation's self-understanding. What Taylor sums up in his speech, therefore, is a brief résumé of his main interests as they apply to ongoing social challenges.

As many Anglophone societies are impacted upon more and more by the effects of an unrestrained global capitalism that has no concern for community, meaningful work, secure incomes or social inclusion, Taylor's message becomes increasingly important. In a time when the social isolation of many citizens is becoming more entrenched, including the elderly, the unemployed, and those economically marginalised by higher costs of living and less secure forms of work, Taylor's project encourages pause for thought about the social conditions and political processes that underlie the West's rush for consumerism and profit at the expense of social solidarity and fairness. The effects of this are becoming more apparent in the political processes of some countries, where populist leaders are challenging the dominant political parties, but doing so through a politics of fear that focuses on migrants and employment insecurity. And beyond the Anglophone societies of the West the effects of ecological damage caused by industrialised countries, along with the ever widening gulf between the rich and the rest that is the hallmark of capitalism when it is left uncontrolled, can be seen tearing apart countries in the developing world, and attests to the kinds of alienation and corruption that stands in stark contrast to Taylor's views on authenticity and a moral order of mutual benefit. Although Taylor's work may seem to be abstract at times in its philosophical sophistication, we can take on board the lessons he gives by example in his life's work, to blend political thought with direct political action that seeks to make a difference.

Bibliography

Abbey, Ruth (2000). *Charles Taylor*. Teddington: Acumen Press.

Abbey, Ruth (ed.) (2004). *Charles Taylor*. Cambridge: Cambridge University Press.

Abbey, Ruth (2006). 'Back to Baczko', *European Journal of Political Theory* 5(3): 355–64.

Abbey, Ruth (2009). '*Plus Ça Change*: Charles Taylor on Accommodating Quebec's Minority Cultures', *Thesis Eleven* 99, November: 71–92.

Abbey, Ruth (2010). '*A Secular Age*: The Missing Question Mark', in Ian Leask (ed.), *The Taylor Effect: Responding to A Secular Age*. Newcastle upon Tyne: Cambridge Scholars, pp. 8–25.

Abbey, Ruth (2014). 'Theorizing Secularity 3: Authenticity, Ontology, Fragilization', in Carlos D. Colorado and Justin D. Klassen (eds) *Aspiring to Fullness in a Secular Age: Essays on Religion and Theology in the Work of Charles Taylor*. Notre Dame, IN: University of Notre Dame Press, pp. 98–124.

Alexander, Jeffrey C. (1995). *Fin de Siècle Social Theory: Relativism, Reduction, and the Problem of Reason*. London: Verso.

Althusser, Louis [1969] (2005). *For Marx*. Trans. Ben Brewster. London: Verso.

Anderson, Benedict (2006). *Imagined Communities: Reflections on the Origin and Spread of Nationalism*. Rev. Ed. London: Verso.

Appiah, Anthony, K. (1994). 'Identity, Authenticity, Survival: Multicultural Societies and Social Reproduction', in Amy Gutmann (ed.) *Multiculturalism: Examining the Politics of Recognition*. Princeton, NJ: Princeton University Press, pp. 149–64.

Arendt, Hannah (1958). *The Human Condition*. Chicago, IL: University of Chicago Press.

Arnason, Johann Pall (1991). 'Modernity as Project and as Field of Tensions', in A. Honneth and H. Joas (eds) *Communicative Action*. Cambridge: Polity Press, pp. 181–213.

Arnason, Johann Pall (1993). *The Future that Failed*. London: Routledge.

Arnason, Johann Pall (2002). 'The Multiplication of Modernity', in E. Ben-Rafael (ed.) *Identity, Culture and Globalization*. Brill: Leiden, pp. 130–54.

Asad, Talal (2003). *Formations of the Secular: Christianity, Islam, Modernity*. Stanford, CA: Stanford University Press.

Ashiwa, Yoshiko and David L. Wank (2009). *Making Religion, Making the State: The Politics of Religion in Modern China*. Stanford, CA: Stanford University Press.

Auden, W. H. and Norman Holmes Pearson (1978). *The Portable Romantic Poets*. New York: Viking.

Baczko, Bronislaw (1984). *Les Imaginaires Sociaux*. Paris: Payet.

Beck, Ulrich and Elisabeth Beck-Gernsheim (2002). *Individualization*. London: Sage.

Bellah, Robert N. (2005). 'What is Axial about the Axial Age?', *Archives Européennes de Sociologie*, 46 (1): 69–89.

Bellah, Robert N. (2010). 'Confronting Modernity: Maruyama Masao, Jürgen Habermas, and Charles Taylor', in Michael Warner, Jonathan VanAntwerpen and Craig Calhoun (eds) *Varieties of Secularism in a Secular Age*. Cambridge, MA: Harvard University Press, pp. 32–53.

Bellah, Robert N. (2011). *Religion and Human Evolution: From the Paleolithic to the Axial Age*. Cambridge, MA: Harvard University Press.

Bellah, Robert N. and Hans Joas (eds) (2012). *The Axial Age and Its Consequences*. Cambridge, MA: Harvard University Press.

Berger, Peter L. (1999). *The Desecularization of the World: Resurgent Religion and World Politics*. Grand Rapids, MI: William B. Erdmans.

Berlin, Isaiah (1969). *Four Essays on Liberty*. Oxford: Oxford University Press.

Berlin, Isaiah (1986). *Four Essays on Liberty*. Oxford: Oxford University Press.

Berlin, Isaiah (1994). 'Introduction', in James Tully (ed.) *Philosophy in an Age of Pluralism: The Philosophy of Charles Taylor in Question*. Cambridge: Cambridge University Press, pp. 1–3.

Berlin, Isaiah (1998). *The Proper Study of Mankind*. London: Pimlico.

Blanning, Tim (2011). *The Romantic Revolution: A History*. New York: Modern Library.

Bohmann, U. and D. Montera (2014). 'History, Critique, Social Change and Democracy – An Interview with Charles Taylor', *Constellations* 21 (1): 3–15.

Boltanski, Luc and Eve Chiapello (2005). *The New Spirit of Capitalism*. London: Verso.

Bourdieu, Pierre (1990). *The Logic of Practice*. Polity Press: Cambridge.

Bourdieu, Pierre (2010). *Sociology is a Martial Art: Political Writings*. Gisèle Sapiro (ed.) New York: The New Press.

Brown, Callum G. (2001). *The Death of Christian Britain: Understanding Secularisation 1800–2000*. London: Routledge.

Browne, Craig (2006). 'A Moral Order of Mutual Benefit', *Thesis Eleven* 86: 114–25.

Browne, Craig (2008). 'The End of Immanent Critique?', *European Journal of Social Theory* 11 (1): 5–24.

Browne, Craig (2009). 'Democracy, Religion and Revolution', *Thesis Eleven* 99: 27–47.

Browne, Craig (2010). 'Democratic Justice as Intersubjective Freedoms', *Thesis Eleven* 101: 53–62.

Browne, Craig (2014a). 'Introduction to "Whatever Works": Political Philosophy and Sociology: Luc Boltanski in Conversation with Craig Browne', in Simon Susen and Bryan Turner (eds) *Luc Boltanksi: Critical Perspectives*, London: Anthem Press, pp. 541–9.

Browne, Craig (2014b). 'Between Creative Democracy and Democratic Creativity', in V. Karalis (ed.) *Castoriadis and Radical Democracy*. Leiden: Brill, pp. 196–217.

Browne, Craig (2015). 'Half-positions and Social Contestation: On the Dynamics of Exclusionary Integration', in B. Bringel and J. M. Domingues (eds.) *Global Modernity and Social Contestation*. London: Sage, pp. 185–202.

Browne, Craig (2016). 'Critiques of Identity and the Permutations of the Capitalist Imaginary', *Social Imaginaries* 2 (1): 95–118.

Browne, Craig (2017a). *Critical Social Theory*. London: Sage.

Browne, Craig (2017b). *Habermas and Giddens on Praxis and Modernity: A Constructive Comparison*. London: Anthem Press.

Bruce, Steve (1996). *Religion in the Modern World: From Cathedrals to Cults*. Oxford: Oxford University Press.

Bruce, Steve (2011). *Secularization: In Defence of an Unfashionable Theory*. Oxford: Oxford University Press.

Burchardt, Marian and Monika Wohlrab-Sahr (2013). '"Multiple Secularities: Religion and Modernity in the Global Age" – Introduction', *International Sociology* 28 (6): 605-11.

Burckhardt, Jacob (1958). *The Civilization of the Renaissance in Italy*. New York: Harper and Row.

Butler, Jon (2010). 'Disquieted History in *A Secular Age*', in Michael Warner, Jonathan VanAntwerpen and Craig Calhoun (eds) *Varieties of Secularism in a Secular Age*. Cambridge, MA: Harvard University Press, pp. 193–216.

Butler, Judith, Jürgen Habermas, Charles Taylor and Cornell West (2011). *The Power of Religion in the Public Sphere*. New York: Columbia University Press.

Campbell, James (1999). *This is the Beat Generation: New York – San Francisco – Paris*. London: Secker & Warburg.

Casanova, José (1994). *Public Religions in the Modern World*. Chicago, IL: University of Chicago Press.

Casanova, José (2010). 'A Secular Age: Dawn or Twilight?', in Michael Warner, Jonathan VanAntwerpen and Craig Calhoun (eds) *Varieties of Secularism in a Secular Age*. Cambridge, MA: Harvard University Press, pp. 265–81.

Casanova, José (2011). 'The Secular, Secularizations, Secularisms', in Craig Calhoun, Mark Juergensmeyer and Jonathan VanAntwerpen (eds) *Rethinking Secularism*. New York: Oxford University Press, pp. 54–74.

Casanova, José (2012). 'Religion, the Axial Age, and Secular Modernity in Bellah's Theory of Religious Evolution', in Robert N. Bellah and Hans Joas (eds) *The Axial Age and Its Consequences*. Cambridge, MA: Harvard University Press, pp. 191–221.

Casanova, José (2016). 'Secularism and Religious and Spiritual Forms of Belonging', in Conversation with Charles Taylor. Talk given at the Australian Catholic University, North Sydney Campus, 29 April.

Castoriadis, Cornelius (1987). *The Imaginary Institution of Society*. Cambridge: Polity.

Castoriadis, Cornelius (1991). *Philosophy, Politics, Autonomy*. D. A. Curtis (ed.), Oxford: Oxford University Press.

Castoriadis, Cornelius (1997a). *World in Fragments*. Stanford, CA: Stanford University Press.

Castoriadis, Cornelius (1997b). 'From Ecology to Autonomy', in D. Curtis (ed.) *The Castoriadis Reader*. Oxford: Blackwell, pp. 239–52.

Chadwick, Owen (1975). *The Secularization of the European Mind in the Nineteenth Century*. Cambridge: University of Cambridge Press.

Chakrabarty, Dipresh (2000). *Provincializing Europe*. Princeton, NJ: Princeton University Press.

Coleridge, Samuel Taylor (1954). *Biographia Literaria*. London: Oxford University Press.

Connolly, William E. (2004). 'Catholicism and Philosophy: A Nontheistic Appreciation', in Ruth Abbey (ed.) *Charles Taylor*. New York: Cambridge University Press, pp. 166–86.

Davie, Grace (1994). *Religion in Britain since 1945: Believing without Belonging*. Oxford: Blackwell.

Davie, Grace (2000). *Religion in Modern Europe: A Memory Mutates*. Oxford: Oxford University Press.

Deranty, Jean-Philippe and Emanuel Renault (2007). 'Politicizing Honneth's Ethics of Recognition', *Thesis Eleven* 88: 92–111.

Domingues, José Maurício (1995). *Sociological Theory and Collective Subjectivity*, London: Macmillan.

Domingues, José Maurício (1999). 'Evolution, History and Collective Subjectivity', *Current Sociology* 47 (3): 1–34.

Domingues, José Maurício (2000). *Social Creativity, Collective Subjectivity and Contemporary Modernity*. Houndsmills: Macmillan.

Driver, Julia (2014). 'Gertrude Elizabeth Margaret Anscombe', *The Stanford Encyclopedia of Philosophy* (Winter Edition), Edward N. Zalta (ed.), <http://plato.stanford.edu/archives/win2014/entries/anscombe/> (last accessed 30 August 2017).

Duffy, Eamon (2005). *The Stripping of the Altars: Traditional Religion in England 1400–1580*. 2nd Ed. New Haven, CT: Yale University Press.

Durkheim, Émile [1912] (1995). *The Elementary Forms of Religious Life*. Trans. Karen E. Fields. New York: Free Press.

Durkheim, Émile (1964). *The Division of Labor in Society*. Free Press: New York.

Dworkin, Ronald (1977). *Taking Rights Seriously*. London: Duckworth.

Edelstein, Dan (2010). *The Enlightenment: A Genealogy*. Chicago, IL: University of Chicago Press.

Eisenstadt, Shmuel Noah (ed.) (1986). *The Origins and Diversity of the Axial Age Civilizations*. Albany, NY: State University of New York Press.

Eisenstadt, Shmuel Noah (1996). *Japanese Civilization: A Comparative View*. Chicago, IL: University of Chicago Press.

Eisenstadt, Shmuel Noah (1999a). *Fundamentalism, Sectarianism, and Revolution*. Cambridge: Cambridge University Press.

Eisenstadt, Shmuel Noah (1999b). 'Multiple Modernities in an Age of Globalization', *Canadian Journal of Sociology* 24 (2): 283–95.

Eisenstadt, Shmuel Noah (2000). 'Multiple Modernities', *Daedalus* 1: 1–29.

Eisenstadt, Shmuel Noah (2001). 'The Civilizational Dynamic of Modernity: Modernity as a Distinct Civilization', *International Sociology* 16: 320–40.

Eisenstadt, Shmuel Noah, Dominic Sachsenmaier and Jens Riedel (eds) (2002). *Reflections on Multiple Modernities: European, Chinese and Other Interpretations*. Leiden: Brill.

Elias, Norbert (1994). *The Civilizing Process*. Trans. Edmund Jephcott. Oxford: Blackwell.

Fanon, Frantz (1967). *The Wretched of the Earth*. Harmondsworth: Penguin.

Fanon, Frantz (1986). *Black Skin, White Masks*. London: Pluto Press.

Farrell, James J. (1997). *The Spirit of the Sixties: Making Postwar Radicalism*. New York: Routledge.

Foucault, Michel (1970). *The Order of Things: An Archaeology of the Human Sciences*. London: Tavistock Publications.

Foucault, Michel (1991). 'Nietzsche, Genealogy, History', in Paul Rabinow (ed.) *The Foucault Reader*. Harmondsworth: Penguin, pp. 76–100.

Frank, Manfred (2004). *The Philosophical Foundations of German Romanticism*. Albany, NY: State University of New York Press.

Fraser, Nancy (1995). 'From Redistribution to Recognition? Dilemmas of Justice in a "Post-Socialist" Age', *New Left Review* 212: 68–93.

Fraser, Nancy (2003a). 'Social Justice in the Age of Identity Politics: Redistribution, Recognition, and Participation', in N. Fraser and A. Honneth (eds) *Redistribution or Recognition? A Political-Philosophical Exchange*. London: Verso. pp. 7–109.

Fraser, Nancy (2003b). 'Distorted beyond Recognition', in N. Fraser and A. Honneth (eds) *Redistribution or Recognition? A Political-Philosophical Exchange*. London: Verso.

Fraser, Nancy and Honneth, Axel (2003). *Redistribution or Recognition? A Political-Philosophical Exchange*. London: Verso.

Fromm, Erich [1956] (1963). *The Sane Society*. London: Routledge.

Fukuyama, Francis (1992). *The End of History and the Last Man*. Harmondsworth: Penguin.

Gaonkar, Dilip Parameshwar (2002). 'Toward New Imaginaries: An Introduction', *Public Culture* 14 (1): 1–19.

Gauchet, Marcel (1997). *The Disenchantment of the World: A Political History of Religion*. Trans. Oscar Burge. Princeton, NJ: Princeton University Press.

Geertz, Clifford (1994). 'The Strange Estrangement: Taylor and the Natural Sciences', in James Tully (ed.) *Philosophy in an Age of Pluralism: The Philosophy of Charles Taylor in Question*. Cambridge: Cambridge University Press, pp. 83–95.

Giddens, Anthony (1992). *The Transformation of Intimacy*. Cambridge: Polity Press.

Giddens, Anthony (1994). 'Living in a Post-Traditional Society', in U. Beck, A. Giddens and S. Lash (eds) *Reflexive Modernization*. Cambridge: Polity Press, pp. 56–109.

Gräb, Wilhelm (2010). 'The Transformation of Religious Culture within Modern Societies: From Secularization to Postsecularism', in Arie L. Molendijk, Justin Beaumont and Christoph Jedan (eds) *Exploring the Postsecular: The Religious, the Political and the Urban*. Leiden: Brill, pp. 113–29.

Gutmann, Amy (ed.) (2004). *Multiculturalism: Examining the Politics of Recognition*. Princeton, NJ: Princeton University Press.

Gutting, Gary (1999). *Pragmatic Liberalism and the Critique of Modernity*. Cambridge: Cambridge University Press.

Habermas, Jürgen (1974). 'On Social Identity', *Telos* 19: 91–103.

Habermas, Jürgen (1976). *Legitimation Crisis*. London: Heinemann.

Habermas, Jürgen (1983). 'Modernity–An Incomplete Project', in Hal Foster (ed.) *Postmodern Culture*. London: Pluto Press, pp. 3–15.

Habermas, Jürgen (1984). *The Theory of Communicative Action: Volume 1: Reason and the Rationalisation of Society*. Boston: Beacon Press.

Habermas, Jürgen (1987a). *The Theory of Communicative Action, Volume 2: Lifeworld and System*. Cambridge: Polity Press.

Habermas, Jürgen (1987b). *The Philosophical Discourse of Modernity: Twelve Lectures*. Cambridge, MA: MIT Press.

Habermas, Jürgen (1992). *Postmetaphysical Thinking*. Cambridge, MA: MIT Press.

Habermas, Jürgen (1994). 'Struggles for Recognition in the Democratic Constitutional State', in Amy Gutmann (ed.) *Multiculturalism: Examining the Politics of Recognition*. Princeton, NJ: Princeton University Press, pp. 107–48.

Habermas, Jürgen (1996). *Between Facts and Norms: Contributions to a Discourse Theory of Law and Democracy* Cambridge, MA: MIT Press.

Habermas, Jürgen (2006). 'Religion in the Public Sphere', *European Journal of Philosophy* 4 (1): 1–25.

Harvey, David (1990). *The Condition of Postmodernity: An Enquiry into the Origins of Cultural Change.* Oxford: Blackwell.

Heelas, Paul and Linda Woodhead (2005). *The Spiritual Revolution: Why Religion is Giving Way to Spirituality.* Oxford: Blackwell.

Hegel, Georg Wilhelm Friedrich (1967). *Philosophy of Right.* Oxford: Oxford University Press.

Hegel, Georg Wilhelm Friedrich (1977). *Phenomenology of Spirit.* Oxford: Oxford University Press.

Hegel, Georg Wilhelm Friedrich (1979). *System of Ethical Life (1802/3) and First Philosophy of Spirit (Part III of the System of Speculative Philosophy 1803/4).* H. S. Harris and T. M. Knox (eds) Albany, NY: State University of New York Press.

Hegel, Georg Wilhelm Friedrich (1986). *The Jena System, 1804–5: Logic and Metaphysics.* G. Di Giovanni, H. S. Harris, and J. W. Burbidge (eds), Kingston: McGill-Queen's University Press.

Honneth, Axel (1995a). *The Struggle for Recognition: The Moral Grammar of Social Conflicts.* Cambridge: Polity Press.

Honneth, Axel (1995b). *The Fragmented World of the Social: Essays in Social and Political Philosophy.* C. W. Wright (ed.), Albany, NY: State University of New York Press.

Honneth, Axel (2001). 'Recognition or Redistribution? Changing Perspectives on the Moral Order of Society', *Theory, Culture and Society* 18 (2–3): 43–55.

Honneth, Axel (2003a). 'Redistribution as Recognition: A Response to Nancy Fraser', in N. Fraser and A. Honneth (eds) *Redistribution or Recognition? A Political-Philosophical Exchange.* London: Verso, pp. 110–97

Honneth, Axel (2003b). 'The Point of Recognition: A Rejoinder to the Rejoinder', in N. Fraser and A. Honneth (eds) *Redistribution or Recognition? A Political-Philosophical Exchange.* London: Verso, pp. 237–68.

Honneth, Axel (2007). *Disrespect: The Normative Foundations of Critical Theory.* Cambridge: Polity.

Honneth, Axel (2009). *Pathologies of Reason.* New York: Columbia University Press.

Honneth, Axel (2013). *The I in We.* Cambridge: Polity Press.

Honneth, Axel (2014). *Freedom's Right – The Social Foundations of Democratic Life.* Cambridge: Polity Press.

Horkheimer, Max and Theodor Adorno (1972). *Dialectic of Enlightenment.* New York: Herder and Herder.

Huntington, Samuel P. (1991). *The Third Wave: Democratization in the Late Twentieth Century.* Norman, OK: Oklahoma University Press.

Huntington, Samuel P. (1997). *The Clash of Civilizations and the Remaking of World Order*. London: Touchstone Books.

Isserman, Maurice and Michael Kazin (2000). *America Divided: The Civil War of the 1960s*. New York: Oxford University Press.

Jager, Colin (2010). 'This Detail, This History: Charles Taylor's Romanticism', in Michael Warner, Jonathan VanAntwerpen and Craig Calhoun (eds) *Varieties of Secularism in a Secular Age*. Cambridge, MA: Harvard University Press, pp. 166–92.

Jameson, Fredric (1988). *The Ideologies of Theory, Volume 2: The Syntax of History*. London: Routledge.

Jaspers, Karl (1953). *The Origin and Goal of History*. London: Routledge and Kegan Paul.

Jenkins, Philip (2002). *The Next Christendom: The Coming of Global Christianity*. New York: Oxford University Press.

Joas, Hans (1985). *George Herbert Mead: A Contemporary Re-Examination of His Thought*. Cambridge: Polity Press.

Joas, Hans (1998). 'The Autonomy of the Self: The Median Heritage and its Postmodern Challenge', *European Journal of Social Theory* 1 (1): 7–18.

Joas, Hans (2000). *The Genesis of Values*. Cambridge: Polity Press.

Juergensmeyer, Mark (2000). *Terror in the Mind of God: The Global Rise of Religious Violence*. Berkeley, CA: University of California Press.

Kant, Immanuel (1964). *Groundwork of the Metaphysics of Morals*. New York: Harper & Row.

Kaplan, Fred (2009). *1959: The Year Everything Changed*. Hoboken, NJ: John Wiley & Sons.

Kepel, Gilles (1994). *The Revenge of God: The Resurgence of Islam, Christianity and Judaism in the Modern World*. Trans. Alan Braley. Cambridge: Polity.

Leezenberg, Michiel (2010). 'How Ethnocentric is the Concept of the Postsecular?' in Arie L. Molendijk, Justin Beaumont and Christoph Jedan (eds) *Exploring the Postsecular: The Religious, the Political and the Urban*. Leiden: Brill, pp. 91–112.

Lefort, Claude (1986). *The Political Forms of Modern Society: Bureaucracy, Democracy, Totalitarianism*. Polity Press: Cambridge.

Lefort, Claude (1988). *Democracy and Political Theory*. Cambridge: Polity Press.

Lilla, Mark (2007). *The Stillborn God: Religion, Politics, and the Modern West*. New York: Alfred A. Knopf.

Lundin, Roger (1993). *The Culture of Interpretation: Christian Faith and the Postmodern World*. Grand Rapids, MI: Erdmans.

Lyotard, Jean-François (1984). *The Postmodern Condition: A Report on Knowledge*. Minneapolis, MN: The University of Minnesota Press.

McLeod, Hugh (2007). *The Religious Crisis of the 1960s*. Oxford: Oxford University Press.

Madsen, Richard (2011). 'Secularism, Religious Change, and Social Conflict in Asia', in Craig Calhoun, Mark Juergensmeyer and Jonathan VanAntwerpen (eds) *Rethinking Secularism*. New York: Oxford University Press, pp. 248–69.

Mann, Michael (2005). *The Dark Side of Democracy*, Cambridge: Cambridge University Press.

Marcuse, Herbert (1964). *One-Dimensional Man: Studies in the Ideology of Advanced Industrial Society*. Boston, MA: Beacon Press.

Marx, Karl and Friedrich Engels (1977). 'The Communist Manifesto', in D. McLellan (ed.) *Karl Marx: Selected Writings*. Oxford: Oxford University Press: pp. 221–47.

Mead, George Herbert (1934). *Mind, Self and Society*. Chicago, IL: University of Chicago Press.

Merleau-Ponty, Maurice (1962). *The Phenomenology of Perception*. London: Routledge and Kegan Paul.

Milbank, John (2010). 'A Closer Walk on the Wild Side', in Michael Warner, Jonathan VanAntwerpen and Craig Calhoun (eds) *Varieties of Secularism in a Secular Age*. Cambridge, MA: Harvard University Press, pp. 54–82.

Mulhall, Stephen (2004). 'Articulating the Horizon of Liberalism: Taylor's Political Philosophy', in Ruth Abbey (ed.) *Charles Taylor*. Cambridge: Cambridge University Press. pp. 105–26.

Murphy, Peter (2012). *The Collective Imagination. The Creative Spirit of Free Societies*. Farnham: Ashgate.

Nasr, Seyyed Hossein (2003). *Islam: Religion, History, and Civilization*. San Francisco, CA: Harper.

Nietzsche, Friedrich (2013). *On the Genealogy of Morals*. Trans. Michael A. Scarpitti. Harmondsworth: Penguin.

Norris, Pippa and Ronald Inglehart (2004). *Sacred and Secular: Religion and Politics Worldwide*. Cambridge: Cambridge University Press.

O'Shea, Andrew (2010). 'Sources of the Sacred: Strong Pedagogy and the Making of a Secular Age', in Ian Leask (ed.), *The Taylor Effect: Responding to a Secular Age*. Newcastle upon Tyne: Cambridge Scholars, pp. 160–74.

O'Shea, Andrew (2012). *Selfhood and Sacrifice: René Girard and Charles Taylor on the Crisis of Modernity*. London: Continuum.

Putnam, Robert D. and David E. Campbell (2010). *American Grace: How Religion Divides and Unites Us*. New York: Simon & Schuster.

Rawls, John (1971). *A Theory of Justice*. Oxford: Oxford University Press.

Rawls, John (2005). *Political Liberalism*. New York: Columbia University Press.

Redhead, M. (2002). *Charles Taylor: Thinking and Living Deep Diversity*. Lanham, MD: Rowman & Littlefield.

Rorty, Richard (ed.) (1967). *The Linguistic Turn*. Chicago, IL: University of Chicago.

Rousseau, Jean-Jacques (1968). *The Social Contract*. Harmondsworth: Penguin.

Rundell, John (2014). 'Charles Taylor's Search for Transcendence: Mystery, Suffering, Violence', in M. Sharpe and D. Nickelson (eds) *Secularisations and Their Debates: Perspectives on the Return of Religion in the Contemporary West*. Dordrecht: Springer, pp. 199–215.

Sandel, Michael J. (1982). *Liberalism and the Limits of Justice*. Cambridge: Cambridge University Press.

Saul, John Ralston (1997). *The Unconscious Civilization*. Harmondsworth: Penguin.

Sheehan, Jonathan (2010). 'When was Disenchantment? History and the Secular Age', in Michael Warner, Jonathan VanAntwerpen and Craig Calhoun (eds) *Varieties of Secularism in a Secular Age*. Cambridge, MA: Harvard University Press, pp. 217–42.

Skinner, Quentin (1994). 'Modernity and Disenchantment: Some Historical Reflections', in James Tully (ed.) *Philosophy in an Age of Pluralism: The Philosophy of Charles Taylor in Question*. Cambridge: Cambridge University Press, pp. 37–48.

Smith, James K. A. (2014). *How (Not) to be Secular: Reading Charles Taylor*. Grand Rapids, MI: William B. Eerdmans.

Smith, Karl E. (2010). *Meaning, Subjectivity, Society: Making Sense of Modernity*. Leiden: Brill.

Smith, Nicholas H. (2002). *Charles Taylor: Meaning, Morals and Modernity*. Cambridge: Polity.

Smith, Nicholas H. and J.-P. Deranty (eds) (2012). *New Philosophies of Labour: Work and the Social Bond*. Leiden: Brill.

Solomon, Robert C. (1990). *Continental Philosophy since 1750: The Rise and Fall of the Self*. Oxford: Oxford University Press.

Susen, Simon (2016). *The Postmodern Turn*. London: Palgrave Macmillan.

Taylor, Charles (1988). 'Foreword', in A. Honneth and H. Joas (eds) *Social Action and Human Nature*. Cambridge: Cambridge University Press, pp. vii–ix.

Taylor, Charles (1994). 'Justice after Virtue', in John Horton and Susan Mendus (eds) *After MacIntyre: Critical Perspectives on the Work of Alasdair MacIntyre*. Notre Dame, IN: University of Notre Dame, pp. 16–43.

Taylor, Charles (2001). 'Two Theories of Modernity', in D. Gaonkar (ed.) *Alternative Modernities*. Durham: Duke University Press.

Taylor, Charles (2002). 'Modern Social Imaginaries', *Public Culture* 14 (1): 91–124.

Taylor, Charles (2009). 'Reply', *Thesis Eleven* 99 (1): 93–104

Taylor, Charles (2016a). 'Can Secularism Travel?', in Akeel Bilgrami (ed.) *Beyond the Secular West*. New York: Columbia University Press, pp. 1–27.

Taylor, Charles (2016b). 'The Language Animal'. Talk given at the Australian Catholic University, North Sydney Campus, 22 April.

Tocqueville, Alexis de (1955). *The Old Régime and the French Revolution.* New York: Anchor Books.

Tocqueville, Alexis de (2003). *Democracy in America.* London: Penguin Books.

Tully, James (ed.) (1994). *Philosophy in an Age of Pluralism: The Philosophy of Charles Taylor in Question.* Cambridge: Cambridge University Press.

Veer, Peter van der (2001). *Imperial Encounters: Religion and Modernity in India and Britain.* Princeton, NJ: Princeton University Press.

Voltaire, F. (2005). *Miracles and Idolatry.* Harmondsworth: Penguin.

Wagner, Peter (1994). *A Sociology of Modernity: Liberty and Discipline.* London: Routledge.

Wagner, Peter (2008). *Modernity as Experience and Interpretation: A New Sociology of Modernity.* Cambridge: Polity.

Wagner, Peter (2012). *Modernity: Understanding the Present.* Cambridge: Polity.

Walzer, Michael (1994). 'Comment', in Amy Gutmann (ed.) *Multiculturalism: Examining the Politics of Recognition.* Princeton, NJ: Princeton University Press, pp. 99–103.

Warner, Michael (1990). *The Letters of the Republic.* Cambridge, MA: Harvard University Press.

Warner, Michael, Jonathan VanAntwerpen and Craig Calhoun (eds) (2010). *Varieties of Secularism in a Secular Age.* Cambridge, MA: Harvard University Press.

Weber, Max [1930] (1995). *The Protestant Ethic and the Spirit of Capitalism.* Trans. Talcott Parsons. London: Routledge.

Weber, Max (1958). 'Science as a Vocation', in H. H. Gerth and C. Wright Mills (eds) *From Max Weber: Essays in Sociology.* London: Routledge, pp. 129–56.

Weber, Max (2009a). 'Politics as a Vocation', in H. H. Gerth and C. Wright Mills (eds) *From Max Weber: Essays in Sociology*, London: Routledge, pp. 77–128.

Weber, Max (2009b). *From Max Weber: Essays in Sociology.* H. H. Gerth and C. Wright Mills (eds), London: Routledge.

Weigel, George (2005). *Witness to Hope: The Biography of Pope John Paul II.* London: Harper Collins.

White, Stephen K. (1997). 'Weak Ontologies and Liberal Political Reflection', *Political Theory* 25 (4): 502–23.

White, Stephen K. (2000). *Sustaining Affirmation: The Strengths of Weak Ontology in Political Theory.* Princeton, NJ: Princeton University Press.

Wittgenstein, Ludwig (1953). *Philosophical Investigations.* Oxford: Oxford University Press.

Wohlrab-Sahr, Monika and Marian Burchardt (2012). 'Multiple Secularities: Toward a Cultural Sociology of Secular Modernities', *Comparative Sociology* 11: 875–909.

Young, Iris M. (2008). 'Unruly Categories: A Critique of Nancy Fraser's Dual Systems Theory', in K. Olson (ed.) *Adding Insult to Injury: Nancy Fraser Debates Her Critics*. London: Verso, pp. 89–106.

Ẑiẑek, Slavoj (2002). 'The Matrix: Or, the Two Sides of Perversion', in William Irwin (ed.) *The Matrix and Philosophy*, Chicago, IL: Open Court, pp. 240–66.

Zurn, Christopher (2003). 'Identity or Status? Struggles over "Recognition" in Fraser, Honneth and Taylor', *Constellations* 10 (4): 519–37.

Index

1960s, 21–2, 134, 144, 146–9, 161, 167, 169, 178, 194–5
1968, May, 21, 23, 148
9/11, 17, 29
Abbey, Ruth, 14, 105, 151, 167–72, 184–5, 193
Agamben, Giorgio, 76
alienation, 3–4, 8, 22–3, 56, 60–2, 69, 73–6, 101–2, 117, 152, 182, 189, 194–5
Althusser, Louis, 22–3
American Revolutionary War of Independence, 119
analytical philosophy, 16, 17, 34, 67, 72
Ancien Régime, 120, 136
ancient constitution, 84, 126, 191
Ancient Greek polis, 62, 123–6, 128, 137, 191
Anderson, Benedict, 109, 181
Anscombe, Elizabeth, 19
Appiah, Anthony, 53
Aristotelian, 58, 123,
articulation, 38
Asia, 108, 157, 166–7, 172
atomism, 61, 68, 101, 108, 152, 174–5, 191
authenticity (ethics of), 8–9, 14, 26–7, 57, 61–2, 74–7, 80, 88, 94, 101, 105, 146–9, 159, 168–72, 194–6
Axial Age, 130, 137–8, 156, 161

Bazcko, Bronislaw, 109, 111
Beck, Ulrich, 60
Beck-Gernsheim, Elizabeth, 60
behaviourism, 19–20
Bellah, Robert, 14, 152–4, 170
Berger, Peter, 156, 178–9
Berlin, Isaiah, 7, 18–19, 23–4, 51–6
Boltanski, Luc, 60
Bourdieu, Pierre, 111, 190
buffered self, 129, 142–3, 145, 149, 160
Burkhardt, Jacob, 80

Canada, 5–6, 10, 17–24, 27–31, 35–9, 84, 138, 168, 181–2
capitalism, 4, 10–11, 19, 21–3, 27, 32, 60, 65, 74, 124, 147, 162, 189, 196
Casanova, José, 14, 151, 155–7, 164–7, 171–2, 176–9
Castoriadis, Cornelius, 52, 109–11, 110–20, 122–7
Catholicism, 5, 18–19, 29, 31, 153–4, 163, 170, 178, 183
chain of being, 58, 77, 114
Chakrabarty, Dipesh, 118

Chiapello, Eve, 60
China, 137–8, 166–7, 172, 176
Christianity, 18, 26–7, 31, 129, 131, 136, 156–7, 163
Civic Republicanism, 84–6, 105, 108
closed world structure, 109, 127
Cold War, 18, 166–7
Coleridge, Samuel Taylor, 59, 187
collective good, 85, 92, 101
collective right, 99–100
collective subjectivity, 109–10
colonialism, 21, 88–9, 138–9, 164
communication, 37, 43, 66–73, 85–7, 100, 175, 188, 190
communitarianism, 1–2, 8, 10, 15, 17, 43, 57, 71, 79–87, 91, 96, 99, 104–5, 108, 113, 181–2
community, 8, 38, 42–3, 47, 58, 60–1, 63–73, 82–7, 89, 97, 103, 166, 190–1, 196
Condillac, Étienne Bonnot de, 67–8
consciousness, 66
control
  'bottom up,' 81
crisis
  of meaning, 65
Critical Theory, 95, 114
critique
  artistic, 60
  social, 60

Davie, Grace, 141, 156
deconstruction, 74
deism, 130, 135–7, 144–5
democracy, 3, 9–10, 36, 58, 73, 77–106, 120–8, 139, 153, 175, 195
  paradoxes, of 100
democratic ethos, 102
democratic exclusion, 102–4
Derrida, Jacques, 74–6
Descartes, René, 31, 135, 145, 189
despotism, 85
  soft despotism, 101
disenchantment, 6, 12, 64, 86, 110, 139, 143–5, 152–9, 164, 170–1
distributive justice, 97
domestication of nobility, 114–15
Dreyfus, Herbert, 31, 174, 189
Durkheim, Emile, 115, 130–1
Dworkin, Ronald, 90

Eisenstadt, S. N., 111, 137–8, 156, 180
Elias, Norbert, 115, 146
emancipatory politics, 60
embodiment, 31, 47–8, 187, 189–90
English Civil War, 126
Enlightenment, 2, 13, 23, 25, 55, 73, 130–7, 144–8, 159–61, 171, 181, 191–3
ethnic cleansing, 104
Europe, 18, 36, 65, 108, 112, 118, 126, 131, 136, 138, 140–1, 155–7, 164–8, 171, 180, 182
exclusive humanism, 129–30, 136, 143–5, 149, 169–70, 172

expression, 38
expressivism, 9, 21, 23–5, 38, 55–69, 72–4, 77, 105, 111, 159, 194
  expressive individualism, 147–9, 169
  expressivist turn, 57–8, 83

Fanon, Frantz, 89–90
feminism, 39, 89, 122
Foucault, Michel, 59, 74–6, 115, 158
France, 21, 139, 165, 180
Frank, Manfred, 72
Frankfurt, Harry, 45
Frankfurt School, 23, 117
Fraser, Nancy, 87, 94–5, 99
freedom, 1–2, 7–10, 19, 23, 33–54, 56–62, 66, 71–4, 77, 80, 83, 85–8, 94–7, 101, 105, 108, 116, 122, 125–7, 133, 136, 144, 147–9, 153, 174, 176, 180, 193–4
  of religion, 15, 157, 174–81, 183, 191
  self-actualisation, 61–2
  self-expression, 61–2
French Revolution, 9, 12, 69, 73–4, 118–20, 126, 133, 139
  Terror, the, 119
Freud, Sigmund, 147
fullness, 56, 143–5, 159, 162–3, 171, 179
Friedrich, Caspar David, 55

Gauchet, Marcel, 110
Gender, 62, 96, 116, 125
Globalisation, 29, 156, 164
Goethe, Johann Wilhelm, 64
good, the, 36, 47–8, 51, 54, 61, 64, 80, 82–6, 96–7
good life, 90–1
Grotius, Hugo, 112, 114

Habermas, Jürgen, 7, 31, 39, 48–9, 88, 91–4, 100, 110–11, 118, 149, 153, 179
Hegel, Georg Wilhelm, 2–3, 8–9, 13, 16, 22–6, 31, 36, 43, 55–7, 62–6, 69, 72–4, 77, 87, 92–3, 96, 119, 194
  ethical life (Sittlickheit), 77
  on French Revolution, 69–70
  Geist/Spirit, 69
  struggle for recognition, 70
  rational state, 77
Herder, Johannes, 8, 25, 57, 63, 65–8, 77, 159, 187
hermeneutic phenomenology, 33, 34
hermeneutics, 2, 7, 20, 33–4, 42, 48, 96, 114
  fusion of horizons, 99, 104–5
hierarchy, 58, 80, 112, 123
historiography, 14, 151, 153, 158, 160–3
holistic liberalism, 43, 54, 77, 79–80, 86, 105, 107
Honneth, Axel, 7, 10, 87, 92–8
horizons of interpretation, 33, 34, 42
humanism, 20, 130, 144–5
Humboldt, Wilhelm von, 8, 66–7, 77, 187
hypergoods, 4, 159, 174, 193

identity, 6–7, 9, 16, 25, 33–54, 56–62, 70–1, 80, 83–4, 88–9, 92–5, 97–9, 104, 110, 118, 147–9, 175, 179, 182–4, 193, 195

identity (*cont.*)
  collective, 35
  personal identity, 35
  self, 35
identity politics, 10–11, 39, 70, 90, 97
ideology, 22, 114, 116–17, 157, 165, 172, 176
immanent frame, 41, 69, 109, 129, 145–9, 162, 170
individualism, 1, 5, 9, 13, 23, 25, 28, 61, 68, 70, 77, 94, 100, 105, 115, 133–4, 144–9, 162, 168, 174, 189, 195
Industrial Revolution, 131, 145, 171
inescapable frameworks, 33, 40, 41
internal exclusion, 103
intersubjectivity, 49
Islam, 132, 177

Jager, Colin, 159, 171
Japan, 18, 138, 180
Jaspers, Karl, 137, 161

Kant, Immanuel, 19, 48, 71–3, 83, 133–4, 136
  categorical imperative, 40

language, 1–2, 4, 8, 15–16, 22, 24, 28, 30–1, 34–5, 40–51, 56–9, 63, 66–9, 72–7, 82, 93–5, 126, 174–5, 184–91, 193, 195
  designation, 68
Lefort, Claude, 109, 118–21, 127
liberal democracy, 127
liberalism, 2, 7–8, 11, 51, 57, 70, 79–88, 90–1, 100–1, 104–5, 108, 113, 123–6
  holistic, 1, 6–7, 54, 68, 77, 79, 86, 105, 107
liberalism–communitarianism debate, 79–81, 105
life politics, 60
Locke, John
  language, 67, 186
  political theory, 112–13
Lyotard, Jean-François, 28, 76

Machiavelli, Niccolo, 84
Madsen, Richard, 151, 166–7, 172
Mann, Michael, 103
Marcuse, Herbert, 21, 23, 148
market economy, 115
Marx, Karl, 19, 22–3, 63, 72–4, 131, 152
Marxism, 19, 27, 32
Mead, George Herbert, 92–4, 96–7, 190
  concrete other, 94
  generalised other, 94
meaning, 6–9, 12, 18, 26, 33–54, 57, 59, 63–8, 71, 74–7, 80, 87, 93–7, 102–8, 118–25, 130, 147, 153, 163–4, 171, 185–90, 194
Merleau-Ponty, Maurice, 34, 40
Middle Ages, 80, 129, 133, 146, 154, 160, 166
migration, 6, 39, 156, 184
Milbank, John, 14, 154–5, 171
Mill, John Stuart, 57, 131
modernisation, 13, 29, 65, 108, 110, 120, 138, 152, 164, 166, 172
  theory of, 120–1

modernity, 2–4, 7–8, 10–14, 16–17, 21, 24, 26–9, 31, 35, 41, 49, 50–4, 55–78, 80–1, 101, 107–27, 130–2, 138–9, 151–61, 170–81, 194
Montesquieu, 84
moral ontology, 44, 47–8, 53–4, 75, 91
moral order, 3–5, 11, 51, 110–27, 181, 191, 196
multiculturalism, 2, 9–10, 15–17, 20–1, 27, 30–1, 39, 70, 81, 87, 90, 174–5, 181–5, 191
multiple modernities, 10, 12, 109–11, 118–21, 130, 137–8, 156–7, 173, 180
multiple secularities, 173, 180
Murphy, Peter, 110

nationalism, 6, 8, 16, 21, 35, 50, 56–7, 65, 70, 77, 80, 84, 102, 109, 162
  imagined community, 109
natural law, 113
naturalist consciousness, 34
negative liberty, 3, 7, 85–6
Nietzsche, Friedrich, 75–6, 158
Novalis (Friedrich von Hardenberg), 72

objectifying, 45, 61
ordinary life (affirmation of), 13, 25, 38, 116, 131, 154–5
other, the, 92

patriotism, 84–5
philosophical anthropology, 39–40
political culture, 81
polytheism, 154, 167
popular sovereignty, 125–6
porous self, 129, 142–3, 145, 160
positive liberty, 7, 51–4, 86
positivism, 40
postmodernism, 11, 27–8, 32, 74–6, 110, 134
post-secularism, 14, 129, 149, 173, 175, 178, 181
practice, 36, 42, 45, 48, 50–1, 61, 63, 66, 71, 95, 97, 102, 105, 107–8, 110, 112–16, 119, 122, 126,
premodern imaginaries, 58, 61, 80, 95, 112, 115–18, 122, 124, 153
private sphere, 13, 29, 60, 62, 77, 131, 175, 177, 179
proceduralism, 1–3, 8, 41, 48–50, 81–3, 86, 91, 100–5
  procedural liberalism *see* proceduralism
progress, 9–10, 50, 62, 120, 122, 136, 149, 152–3, 158
Protestantism, 115, 146, 178
psychoanalysis, 111
public culture, 108
public goods, 84
public sphere, 20, 88–9, 98, 113, 115, 117–18, 122, 126–7, 131, 141, 145, 153, 175, 177–81, 191

Quebec, 6, 15–16, 18, 21–2, 27–31, 91, 173–6, 179, 181–5, 188, 191
Quinet, Edgar, 120

radical democracy, 128
Rational Choice Theory, 37

rationality, 7, 10, 25, 55–6, 60, 63–7, 71–2, 100, 110, 123, 127, 140, 143, 152–3, 165, 171, 193–4
Rawls, John, 81, 86, 90
  communitarian critics, 81
realism, 1–2, 15, 31, 174, 191
reason, 13, 25, 28, 34, 44–5, 49, 55–6, 60–6, 70–3, 77, 100, 111, 118, 123–4, 130–6, 143, 153–5, 171, 193–4
recognition, 2–4, 7–10, 27, 39, 50, 70, 76–106, 108, 122, 149, 182, 191, 194–5
  of difference, 90
  non-recognition, 89, 94–5
redistribution, 87
reform, 13, 131, 154, 159, 161–3, 167
reformation, 131, 145–6, 152–5, 161, 169
relativism, 28
renaissance, 133, 152, 155, 161, 185–6
republicanism, 85, 126
right, the, 36
rights, of individual, 5, 8–9, 36, 50, 80, 85–92, 98, 103–5, 113–16, 122, 126, 136, 148–9, 180–5
romanticism, 2, 4, 7–9, 16, 23, 42, 55–78, 88, 111, 134–7, 145–52, 159–60, 169–71, 147, 181, 194
  and politics, 65
Rousseau, Jean-Jacques, 8–9, 25, 55, 59–62, 73–4, 88, 93, 119, 136, 147
  disalienation, politics of, 73–4
  the general will, 119
Sandel, Michael, 81
  unencumbered self, 83
Schlegel, Friedrich, 72
science, 2, 19–20, 34, 40, 115, 133, 137, 139–40, 142–5, 152, 155, 160, 164, 166, 181, 186–7
Scientific Revolution, 136, 154–5, 171, 186
Second World War, 18, 147, 169
secularisation, 12–14, 29–30, 107, 118, 127–37, 141, 145, 151–66, 171–2, 175–9, 183
secularism, 1–4, 12, 14–15, 29–30, 41, 129–32, 137, 140–6, 151, 155–7, 160–95
secularity, 12, 41, 47, 118, 129, 141–9, 160, 166–72, 176, 180
self, 2–4, 7–8, 12–13, 16, 21, 24–8, 31, 35, 37–8, 43–9, 51–4, 64–7, 86, 88–98, 101, 110, 113–15, 118, 123, 129, 131–5, 142, 145–9, 152, 159–60, 174–5, 181, 187, 190, 193–5
self-narrative, 7, 25, 38, 43, 48, 190
shared identity space, 104
Sheehan, Jonathan, 161–3, 168, 171
Shelley, Mary, 136–7, 187
Shelley, Percy Bysshe, 55
social, 114
social imaginaries, 10–11, 13, 42, 50, 62, 95, 105–6, 110–11, 125, 127, 163
socialism, 9, 11, 50, 56
solidarity, 8, 64, 80, 84–5, 102, 105, 115, 190, 196

Smith, Adam, 114
Smith, Karl, 43
Smith, Nick, 1, 2, 35, 48–9, 53, 193
stadial consciousness, 14, 159, 163–4
strong evaluations, 45–7, 49
structuralism, 32, 37
struggle for recognition, 38, 70, 87, 92–6
Sturm and Drang, 64
subject, 43; *see also* self
subjectivity, 9, 36–7, 42, 47–8, 55, 59–60, 65–6, 69–72, 80, 88, 109, 142, 151

Tocqueville, de Alexis, 9, 81, 84–6, 100–2, 127–8
totalitarianism, 50, 120–2, 127, 162
transcendence, 12, 74, 109, 127, 137, 159, 162, 170
trans-subjective, 95

United States (of America), 21–2, 139, 156, 164, 168, 171–2, 177–8, 180, 191

Wagner, Peter, 21, 27, 125
Warner, Michael, 118
Weber, Max, 64–5, 115, 139–40, 152–5
Wittgenstein, Ludwig, 19, 66
Wordsworth, William, 55, 59, 159, 187

Zurn, Christopher, 99